Sea-Power

And Other Studies

CYPRIAN BRIDGE

CAMBRIDGE
UNIVERSITY PRESS

CAMBRIDGE UNIVERSITY PRESS

Cambridge, New York, Melbourne, Madrid, Cape Town,
Singapore, São Paolo, Delhi, Mexico City

Published in the United States of America by Cambridge University Press, New York

www.cambridge.org
Information on this title: www.cambridge.org/9781108054201

This edition first published 1910
This digitally printed version 2013

ISBN 978-1-108-05420-1 Paperback

CAMBRIDGE LIBRARY COLLECTION

Books of enduring scholarly value

Naval and Military History

This series includes accounts of sea and land campaigns by eye-witnesses and contemporaries, as well as landmark studies of their social, political and economic impacts. The series focuses mainly on the period from the Renaissance to the end of the Victorian era. It includes major concentrations of material on the American and French revolutions, the British campaigns in South Asia, and nineteenth-century conflicts in Europe, such as the Peninsular and Crimean Wars. Although many of the accounts are semi-official narratives by senior officers and their relatives, the series also includes alternative viewpoints from dissenting leaders, servicemen in the lower ranks, and military wives and civilians caught up in the theatre of war.

Sea-Power

A naval officer from a generation that could spend an average of between 250 and 300 days a year at sea, Sir Cyprian Bridge (1839–1924) used this extensive experience and the knowledge he gained from wide reading to become a highly respected commander, firm in his beliefs and unafraid to voice them. In retirement he became a vocal critic of the drive to build bigger ships, believing that hardware should be subordinate to tactics. A regular contributor to newspapers, he wrote articles on naval history, tactics and strategy. This collection of articles was published in 1910, and includes his well-known paper, first delivered in 1902, setting out the difficulties in maintaining supplies and communications with a fleet based far from home. This work remains relevant to naval historians, and to those interested in how Britain maintained her maritime supremacy into the twentieth century.

Cambridge University Press has long been a pioneer in the reissuing of out-of-print titles from its own backlist, producing digital reprints of books that are still sought after by scholars and students but could not be reprinted economically using traditional technology. The Cambridge Library Collection extends this activity to a wider range of books which are still of importance to researchers and professionals, either for the source material they contain, or as landmarks in the history of their academic discipline.

Drawing from the world-renowned collections in the Cambridge University Library and other partner libraries, and guided by the advice of experts in each subject area, Cambridge University Press is using state-of-the-art scanning machines in its own Printing House to capture the content of each book selected for inclusion. The files are processed to give a consistently clear, crisp image, and the books finished to the high quality standard for which the Press is recognised around the world. The latest print-on-demand technology ensures that the books will remain available indefinitely, and that orders for single or multiple copies can quickly be supplied.

The Cambridge Library Collection brings back to life books of enduring scholarly value (including out-of-copyright works originally issued by other publishers) across a wide range of disciplines in the humanities and social sciences and in science and technology.

SEA-POWER

SEA-POWER

AND OTHER STUDIES

BY

ADMIRAL SIR CYPRIAN BRIDGE, G.C.B.

AUTHOR OF 'THE ART OF NAVAL WARFARE' ETC.

LONDON

SMITH, ELDER & CO., 15 WATERLOO PLACE, S.W.

1910

PREFACE

THE essays collected in this volume are republished in the hope that they may be of some use to those who are interested in naval history. The aim has been to direct attention to certain historical occurrences and conditions which the author ventures to think have been often misunderstood. An endeavour has been made to show the continuity of the operation of sea-power throughout history, and the importance of recognising this at the present day.

In some cases specially relating to our navy at different periods a revision of the more commonly accepted conclusions—formed, it is believed, on imperfect knowledge—is asked for.

It is also hoped that the intimate connection between naval history in the strict sense and military history in the strict sense has been made apparent, and likewise the fact that both are in reality branches of the general history of a nation and not something altogether distinct from and outside it.

In a collection of essays on kindred subjects some repetitions are inevitable, but it is believed that they will be found present only to a moderate extent in the following pages.

My nephew, Mr. J. S. C. Bridge, has very kindly seen the book through the press.

June 1910.

CONTENTS

TEN of the essays included in this volume first appeared in the *Encyclopædia Britannica*, the *Times*, the *Morning Post*, the *National Review*, the *Nineteenth Century and After*, the *Cornhill Magazine*, and the *Naval Annual*. The proprietors of those publications have courteously given me permission to republish them here.

Special mention must be made of my obligation to the proprietors of the *Encyclopædia Britannica* for allowing me to reproduce the essays on 'Sea-Power' and 'The Command of the Sea.' They are the owners of the copyright of both essays, and their courtesy to me is the more marked because they are about to republish them themselves in the forthcoming edition of the *Encyclopædia*.

The paper on 'Naval Strategy and Tactics at the Time of Trafalgar' was read at the Institute of Naval Architects, and that on 'The Supply and Communications of a Fleet' at the Hong-Kong United Service Institution.

SEA-POWER AND OTHER STUDIES

I

SEA-POWER [1]

SEA-POWER is a term used to indicate two distinct, though cognate things. The affinity of these two and the indiscriminate manner in which the term has been applied to each have tended to obscure its real significance. The obscurity has been deepened by the frequency with which the term has been confounded with the old phrase, 'Sovereignty of the sea,' and the still current expression, 'Command of the sea.' A discussion—etymological, or even archæological in character—of the term must be undertaken as an introduction to the explanation of its now generally accepted meaning. It is one of those compound words in which a Teutonic and a Latin (or Romance) element are combined, and which are easily formed and become widely current when the sea is concerned. Of such are 'sea-coast,' 'sea-forces' (the 'land- and sea-forces' used to be a

[1] Written in 1899. (*Encyclopædia Britannica*.)

B

common designation of what we now call the ' Army and Navy '), ' sea-service,' ' sea-serpent,' and ' sea-officer ' (now superseded by ' naval officer '). The term in one form is as old as the fifteenth century. Edward III, in commemoration of the naval victory of Sluys, coined gold ' nobles ' which bore on one side his effigy ' crowned, standing in a large ship, holding in one hand a sword and in the other a shield.' An anonymous poet, who wrote in the reign of Henry VI, says of this coin :

> For four things our noble showeth to me,
> King, ship, and sword, and *power of the sea.*

Even in its present form the term is not of very recent date. Grote[1] speaks of ' the conversion of Athens from a land-power into a sea-power.' In a lecture published in 1883, but probably delivered earlier, the late Sir J. R. Seeley says that ' commerce was swept out of the Mediterranean by the besom of the Turkish sea-power.' [2] The term also occurs in vol. xviii. of the ' Encyclopædia Britannica,' published in 1885. At p. 574 of that volume (art. Persia) we are told that Themistocles was ' the founder of the Attic sea-power.' The sense in which the term is used differs in these extracts. In the first it means what we generally call a ' naval power '—that is to say, a state having a considerable navy in contra-distinction to a ' military power,' a state with a con-siderable army but only a relatively small navy. In

---

[1] *Hist. of Greece*, v. p. 67, published in 1849, but with preface dated 1848.

[2] *Expansion of England*, p. 89.

the last two extracts it means all the elements of the
naval strength of the state referred to ; and this is
the meaning that is now generally, and is likely to
be exclusively, attached to the term owing to the
brilliant way in which it has been elucidated by
Captain A. T. Mahan of the United States Navy in a
series of remarkable works.[1] The double use of the
term is common in German, though in that language
both parts of the compound now in use are Teutonic.
One instance out of many may be cited from the
historian Adolf Holm.[2] He says[3] that Athens, being
in possession of a good naval port, could become
‘ *eine bedeutende Seemacht,*’ i.e. an important naval
power. He also says[4] that Gelon of Syracuse,
besides a large army (*Heer*), had ‘ *eine bedeutende
Seemacht,*’ meaning a considerable navy. The term,
in the first of the two senses, is old in German, as
appears from the following, extracted from Zedler’s
‘ Grosses Universal Lexicon,’ vol. xxxvi : [5] ‘ See-
machten, Seepotenzen, Latin. *summae potestates mari
potentes.*’ ‘ Seepotenzen ’ is probably quite obsolete
now. It is interesting as showing that German no
more abhors Teuto-Latin or Teuto-Romance compounds than English. We may note, as a proof of the
indeterminate meaning of the expression until his
own epoch-making works had appeared, that Mahan

---

[1] *Influence of Sea-power on History*, published 1890 ; *Influence
of Sea-power on the French Revolution and Empire*, 2 vols. 1892 ;
Nelson : the Embodiment of the Sea-power of Great Britain, 2
vols. 1897.
[2] *Griechische Geschichte.* Berlin, 1889.
[3] *Ibid.* ii. p. 37.   [4] *Ibid.* ii. p. 91.
[5] Leipzig und Halle, 1743.

B 2

himself in his earliest book used it in both senses.
He says,[1] ' The Spanish Netherlands ceased to be a
sea-power.' He alludes[2] to the development of a
nation as a 'sea-power,' and[3] to the inferiority of
the Confederate States ' as a sea-power.' Also,[4] he
remarks of the war of the Spanish Succession that
' before it England was one of the sea-powers, after
it she was *the* sea-power without any second.' In all
these passages, as appears from the use of the
indefinite article, what is meant is a naval power,
or a state in possession of a strong navy. The other
meaning of the term forms the general subject of his
writings above enumerated. In his earlier works
Mahan writes ' sea power ' as two words ; but in a
published letter of the 19th February 1897, he joins
them with a hyphen, and defends this formation of
the term and the sense in which he uses it. We may
regard him as the virtual inventor of the term in its
more diffused meaning, for—even if it had been employed by earlier writers in that sense—it is he
beyond all question who has given it general currency.
He has made it impossible for any one to treat of
sea-power without frequent reference to his writings
and conclusions.

There is something more than mere literary
interest in the fact that the term in another language
was used more than two thousand years ago. Before
Mahan no historian—not even one of those who
specially devoted themselves to the narration of

---

[1] *Influence of Sea-power on History*, p. 35.
[2] *Ibid.* p. 42.   [3] *Ibid.* p. 43.   [4] *Ibid.* p. 225.

naval occurrences—had evinced a more correct appreciation of the general principles of naval warfare than Thucydides. He alludes several times to the importance of getting command of the sea. This country would have been saved some disasters and been less often in peril had British writers— taken as guides by the public—possessed the same grasp of the true principles of defence as Thucydides exhibited. One passage in his history is worth quoting. Brief as it is, it shows that on the subject of sea-power he was a predecessor of Mahan. In a speech in favour of prosecuting the war, which he puts into the mouth of Pericles, these words occur :—

οἱ μὲν γὰρ οὐχ ἕξουσιν ἄλλην ἀντιλαβεῖν ἀμαχεί, ἡμῖν δέ ἐστι γῆ πολλὴ καὶ ἐν νήσοις καὶ κατ' ἤπειρον· μέγα γὰρ τὸ τῆς θαλάσσης κράτος. The last part of this extract, though often translated ' command of the sea,' or ' dominion of the sea,' really has the wider meaning of sea-power, the ' power of the sea ' of the old English poet above quoted. This wider meaning should be attached to certain passages in Herodotus,[1] which have been generally interpreted ' commanding the sea,' or by the mere titular and honorific ' having the dominion of the sea.' One editor of Herodotus, Ch. F. Baehr, did, however, see exactly what was meant, for, with reference to the allusion to Polycrates, he says, *classe maximum valuit*. This is perhaps as exact a definition of sea-power as could be given in a sentence.

[1] *Herodotus*, lii. 122 in two places ; v. 83.

It is, however, impossible to give a definition which would be at the same time succinct and satisfactory. To say that ' sea-power ' means the sum-total of the various elements that go to make up the naval strength of a state would be in reality to beg the question. Mahan lays down the ' principal conditions affecting the sea-power of nations,' but he does not attempt to give a concise definition of it. Yet no one who has studied his works will find it difficult to understand what it indicates.

Our present task is to put readers in possession of the means of doing this. The best, indeed—as Mahan has made us see—the only effective way of attaining this object is to treat the matter historically. Whatever date we may agree to assign to the formation of the term itself, the idea—as we have seen—is as old as history. It is not intended to give a condensed history of sea-power, but rather an analysis of the idea and what it contains, illustrating this analysis with examples from history ancient and modern. It is important to know that it is not something which originated in the middle of the seventeenth century, and having seriously affected history in the eighteenth, ceased to have weight till Captain Mahan appeared to comment on it in the last decade of the nineteenth. With a few masterly touches Mahan, in his brief allusion to the second Punic war, has illustrated its importance in the struggle between Rome and Carthage. What has to be shown is that the principles which he has laid down in that case, and in cases much more modern, are true and have been true always and everywhere. Until this is perceived there is much history which cannot be understood, and yet it is essential to our welfare as a maritime people that we should understand it thoroughly. Our failure to understand it has more than once brought us, if not to the verge of destruction, at any rate within a short distance of serious disaster.

SEA-POWER IN ANCIENT TIMES

The high antiquity of decisive naval campaigns is amongst the most interesting features of international conflicts. Notwithstanding the much greater frequency of land wars, the course of history has been profoundly changed more often by contests on the water. That this has not received the notice it deserved is true, and Mahan tells us why. 'Historians generally,' he says, 'have been unfamiliar with the conditions of the sea, having as to it neither special interest nor special knowledge ; and the profound determining influence of maritime strength on great issues has consequently been overlooked.' Moralising on that which might have been is admittedly a sterile process ; but it is sometimes necessary to point, if only by way of illustration, to a possible alternative. As in modern times the fate of India and the fate of North America were determined by sea-power, so also at a very remote epoch sea-power decided whether or not Hellenic colonisation was to take root in, and Hellenic culture to dominate, Central and Northern Italy as it dominated Southern Italy, where traces of it are extant to this day. A moment's consideration will enable us to see how different the history of the world would have been had a Hellenised city grown and prospered on the Seven Hills. Before the Tarquins were driven out of Rome a Phocœan fleet was encountered (537 B.C.) off Corsica by a combined force of Etruscans and Phœnicians, and was so handled that the Phocœans abandoned the island and settled on the coast of Lucania.[1] The enterprise of their navigators had built up for the Phœnician cities and their great off-shoot Carthage, a sea-power which enabled them to gain the practical sovereignty of the sea to the west of Sardinia and Sicily. The control of these waters was the object of prolonged and memorable struggles, for on it— as the result showed—depended the empire of the world. From very remote times the consolidation and expansion, from within outwards, of great continental states have had serious consequences for mankind when they were accompanied by the acquisition of a coast-line and the absorption of a maritime population. We shall find that the process loses none of its importance in recent years. ' The ancient empires,' says the historian of Greece, Ernst Curtius, ' as long as no foreign elements had intruded into them, had an invincible horror of the

---

[1] Mommsen, *Hist. Rome*, English trans., i. p. 153.

water.' When the condition, which Curtius notices in parenthesis, arose, the 'horror' disappeared. There is something highly significant in the uniformity of the efforts of Assyria, Egypt, Babylon, and Persia to get possession of the maritime resources of Phœnicia. Our own immediate posterity will, perhaps, have to reckon with the results of similar efforts in our own day. It is this which gives a living interest to even the very ancient history of sea-power, and makes the study of it of great practical importance to us now. We shall see, as we go on, how the phenomena connected with it reappear with striking regularity in successive periods. Looked at in this light, the great conflicts of former ages are full of useful, indeed necessary, instruction.

In the first and greatest of the contests waged by the nations of the East against Europe—the Persian wars—sea-power was the governing factor. Until Persia had expanded to the shores of the Levant the European Greeks had little to fear from the ambition of the great king. The conquest of Egypt by Cambyses had shown how formidable that ambition could be when supported by an efficient navy. With the aid of the naval forces of the Phœnician cities the Persian invasion of Greece was rendered comparatively easy. It was the naval contingents from Phœnicia which crushed the Ionian revolt. The expedition of Mardonius, and still more that of Datis and Artaphernes, had indicated the danger threatening Greece when the master of a great army was likewise the master of a great navy. Their defeat at Marathon was not likely to, and as a matter of fact did not, discourage the Persians from further attempts at aggression. As the advance of Cambyses into Egypt had been flanked by a fleet, so also was that of Xerxes into Greece. By the good fortune sometimes vouchsafed to a people which, owing to its obstinate opposition to, or neglect of, a wise policy, scarcely deserves it, there appeared at Athens an influential citizen who understood all that was meant by the term sea-power. Themistocles saw more clearly than any of his contemporaries that, to enable Athens to play a leading part in the Hellenic world, she needed above all things a strong navy. ' He had already in his eye the battle-field of the future.' He felt sure that the Persians would come back, and come with such forces that resistance in the open field would be out of the question. One scene of action remained—the sea. Persuaded by him the Athenians increased their navy, so that of the 271 vessels comprising the Greek fleet at Artemisium, 147 had been provided by Athens, which also sent a large reinforcement after the first action. Though no one has ever surpassed Themistocles in the faculty of correctly estimating the importance of sea-power, it was understood by Xerxes as clearly as by him that the issue of the war depended upon naval operations. The arrangements made under the Persian monarch's direction, and his very personal movements, show that this was his view. He felt, and probably expressed the feeling, exactly as—in the war of American Independence—Washington did in the words, ' Whatever efforts are made by the land armies, the navy must have the casting vote in the present contest.' The decisive event was the naval action of Salamis. To have made certain of success, the Persians should have first obtained a command of the Ægean, as complete for all practical purposes as the French and English had of the sea generally in the war against Russia of 1854-56. The Persian sea-power was not equal to the task. The fleet of the great king was numerically stronger than that of the Greek allies ; but it has been proved many times that naval efficiency does not depend on numerical superiority alone. The choice sections of the Persian fleet were the contingents of the Ionians and Phœnicians. The former were half-hearted or disaffected ; whilst the latter were, at best, not superior in skill, experience, and valour to the Greek sailors. At Salamis Greece was saved not only from the ambition and vengeance of Xerxes, but also and for many centuries from oppression by an Oriental conqueror. Persia did not succeed against the Greeks, not because she had no sea-power, but because her sea-power, artificially built up, was inferior to that which was a natural element of the vitality of her foes. Ionia was lost and Greece in the end enslaved, because the quarrels of Greeks with Greeks led to the ruin of their naval states.

The Peloponnesian was largely a naval war. The confidence of the Athenians in their sea-power had a great deal to do with its outbreak. The immediate occasion of the hostilities, which in time involved so many states, was the opportunity offered by the conflict between Corinth and Corcyra of increasing the sea-power of Athens. Hitherto the Athenian naval predominance had been virtually confined to the Ægean Sea. The Corcyræan envoy, who pleaded for help at Athens, dwelt upon the advantage to be derived by the Athenians from alliance with a naval state occupying an important situation 'with respect to the western regions towards which the views of the Athenians had for some time been directed.'[1] It was the 'weapon of her sea-power,' to adopt Mahan's phrase, that enabled Athens to maintain the great conflict in which she was engaged. Repeated invasions of her territory, the ravages of disease amongst her people, and the rising disaffection of her allies had been more than made up for by her predominance on the water. The scale of the subsequent Syracusan expedition showed how vigorous Athens still was down to the interruption of the war by the peace of Nicias. The great expedition just mentioned over-taxed her strength. Its failure brought about the ruin of the state. It was held by contemporaries, and has been held in our own day, that the Athenian defeat at Syracuse was due to the omission of the government at home to keep the force in Sicily properly supplied and reinforced. This explanation of failure is given in all ages, and should always

[1] Thirwall, *Hist. Greece*, iii. p. 96.

be suspected. The friends of unsuccessful generals and admirals always offer it, being sure of the support of the political opponents of the administration. After the despatch of the supporting expedition under Demosthenes and Eurymedon, no further great reinforcement, as Nicias admitted, was possible. The weakness of Athens was in the character of the men who swayed the popular assemblies and held high commands. A people which remembered the administration of a Pericles, and yet allowed a Cleon or an Alcibiades to direct its naval and military policy, courted defeat. Nicias, notwithstanding the possession of high qualities, lacked the supreme virtue of a commander —firm resolution. He dared not face the obloquy consequent on withdrawal from an enterprise on which the popular hopes had been fixed ; and therefore he allowed a reverse to be converted into an overwhelming disaster. ' The complete ruin of Athens had appeared, both to her enemies and to herself, impending and irreparable. But so astonishing, so rapid, and so energetic had been her rally, that [a year after Syracuse] she was found again carrying on a terrible struggle.'[1] Nevertheless her sea-power had indeed been ruined at Syracuse. Now she could wage war only ' with impaired resources and on a purely defensive system.' Even before Arginusæ it was seen that ' superiority of nautical skill had passed to the Peloponnesians and their allies.'[2]

[1] Grote, *Hist. Greece*, v. p. 354.   [2] *Ibid.* p. 503.

The great, occasionally interrupted, and prolonged contest between Rome and Carthage was
a sustained effort on the part of one to gain and
of the other to keep the control of the Western
Mediterranean. So completely had that control
been exercised by Carthage, that she had anticipated
the Spanish commercial policy in America. The
Romans were precluded by treaties from trading
with the Carthaginian territories in Hispania, Africa,
and Sardinia. Rome, as Mommsen tells us, ' was
from the first a maritime city and, in the period of
its vigour, never was so foolish or so untrue to its
ancient traditions as wholly to neglect its war
marine and to desire to be a mere continental power.'
It may be that it was lust of wealth rather than
lust of dominion that first prompted a trial of
strength with Carthage. The vision of universal
empire could hardly as yet have formed itself
in the imagination of a single Roman. The area
of Phœnician maritime commerce was vast enough
both to excite jealousy and to offer vulnerable
points to the cupidity of rivals. It is probable
that the modern estimate of the sea-power of
Carthage is much exaggerated. It was great by
comparison, and of course overwhelmingly great
when there were none but insignificant competitors
to challenge it. Mommsen holds that, in the fourth
and fifth centuries after the foundation of Rome,
' the two main competitors for the dominion of
the Western waters ' were Carthage and Syracuse.
' Carthage,' he says, ' had the preponderance, and

Syracuse sank more and more into a second-rate naval power. The maritime importance of the Etruscans was wholly gone. . . . Rome itself was not exempt from the same fate; its own waters were likewise commanded by foreign fleets.' The Romans were for a long time too much occupied at home to take much interest in Mediterranean matters. The position of the Carthaginians in the western basin of the Mediterranean was very like that of the Portuguese long afterwards in India. The latter kept within reach of the sea ; ' nor did their rule ever extend a day's march from their ships.' [1] ' The Carthaginians in Spain,' says Mommsen, ' made no effort to acquire the interior from the warlike native nations ; they were content with the possession of the mines and of stations for traffic and for shell and other fisheries.' Allowance being made for the numbers of the classes engaged in administration, commerce, and supervision, it is nearly certain that Carthage could not furnish the crews required by both a great war-navy and a great mercantile marine. No one is surprised on finding that the land-forces of Carthage were composed largely of alien mercenaries. We have several examples from which we can infer a parallel, if not an identical, condition of her maritime resources. How, then, was the great Carthaginian carrying-trade provided for ? The experience of more than one country will enable us to answer this

[1] R. S. Whiteway, *Rise of the Portuguese Power in India* p. 12. Westminster, 1899.

question. The ocean trade of those off-shoots or dependencies of the United Kingdom, viz. the United States, Australasia, and India, is largely or chiefly conducted by shipping of the old country. So that of Carthage was largely conducted by old Phœnicians. These may have obtained a 'Carthaginian Register,' or the contemporary equivalent ; but they could not all have been purely Carthaginian or Liby-Phœnician. This must have been the case even more with the war-navy. British India for a considerable time possessed a real and indeed highly efficient navy ; but it was officered entirely and manned almost entirely by men from the 'old country.' Moreover, it was small. The wealth of India would have sufficed to furnish a larger material element ; but, as the country could not supply the *personnel*, it would have been absurd to speak of the sea-power of India apart from that of England. As soon as the Romans chose to make the most of their natural resources the maritime predominance of Carthage was doomed. The artificial basis of the latter's sea-power would not enable it to hold out against serious and persistent assaults. Unless this is perceived it is impossible to understand the story of the Punic wars. Judged by every visible sign of strength, Carthage, the richer, the more enterprising, ethnically the more predominant amongst her neighbours, and apparently the more nautical, seemed sure to win in the great struggle with Rome which, by the conditions of the case, was to be waged largely on the water.

Yet those who had watched the struggles of the Punic city with the Sicilian Greeks, and especially that with Agathocles, must have seen reason to cherish doubts concerning her naval strength. It was an anticipation of the case of Spain in the age of Philip II. As the great Elizabethan seamen discerned the defects of the Spanish naval establishment, so men at Rome discerned those of the Carthaginian. Dates in connection with this are of great significance. A comprehensive measure, with the object of 'rescuing their marine from its condition of impotence,' was taken by the Romans in the year 267 B.C. Four *quæstores classici*—in modern naval English we may perhaps call them port - admirals — were nominated, and one was stationed at each of four ports. The objects of the Roman Senate, so Mommsen tells us, were very obvious. They were ' to recover their independence by sea, to cut off the maritime communications of Tarentum, to close the Adriatic against fleets coming from Epirus, and to emancipate themselves from Carthaginian supremacy.' Four years afterwards the first· Punic war began. It was, and had to be, largely a naval contest. The Romans waged it with varying fortune, but in the end triumphed by means of their sea-power. ' The sea was the place where all great destinies were decided.' [1] The victory of Catulus over the Carthaginian fleet off the Ægatian Islands decided the war and left to the Romans the possession of Sicily and the power

[1] J. H. Burton, *Hist. of Scotland*, 1873, vol. i. p. 318.

of possessing themselves of Sardinia and Corsica. It would be an interesting and perhaps not a barren investigation to inquire to what extent the decline of the mother states of Phœnicia, consequent on the campaigns of Alexander the Great, had helped to enfeeble the naval efficiency of the Carthaginian defences. One thing was certain. Carthage had now met with a rival endowed with natural maritime resources greater than her own. That rival also contained citizens who understood the true importance of sea-power. ' With a statesmanlike sagacity from which succeeding generations might have drawn a lesson, the leading men of the Roman Commonwealth perceived that all their coast-fortifications and coast-garrisons would prove inadequate unless the war-marine of the state were again placed on a footing that should command respect.'[1] It is a gloomy reflection that the leading men of our own great maritime country could not see this in 1860. A thorough comprehension of the events of the first Punic war enables us to solve what, until Mahan wrote, had been one of the standing enigmas of history, viz. Hannibal's invasion of Italy by land instead of by sea in the second Punic war. Mahan's masterly examination of this question has set at rest all doubts as to the reason of Hannibal's action.[2] The naval predominance in the western basin of the Mediterranean acquired by Rome had never been lost. Though modern historians, even those belonging to a maritime

[1] Mommsen, i. p. 427.   [2] *Inf. on Hist.*, pp. 13–21.

country, may have failed to perceive it, the Carthaginians knew well enough that the Romans were too strong for them on the sea. Though other forces co-operated to bring about the defeat of Carthage in the second Punic war, the Roman navy, as Mahan demonstrates, was the most important. As a navy, he tells us in words like those already quoted, ' acts on an element strange to most writers, as its members have been from time immemorial a strange race apart, without prophets of their own, neither themselves nor their calling understood, its immense determining influence on the history of that era, and consequently upon the history of the world, has been overlooked.'

The attainment of all but universal dominion by Rome was now only a question of time. ' The annihilation of the Carthaginian fleet had made the Romans masters of the sea.' [1] A lodgment had already been gained in Illyricum, and countries farther east were before long to be reduced to submission. A glance at the map will show that to effect this the command of the eastern basin of the Mediterranean, like that of the western, must be secured by the Romans. The old historic navies of the Greek and Phœnician states had declined. One considerable naval force there was which, though it could not have prevented, was strong enough to have delayed the Roman progress eastwards. This force belonged to Rhodes, which in the years immediately following the close of the second Punic war reached

[1] Schmitz, *Hist. Rome*, p. 256.

its highest point as a naval power.[1] Far from trying
to obstruct the advance of the Romans the Rhodian
fleet helped it. Hannibal, in his exile, saw the necessity of being strong on the sea if the East was to be
saved from the grasp of his hereditary foe ; but the
resources of Antiochus, even with the mighty co-
operation of Hannibal, were insufficient. In a later
and more often-quoted struggle between East and
West—that which was decided at Actium—sea-
power was again seen to ' have the casting vote.'
When the whole of the Mediterranean coasts became
part of a single state the importance of the navy was
naturally diminished ; but in the struggles within
the declining empire it rose again at times. The
contest of the Vandal Genseric with Majorian and the
African expedition of Belisarius—not to mention
others—were largely influenced by the naval operations.[2]

SEA-POWER IN THE MIDDLE AGES

A decisive event, the Mohammedan conquest of
Northern Africa from Egypt westwards, is unintel-
ligible until it is seen how great a part sea-power
played in effecting it. Purely land expeditions, or
expeditions but slightly supported from the sea, had
ended in failure. The emperor at Constantinople
still had at his disposal a fleet capable of keeping open
the communications with his African province. It
took the Saracens half a century (647-698 A.D.) to

---

[1] C. Torr, *Rhodes in Ancient Times*, p. 40.
[2] Gibbon, *Dec. and Fall*, chaps. xxxvi. xli

win ' their way along the coast of Africa as far as the Pillars of Hercules ' ;[1] and, as Gibbon tells us, it was not till the Commander of the Faithful had prepared a great expedition, this time by sea as well as by land, that the Saracenic dominion was definitely established. It has been generally assumed that the Arabian conquerors who, within a few years of his death, spread the faith of Mohammed over vast regions, belonged to an essentially non-maritime race ; and little or no stress has been laid on the extent to which they relied on naval support in prosecuting their conquests. In parts of Arabia, however, maritime enterprise was far from non-existent ; and when the Mohammedan empire had extended outwards from Mecca and Medina till it embraced the coasts of various seas, the consequences to the neighbouring states were as serious as the rule above mentioned would lead us to expect that they would be. ' With the conquest of Syria and Egypt a long stretch of sea-board had come into the Saracenic power ; and the creation and maintenance of a navy for the protection of the maritime ports as well as for meeting the enemy became a matter of vital importance. Great attention was paid to the manning and equipment of the fleet.'[2] At first the fleet was manned by sailors drawn from the Phœnician towns where nautical energy was not yet quite extinct ; and later the crews were recruited from Syria, Egypt, and the coasts of Asia Minor. Ships were built at most

[1] Hallam, *Mid. Ages*, chap. vi.
[2] Ameer Ali, Syed, *Short Hist. Saracens*, p. 442

of the Syrian and Egyptian ports, and ' also at Obolla
and Bushire on the Persian Gulf,' whilst the mercantile marine and maritime trade were fostered
and encouraged. The sea-power thus created was
largely artificial. It drooped—as in similar cases—
when the special encouragement was withdrawn.
' In the days of Arabian energy,' says Hallam, ' Constantinople was twice, in 668 and 716, attacked
by great naval armaments.' The same authority
believes that the abandonment of such maritime
enterprises by the Saracens may be attributed to
the removal of the capital from Damascus to Bagdad.
The removal indicated a lessened interest in the
affairs of the Mediterranean Sea, which was now left
by the administration far behind. ' The Greeks in
their turn determined to dispute the command of the
sea,' with the result that in the middle of the tenth
century their empire was far more secure from its
enemies than under the first successors of Heraclius.
Not only was the fall of the empire, by a rational
reliance on sea-power, postponed for centuries, but
also much that had been lost was regained. ' At the
close of the tenth century the emperors of Constantinople possessed the best and greatest part ' of
Southern Italy, part of Sicily, the whole of what is
now called the Balkan Peninsula, Asia Minor, with
some parts of Syria and Armenia.[1]

Neglect of sea-power by those who can be reached
by sea brings its own punishment. Whether
neglected or not, if it is an artificial creation it is

[1] Hallam, chap. vi. ; Gibbon, chap. li.

nearly sure to disappoint those who wield it when it encounters a rival power of natural growth. How was it possible for the Crusaders, in their various expeditions, to achieve even the transient success that occasionally crowned their efforts ? How did the Christian kingdom of Jerusalem contrive to exist for more than three-quarters of a century ? Why did the Crusades more and more become maritime expeditions ? The answer to these questions is to be found in the decline of the Mohammedan naval defences and the rising enterprise of the seafaring people of the West. Venetians, Pisans, and Genoese transported crusading forces, kept open the communications of the places held by the Christians, and hampered the operations of the infidels. Even the great Saladin failed to discern the important alteration of conditions. This is evident when we look at the efforts of the Christians to regain the lost kingdom. Saladin ' forgot that the safety of Phœnicia lay in immunity from naval incursions, and that no victory on land could ensure him against an influx from beyond the sea.' [1] Not only were the Crusaders helped by the fleets of the maritime republics of Italy, they also received reinforcements by sea from western Europe and England, on the ' arrival of *Malik Ankiltar* (Richard Cœur de Lion) with twenty shiploads of fighting men and munitions of war.'

Participation in the Crusades was not a solitary proof of the importance of the naval states of Italy. That they had been able to act effectively in the

[1] Ameer Ali, Syed, pp. 359, 360.

Levant may have been in some measure due to the weakening of the Mohammedans by the disintegration of the Seljukian power, the movements of the Moguls, and the confusion consequent on the rise of the Ottomans. However that may have been, the naval strength of those Italian states was great absolutely as well as relatively. Sismondi, speaking of Venice, Pisa, and Genoa, towards the end of the eleventh century, says ' these three cities had more vessels on the Mediterranean than the whole of Christendom besides.' [1] Dealing with a period two centuries later, he declares it ' difficult to comprehend how two simple cities could put to sea such prodigious fleets as those of Pisa and Genoa.' The difficulty disappears when we have Mahan's explanation. The maritime republics of Italy—like Athens and Rhodes in ancient, Catalonia in mediæval, and England and the Netherlands in more modern times —were ' peculiarly well fitted, by situation and resources, for the control of the sea by both war and commerce.' As far as the western Mediterranean was concerned, Genoa and Pisa had given early proofs of their maritime energy, and fixed themselves, in succession to the Saracens, in the Balearic Isles, Sardinia, and Corsica. Sea-power was the Themistoclean instrument with which they made a small state into a great one.

A fertile source of dispute between states is the acquisition of territory beyond sea. As others have done before and since, the maritime republics of Italy

[1] *Ital. Republics*, English ed., p. 29.

quarrelled over this. Sea-power seemed, like Saturn, to devour its own children. In 1284, in a great sea-fight off Meloria, the Pisans were defeated by the Genoese with heavy loss, which, as Sismondi states, ' ruined the maritime power ' of the former. From that time Genoa, transferring her activity to the Levant, became the rival of Venice. The fleets of the two cities in 1298 met near Cyprus in an encounter, said to be accidental, that began ' a terrible war which for seven years stained the Mediterranean with blood and consumed immense wealth.' In the next century the two republics, ' irritated by commercial quarrels '—like the English and Dutch afterwards—were again at war in the Levant. Sometimes one side, sometimes the other was victorious ; but the contest was exhausting to both, and especially to Venice. Within a quarter of a century they were at war again. Hostilities lasted till the Genoese met with the crushing defeat of Chioggia. ' From this time,' says Hallam, ' Genoa never commanded the ocean with such navies as before ; her commerce gradually went into decay ; and the fifteenth century, the most splendid in the annals of Venice, is till recent times the most ignominious in those of Genoa.' Venice seemed now to have no naval rival, and had no fear that anyone could forbid the ceremony in which the Doge, standing in the bows of the *Bucentaur*, cast a ring into the Adriatic with the words, *Desponsamus te, Mare, in signum veri perpetuique dominii*. The result of the combats at Chioggia, though fatal to it in the long-run, did not at once

destroy the naval importance of Genoa.   A remarkable characteristic of sea-power is the delusive
manner in which it appears to revive after a great
defeat.   The Persian navy occasionally made a brave
show afterwards ; but in reality it had received at
Salamis a mortal wound.   Athens seemed strong
enough on the sea after the catastrophe of Syracuse ;
but, as already stated, her naval power had been
given there a check from which it never completely
recovered.   The navy of Carthage had had similar
experience ; and, in later ages, the power of the
Turks was broken at Lepanto and that of Spain at
Gravelines notwithstanding deceptive appearances
afterwards.   Venice was soon confronted on the sea
by a new rival.   The Turkish naval historian, Haji
Khalifeh,[1] tells us that, ' After the taking of Constantinople, when they [the Ottomans] spread their
conquests over land and sea, it became necessary to
build ships and make armaments in order to subdue
the fortresses and castles on the Rumelian and
Anatolian shores, and in the islands of the Mediterranean.'   Mohammed II established a great naval
arsenal at Constantinople.   In 1470 the Turks, ' for
the first time, equipped a fleet with which they drove
that of the Venetians out of the Grecian seas.'[2]   The
Turkish wars of Venice lasted a long time.   In that
which ended in 1503 the decline of the Venetians'
naval power was obvious.   ' The Mussulmans had
made progress in naval discipline ; the Venetian fleet

[1] *Maritime Wars of the Turks*, Mitchell's trans., p. 12.
[2] Sismondi, p. 256.

could no longer cope with theirs.' Henceforward it was as an allied contingent of other navies that that of Venice was regarded as important. Dyer[1] quotes a striking passage from a letter of Æneas Sylvius, afterwards Pope Pius II, in which the writer affirms that, if the Venetians are defeated, Christendom will not control the sea any longer ; for neither the Catalans nor the Genoese, without the Venetians, are equal to the Turks.

SEA-POWER IN THE SIXTEENTH AND SEVENTEENTH CENTURIES

The last-named people, indeed, exemplified once more the rule that a military state expanding to the sea and absorbing older maritime populations becomes a serious menace to its neighbours. Even in the fifteenth century Mohammed II had made an attack on Southern Italy ; but his sea-power was not equal to the undertaking. Suleymân the Magnificent directed the Ottoman forces towards the West. With admirable strategic insight he conquered Rhodes, and thus freed himself from the danger of a hostile force on his flank. ' The centenary of the conquest of Constantinople was past, and the Turk had developed a great naval power besides annexing Egypt and Syria.'[2] The Turkish fleets, under such leaders as Khair-ad-din (Barbarossa), Piale, and Dragut, seemed to command the Mediterranean including its western basin ; but the repulse

[1] *Hist. Europe*, i. p. 85.
[2] Seeley, *British Policy*, i. p. 143.

at Malta in 1565 was a serious check, and the defeat at Lepanto in 1571 virtually put an end to the prospect of Turkish maritime dominion. The predominance of Portugal in the Indian Ocean in the early part of the sixteenth century had seriously diminished the Ottoman resources. The wealth derived from the trade in that ocean, the Persian Gulf, and the Red Sea, had supplied the Mohammedans with the sinews of war, and had enabled them to contend with success against the Christians in Europe. 'The main artery had been cut when the Portuguese took up the challenge of the Mohammedan merchants of Calicut, and swept their ships from the ocean.' [1] The sea-power of Portugal wisely employed had exercised a great, though unperceived, influence. Though enfeebled and diminishing, the Turkish navy was still able to act with some effect in the seventeenth century. Nevertheless, the sea-power of the Turks ceased to count as a factor of importance in the relations between great states.

In the meantime the state which had a leading share in winning the victory of Lepanto had been growing up in the West. Before the union of its crown with that of Castile and the formation of the Spanish monarchy, Aragon had been expanding till it reached the sea. It was united with Catalonia in the twelfth century, and it conquered Valencia in the thirteenth. Its long line of coast opened the

---

[1] Whiteway, p. 2.

way to an extensive and flourishing commerce ; and
an enterprising navy indemnified the nation for the
scantiness of its territory at home by the important
foreign conquests of Sardinia, Sicily, Naples, and
the Balearic Isles. Amongst the maritime states of
the Mediterranean Catalonia had been conspicuous.
She was to the Iberian Peninsula much what
Phœnicia had been to Syria. The Catalan navy had
disputed the empire of the Mediterranean with the
fleets of Pisa and Genoa. The incorporation of
Catalonia with Aragon added greatly to the strength
of that kingdom. The Aragonese kings were wise
enough to understand and liberal enough to foster
the maritime interests of their new possessions.[1]
Their French and Italian neighbours were to feel,
before long, the effect of this policy ; and when the
Spanish monarchy had been consolidated, it was felt
not only by them, but by others also. The more
Spanish dominion was extended in Italy, the more
were the naval resources at the command of Spain
augmented. Genoa became ' Spain's water-gate
to Italy. . . . Henceforth the Spanish crown found
in the Dorias its admirals ; their squadron was
permanently hired to the kings of Spain.' Spanish
supremacy at sea was established at the expense of
France.[2] The acquisition of a vast domain in the
New World had greatly developed the maritime
activity of Castile, and Spain was as formidable
on the ocean as in the Mediterranean. After

[1] Prescott, *Ferdinand and Isabella*, Introd. sects. i. ii.
[2] G. W. Prothero, in M. Hume's *Spain*, 1479–1788, p. 65.

Portugal had been annexed the naval forces of that country were added to the Spanish, and the great port of Lisbon became available as a place of equipment and as an additional base of operations for oceanic campaigns. The fusion of Spain and Portugal, says Seeley, 'produced a single state of unlimited maritime dominion. . . . Henceforth the whole New World belonged exclusively to Spain.' The story of the tremendous catastrophe—the defeat of the Armada—by which the decline of this dominion was heralded is well known. It is memorable, not only because of the harm it did to Spain, but also because it revealed the rise of another claimant to maritime pre-eminence—the English nation. The effects of the catastrophe were not at once visible. Spain still continued to look like the greatest power in the world ; and, though the English seamen were seen to be something better than adventurous pirates—a character suggested by some of their recent exploits—few could have comprehended that they were engaged in building up what was to be a sea-power greater than any known to history.

They were carrying forward, not beginning the building of this. 'England,' says Sir J. K. Laughton, ' had always believed in her naval power, had always claimed the sovereignty of the Narrow Seas ; and more than two hundred years before Elizabeth came to the throne, Edward III had testified to his sense of its importance by ordering a gold coinage bearing a device showing the armed strength and sovereignty of England based on the sea.'[1] It is impossible to make intelligible the course of the many wars which the English waged with the French in the Middle Ages unless the true naval position of the former is rightly appreciated. Why were Crécy, Poitiers, Agincourt—not to mention other combats—fought, not on English, but on continental soil? Why during the so-called 'Hundred Years' War' was England in reality the invader and not the invaded? We of the present generation are at last aware of the significance of naval defence, and know that, if properly utilised, it is the best security against invasion that a sea-surrounded state can enjoy. It is not, however, commonly remembered that the same condition of security existed and was properly valued in mediæval times. The battle of Sluys in 1340 rendered invasion of England as impracticable as did that of La Hogue in 1692, that of Quiberon Bay in 1759, and that of Trafalgar in 1805; and it permitted, as did those battles, the transport of troops to the continent to support our allies in wars which, had we not been strong at sea, would have been waged on the soil of our own country. Our early continental wars, therefore, are proofs of the long-established efficiency of our naval defences. Notwithstanding the greater attention paid, within the last dozen years or so, to naval affairs, it is doubtful if the country generally even yet recognises the extent to which its security depends upon a good

[1] *Armada*, Introd. (Navy Records Society).

fleet as fully as our ancestors did nearly seven
centuries ago.   The narrative of our pre-Elizabethan
campaigns is interesting merely as a story ; and,
when told—as for instance D. Hannay has told it in
the introductory chapters of his 'Short History of
the Royal Navy'—it will be found instructive and
worthy of careful study at the present day.   Each
of the principal events in our early naval campaigns
may be taken as an illustration of the idea conveyed
by the term ' sea-power,' and of the accuracy with
which its meaning was apprehended at the time.
To take a very early case, we may cite the defeat of
Eustace the Monk by Hubert de Burgh in 1217.
Reinforcements and supplies had been collected at
Calais for conveyance to the army of Prince Louis
of France and the rebel barons who had been defeated
at Lincoln.   The reinforcements tried to cross the
Channel under the escort of a fleet commanded
by Eustace.   Hubert de Burgh, who had stoutly
held Dover for King John, and was faithful
to the young Henry III, heard of the enemy's
movements.   ' If these people land,' said he,
' England is lost ; let us therefore boldly meet
them.'   He reasoned in almost the same words as
Raleigh about four centuries afterwards, and
undoubtedly ' had grasped the true principles of
the defence of England.'   He put to sea and defeated
his opponent.   The fleet on which Prince Louis and
the rebellious barons had counted was destroyed ;
and with it their enterprise.   ' No more admirably
planned, no more fruitful battle has been fought by

Englishmen on water.'[1]   As introductory to a long series of naval operations undertaken with a like object, it has deserved detailed mention here.

The sixteenth century was marked by a decided advance in both the development and the application of sea-power. Previously its operation had been confined to the Mediterranean or to coast waters outside it. Spanish or Basque seamen— by their proceedings in the English Channel—had proved the practicability of, rather than been engaged in, ocean warfare. The English, who withstood them, were accustomed to seas so rough, to seasons so uncertain, and to weather so boisterous, that the ocean had few terrors for them. All that was wanting was a sufficient inducement to seek distant fields of action and a development of the naval art that would permit them to be reached. The discovery of the New World supplied the first; the consequently increased length of voyages and of absence from the coast led to the second. The world had been moving onwards in other things as well as in navigation. Intercommunication was becoming more and more frequent. What was done by one people was soon known to others. It is a mistake to suppose that, because the English had been behindhand in the exploration of remote regions, they were wanting in maritime enterprise. The career of the Cabots would of itself suffice to render such a supposition doubtful. The English had two good reasons for postponing voyages to and

[1] Hannay, p. 7.

D

settlement in far-off lands. They had their hands
full nearer home ; and they thoroughly, and as it
were by instinct, understood the conditions on which
permanent expansion must rest. They wanted to
make sure of the line of communication first. To
effect this a sea-going marine of both war and
commerce and, for further expansion, stations on
the way were essential. The chart of the world
furnishes evidence of the wisdom and the thorough-
ness of their procedure. Taught by the experience
of the Spaniards and the Portuguese, when un-
impeded by the political circumstances of the time,
and provided with suitable equipment, the English
displayed their energy in distant seas. It now
became simply a question of the efficiency of sea-
power. If this was not a quality of that of the
English, then their efforts were bound to fail ; and,
more than this, the position of their country,
challenging as it did what was believed to be the
greatest of maritime states, would have been
altogether precarious. The principal expeditions
now undertaken were distinguished by a characteristic peculiar to the people, and not to be
found in connection with the exploring or colonising
activity of most other great nations even down to
our own time. They were really unofficial speculations in which, if the Government took part at all,
it was for the sake of the profit expected and almost,
if not exactly, like any private adventurer. The
participation of the Government, nevertheless,
had an aspect which it is worth while to note. It

conveyed a hint—and quite consciously—to all whom it might concern that the speculations were ' under-written ' by the whole sea-power of England. The forces of more than one state had been used to protect its maritime trade from the assaults of enemies in the Mediterranean or in the Narrow Seas. They had been used to ward off invasion and to keep open communications across not very extensive areas of water. In the sixteenth century they were first relied upon to support distant commerce, whether carried on in a peaceful fashion or under aggressive forms. This, naturally enough, led to collisions. The contention waxed hot, and was virtually decided when the Armada shaped course to the northward after the fight off Gravelines.

The expeditions against the Spanish Indies and, still more, those against Philip II's peninsular territory, had helped to define the limitations of sea-power. It became evident, and it was made still more evident in the next century, that for a great country to be strong it must not rely upon a navy alone. It must also have an adequate and properly organised mobile army. Notwithstanding the number of times that this lesson has been repeated, we have been slow to learn it. It is doubtful if we have learned it even yet. English seamen in all ages seem to have mastered it fully ; for they have always demanded—at any rate for upwards of three centuries—that expeditions against foreign territory over-sea should be accompanied by a proper number of land-troops. On the other hand, the necessity of organising the army of a maritime insular state, and of training it with the object of rendering effective aid in operations of the kind in question, has rarely been perceived and acted upon by others. The result has been a long series of inglorious or disastrous affairs like the West Indies voyage of 1595–96, the Cadiz expedition of 1625, and that to the Ile de Ré of 1627. Additions might be made to the list. The failures of joint expeditions have often been explained by alleging differences or quarrels between the naval and the military commanders. This way of explaining them, however, is nothing but the inveterate critical method of the streets by which cause is taken for effect and effect for cause. The differences and quarrels arose, no doubt; but they generally sprang out of the recriminations consequent on, not producing, the want of success. Another manifestation of the way in which sea-power works was first observed in the seventeenth century. It suggested the adoption of, and furnished the instrument for, carrying out a distinct maritime policy. What was practically a standing navy had come into existence. As regards England this phenomenon was now of respectable age. Long voyages and cruises of several ships in company had been frequent during the latter half of the sixteenth century and the early part of the seventeenth. Even the grandfathers of the men who sailed with Blake and Penn in 1652 could not have known a time when ships had never crossed the ocean, and squadrons kept together for months had never cruised. However imperfect it may have been, a system of provisioning ships and supplying them with stores, and of preserving discipline amongst their crews, had been developed, and had proved fairly satisfactory. The Parliament and the Protector in turn found it necessary to keep a considerable number of ships in commission, and make them cruise and operate in company. It was not till well on in the reign of Queen Victoria that the man-of-war's man was finally differentiated from the merchant seaman ; but two centuries before some of the distinctive marks of the former had already begun to be noticeable. There were seamen in the time of the Commonwealth who rarely, perhaps some who never, served afloat except in a man-of-war. Some of the interesting naval families which were settled at Portsmouth and the eastern ports, and which—from father to son—helped to recruit the ranks of our bluejackets till a date later than that of the launch of the first ironclad, could carry back their professional genealogy to at least the days of Charles II, when, in all probability, it did not first start. Though landsmen continued even after the civil war to be given naval appointments, and though a permanent corps, through the ranks of which every one must pass, had not been formally established, a body of real naval officers—men who could handle their ships, supervise the working of the armament, and exercise military command—had been formed.

A navy, accordingly, was now a weapon of undoubted keenness, capable of very effective use by any one who knew how to wield it.   Having tasted the sweets of intercourse with the Indies, whether in the occupation of Portugal or of Spain, both English and Dutch were desirous of getting a larger share of them.   English maritime commerce had increased and needed naval protection.   If England was to maintain the international position to which, as no one denied, she was entitled, that commerce must be permitted to expand.   The minds of men in western Europe, moreover, were set upon obtaining for their country territories in the New World, the amenities of which were now known.   From the reign of James I the Dutch had shown great jealousy of English maritime enterprise.   Where it was possible, as in the East Indian Archipelago, they had destroyed it.   Their naval resources were great enough to let them hold English shipping at their mercy, unless a vigorous effort were made to protect it.   The Dutch conducted the carrying trade of a great part of the world, and the monopoly of this they were resolved to keep, while the English were resolved to share in it.   The exclusion of the English from every trade-route, except such as ran by their own coast or crossed the Narrow Seas, seemed a by no means impossible contingency.   There seemed also to be but one way of preventing it, viz. by war.   The supposed unfriendliness of the Dutch, or at least of an important party amongst them, to the regicide Government in England helped to force the conflict. The Navigation Act of 1651 was passed and regarded as a covert declaration of hostilities. So the first Dutch war began. It established our claim to compete for the position of a great maritime commercial power.

The rise of the sea-power of the Dutch, and the magnitude which it attained in a short time and in the most adverse circumstances, have no parallel in history. The case of Athens was different, because the Athenian power had not so much been unconsciously developed out of a great maritime trade, as based on a military marine deliberately and persistently fostered during many years. Thirlwall believes that it was Solon who ' laid the foundations of the Attic navy,' [1] a century before Salamis. The great achievement of Themistocles was to convince his fellow-citizens that their navy ought to be increased. Perhaps the nearest parallel with the power of the Dutch was presented by that of Rhodes, which rested largely on a carrying trade. The Rhodian undertakings, however, were by comparison small and restricted in extent. Motley declares of the Seven United Provinces that they ' commanded the ocean,' [2] and that it would be difficult to exaggerate the naval power of the young Commonwealth. Even in the days of Spain's greatness English seamen positively declined to admit that she was stronger than England on the sea ; and the story of the Armada justified their view. Our first two Dutch wars were, therefore,

[1] *Hist. Greece*, ii. p. 52.   [2] *United Netherlands*, ii. p. 132.

contests between the two foremost naval states of the world for what was primarily a maritime object. The identity of the cause of the first and of the second war will be discerned by any one who compares what has been said about the circumstances leading to the former, with Monk's remark as to the latter. He said that the English wanted a larger share of the trade enjoyed by the Dutch. It was quite in accordance with the spirit of the age that the Dutch should try to prevent, by force, this want from being satisfied. Anything like free and open competition was repugnant to the general feeling. The high road to both individual wealth and national prosperity was believed to lie in securing a monopoly. Merchants or manufacturers who called for the abolition of monopolies granted to particular courtiers and favourites had not the smallest intention, on gaining their object, of throwing open to the enterprise of all what had been monopolised. It was to be kept for the exclusive benefit of some privileged or chartered company. It was the same in greater affairs. As Mahan says, ' To secure to one's own people a disproportionate share of the benefits of sea commerce every effort was made to exclude others, either by the peaceful legislative methods of monopoly or prohibitory regulations, or, when these failed, by direct violence.' The apparent wealth of Spain was believed to be due to the rigorous manner in which foreigners were excluded from trading with the Spanish over-sea territories. The skill and enterprise of the Dutch having enabled them to force themselves into this trade, they were determined to keep it to themselves. The Dutch East India Company was a powerful body, and largely dictated the maritime policy of the country. We have thus come to an interesting point in the historical consideration of sea-power. The Elizabethan conflict with Spain had practically settled the question whether or not the expanding nations were to be allowed to extend their activities to territories in the New World. The first two Dutch wars were to settle the question whether or not the ocean trade of the world was to be open to any people qualified to engage in it. We can see how largely these were maritime questions, how much depended on the solution found for them, and how plain it was that they must be settled by naval means.

Mahan's great survey of sea-power opens in 1660, midway between the first and second Dutch wars. ' The sailing-ship era, with its distinctive features,' he tells us, ' had fairly begun.' The art of war by sea, in its more important details, had been settled by the first war. From the beginning of the second the general features of ship design, the classification of ships, the armament of ships, and the handling of fleets, were to remain without essential alteration until the date of Navarino. Even the tactical methods, except where improved on occasions by individual genius, altered little. The great thing was to bring the whole broadside force to bear on an enemy. Whether this was to be impartially distributed throughout the hostile line or concentrated on one part of it depended on the character of particular admirals. It would have been strange if a period so long and so rich in incidents had afforded no materials for forming a judgment on the real significance of sea-power. The text, so to speak, chosen by Mahan is that, notwithstanding the changes wrought in naval *matériel* during the last half-century, we can find in the history of the past instructive illustrations of the general principles of maritime war. These illustrations will prove of value not only ' in those wider operations which embrace a whole theatre of war,' but also, if rightly applied, ' in the tactical use of the ships and weapons ' of our own day. By a remarkable coincidence the same doctrine was being preached at the same time and quite independently by the late Vice-Admiral Philip Colomb in his work on ' Naval Warfare.' As a prelude to the second Dutch war we find a repetition of a process which had been adopted somewhat earlier. That was the permanent conquest of trans-oceanic territory. Until the seventeenth century had well begun, naval, or combined naval and military, operations against the distant possessions of an enemy had been practically restricted to raiding or plundering attacks on commercial centres. The Portuguese territory in South America having come under Spanish dominion in consequence of the annexation of Portugal to Spain, the Dutch—as the power of the latter country declined—attempted to reduce part of that territory into permanent possession. This improvement on the practice of Drake and others was soon seen to be a game at which more than one could play. An expedition sent by Cromwell to the West Indies seized the Spanish island of Jamaica, which has remained in the hands of its conquerors to this day. In 1664 an English force occupied the Dutch North American settlements on the Hudson. Though the dispossessed rulers were not quite in a position to throw stones at sinners, this was rather a raid than an operation of recognised warfare, because it preceded the formal outbreak of hostilities. The conquered territory remained in English hands for more than a century, and thus testified to the efficacy of a sea-power which Europe had scarcely begun to recognise. Neither the second nor the third Dutch war can be counted amongst the occurrences to which Englishmen may look back with unalloyed satisfaction ; but they, unquestionably, disclosed some interesting manifestations of sea-power. Much indignation has been expressed concerning the corruption and inefficiency of the English Government of the day, and its failure to take proper measures for keeping up the navy as it should have been kept up. Some, perhaps a good deal, of this indignation was deserved ; but it would have been nearly as well deserved by every other government of the day. Even in those homes of political virtue where the administrative machinery was worked by or in the interest of speculating capitalists and privileged companies, the accumulating evidence of late years has proved that everything was not considered to be, and as a matter of fact was not, exactly as it ought to have been. Charles II and his brother, the Duke of York, have been held up to obloquy because they thought that the coast of England could be defended against a naval enemy better by fortifications than by a good fleet and, as Pepys noted, were ' not ashamed of it.' The truth is that neither the king nor the duke believed in the power of a navy to ward off attack from an island. This may have been due to want of intellectual capacity ; but it would be going a long way to put it down to personal wickedness. They have had many imitators, some in our own day. The huge forts which stud the coast of the United Kingdom, and have been erected within the memory of the present generation, are monuments, likely to last for many years, of the inability of people, whom no one could accuse of being vicious, to rate sea-power at its proper value. It is much more likely that it was owing to a reluctance to study questions of naval defence as industriously as they deserved, and to that moral timidity which so often tempts even men of proved physical courage to undertake the impossible task of making themselves absolutely safe against hostile efforts at every point.

Charles II has also been charged with indifference to the interests of his country, or worse, because during a great naval war he adopted the plan of trying to weaken the enemy by destroying his commerce. The king ' took a fatal resolution of laying up his great ships and keeping only a few frigates on the cruise.' It is expressly related that this was not Charles's own idea, but that it was urged upon him by advisers whose opinion probably seemed at the time as well worth listening to as that of others. Anyhow, if the king erred, as he undoubtedly did, he erred in good company. Fourteen hundred years earlier the statesmen who conducted the great war against Carthage, and whose astuteness has been the theme of innumerable panegyrics since, took the same 'fatal resolution.' In the midst of the great struggle they ' did away with the fleet. At the most they encouraged privateering; and with that view placed the war-vessels of the State at the disposal of captains who were ready to undertake a corsair warfare on their own account.' [1] In much later times this method has had many and respectable defenders. Mahan's works are, in a sense, a formal warning to his fellow-citizens not to adopt it. In France, within the last years of the nineteenth century, it found, and appears still to find, adherents enough to form a school. The reappearance of belief in demonstrated impossibilities is a recognised incident in human history ; but it is usually confined to the emotional or the vulgar. It is serious and filled with menaces of disaster when it is held by men thought fit to administer the affairs of a nation or advise concerning its defence. The third Dutch war may not have settled directly the position of England in the maritime world ; but

[1] Mommsen, ii. p. 52.

it helped to place that country above all other maritime states,—in the position, in fact, which Great Britain, the United Kingdom, the British Empire, whichever name may be given it, has retained up to the present. It also manifested in a very striking form the efficacy of sea-power. The United Provinces, though attacked by two of the greatest monarchies in the world, France and England, were not destroyed. Indeed, they preserved much of their political importance in the State system of Europe. The Republic ' owed this astonishing result partly to the skill of one or two men, but mainly to its sea-power.' The effort, however, had undermined its strength and helped forward its decline.

The war which was ended by the Peace of Ryswick in 1697 presents two features of exceptional interest : one was the havoc wrought on English commerce by the enemy ; the other was Torrington's conduct at and after the engagement off Beachy Head. Mahan discusses the former with his usual lucidity. At no time has war against commerce been conducted on a larger scale and with greater results than during this period. We suffered ' infinitely more than in any former war.' Many of our merchants were ruined ; and it is affirmed that the English shipping was reduced to the necessity of sailing under the Swedish and Danish flags. The explanation is that Louis XIV made great efforts to keep up powerful fleets. Our navy was so fully occupied in watching these that no ships could be spared to protect our maritime trade. This is only another way of saying that our commerce had increased so largely that the navy was not strong enough to look after it as well as oppose the enemy's main force. Notwithstanding our losses we were on the winning side in the conflict. Much misery and ruin had been caused, but not enough to affect the issue of the war.

Torrington's proceedings in July 1690 were at the time the subject of much angry debate. The debate, still meriting the epithet angry, has been renewed within the last few years. The matter has to be noticed here, because it involves the consideration of a question of naval strategy which must be understood by those who wish to know the real meaning of the term sea-power, and who ought to learn that it is not a thing to be idly risked or thrown away at the bidding of the ignorant and the irresponsible. Arthur Herbert, Earl of Torrington— the later peerage is a viscounty held by the Byng family—was in command of the allied English and Dutch fleet in the Channel. ' The disparity of force,' says Mahan, ' was still in favour of France in 1690, but it was not so great as the year before.' We can measure the ability of the then English Government for conducting a great war, when we know that, in its wisdom, it had still further weakened our fleet by dividing it (Vice-Admiral Killigrew having been sent to the Mediterranean with a squadron), and had neglected, and indeed refused when urged, to take the necessary steps to repair this error. The

Government having omitted, as even British Governments sometimes do, to gain any trustworthy intelligence of the strength or movements of the enemy, Torrington suddenly found himself confronted by a considerably superior French fleet under Tourville, one of the greatest of French sea-officers. Of late years the intentions of the French have been questioned ; but it is beyond dispute that in England at the time Tourville's movements were believed to be preliminary to invasion. Whether Tourville deliberately meant his movement to cover an invasion or not, invasion would almost certainly have followed complete success on his part ; otherwise his victory would have been without any valuable result. Torrington saw that as long as he could keep his own fleet intact, he could, though much weaker than his opponent, prevent him from doing serious harm. Though personally not a believer in the imminence of invasion, the English admiral knew that ' most men were in fear that the French would invade.' His own view was, ' that whilst we had a fleet in being they would not dare to make an attempt.' Of late years controversy has raged round this phrase, ' a fleet in being,' and the strategic principle which it expresses. Most seamen were at the time, have been since, and still are in agreement with Torrington. This might be supposed enough to settle the question. It has not been allowed, however, to remain one of purely naval strategy. It was made at the time a matter of party politics. This is why it is so necessary that

in a notice of sea-power it should be discussed.
Both as a strategist and as a tactician Torrington
was immeasurably ahead of his contemporaries.
The only English admirals who can be placed above
him are Hawke and Nelson. He paid the penalty
of his pre-eminence : he could not make ignorant
men and dull men see the meaning or the advantages
of his proceedings. Mahan, who is specially qualified
to do him full justice, does not devote much space
in his work to a consideration of Torrington's
case, evidently because he had no sufficient materials
before him on which to form a judgment. The
admiral's character had been taken away already
by Macaulay, who did have ample evidence before
him. William III, with all his fine qualities, did
not possess a military genius quite equal to that of
Napoleon ; and Napoleon, in naval strategy, was
often wrong. William III understood that subject
even less than the French emperor did ; and his
favourites were still less capable of understanding it.
Consequently Torrington's action has been put down
to jealousy of the Dutch. There have been people
who accused Nelson of being jealous of the naval
reputation of Caracciolo ! The explanation of
Torrington's conduct is this :—He had a fleet so
much weaker than Tourville's that he could not fight
a general action with the latter without a practical
certainty of getting a crushing defeat. Such a result
would have laid the kingdom open : a defeat of the
allied fleet, says Mahan, ' if sufficiently severe, might
involve the fall of William's throne in England.'

E

Given certain movements of the French fleet, Torrington might have manœuvred to slip past it to the westward and join his force with that under Killigrew, which would make him strong enough to hazard a battle. This proved impracticable. There was then one course left. To retire before the French, but not to keep far from them. He knew that, though not strong enough to engage their whole otherwise unemployed fleet with any hope of success, he would be quite strong enough to fight and most likely beat it, when a part of it was trying either to deal with our ships to the westward or to cover the disembarkation of an invading army. He, therefore, proposed to keep his fleet ' in being ' in order to fall on the enemy when the latter would have two affairs at the same time on his hands. The late Vice-Admiral Colomb rose to a greater height than was usual even with him in his criticism of this campaign. What Torrington did was merely to reproduce on the sea what has been noticed dozens of times on shore, viz. the menace by the flanking enemy. In land warfare this is held to give exceptional opportunities for the display of good generalship, but, to quote Mahan over again, a navy ' acts on an element strange to most writers, its members have been from time immemorial a strange race apart, without prophets of their own, neither themselves nor their calling understood.' Whilst Torrington has had the support of seamen, his opponents have been landsmen. For the crime of being a good strategist he was brought before a court-martial, but acquitted. His sovereign, who had been given the crowns of three kingdoms to defend our laws, showed his respect for them by flouting a legally constituted tribunal and disregarding its solemn finding. The admiral who had saved his country was forced into retirement. Still, the principle of the ' fleet in being ' lies at the bottom of all sound strategy.

Admiral Colomb has pointed out a great change of plan in the later naval campaigns of the seventeenth century. Improvements in naval architecture, in the methods of preserving food, and in the arrangements for keeping the crews healthy, permitted fleets to be employed at a distance from their home ports for long continuous periods. The Dutch, when allies of the Spaniards, kept a fleet in the Mediterranean for many months. The great De Ruyter was mortally wounded in one of the battles there fought. In the war of the Spanish Succession the Anglo-Dutch fleet found its principal scene of action eastward of Gibraltar. This, as it were, set the fashion for future wars. It became a kind of tacitly accepted rule that the operation of British sea-power was to be felt in the enemy's rather than in our own waters. The hostile coast was regarded strategically as the British frontier, and the sea was looked upon as territory which the enemy must be prevented from invading. Acceptance of this principle led in time to the so-called ' blockades ' of Brest and Toulon. The name was misleading. As Nelson took care to explain, there was no desire

to keep the enemy's fleet in ; what was desired was
to be near enough to attack it if it came out.   The
wisdom of the plan is undoubted.   The hostile navy
could be more easily watched and more easily
followed if it put to sea.   To carry out this plan
a navy stronger in number of ships or in general
efficiency than that of the enemy was necessary to us.
With the exception of that of American Independence, which will therefore require special notice, our
subsequent great wars were conducted in accordance
with the rule.

Sea-power in the Eighteenth Century and Early Part of the Nineteenth Century

In the early part of the eighteenth century there
was a remarkable manifestation of sea-power in the
Baltic.   Peter the Great, having created an efficient
army, drove the Swedes from the coast provinces
south of the Gulf of Finland.   Like the earlier monarchies of which we have spoken, Russia, in the
Baltic at least, now became a naval state.   A
large fleet was built, and, indeed, a considerable
navy established.   It was a purely artificial creation,
and showed the merits and defects of its character.
At first, and when under the eye of its creator,
it was strong ; when Peter was no more it dwindled
away and, when needed again, had to be created
afresh.   It enabled Peter the Great to conquer the
neighbouring portion of Finland, to secure his coast
territories, and to dominate the Baltic.   In this he

was assisted by the exhaustion of Sweden consequent on her endeavours to retain, what was no longer possible, the position of a *quasi* great power which she had held since the days of Gustavus Adolphus. Sweden had been further weakened, especially as a naval state, by almost incessant wars with Denmark, which prevented all hope of Scandinavian pre-dominance in the Baltic, the control of which sea has in our own days passed into the hands of another state possessing a quickly created navy—the modern German empire.

The war of the Spanish Succession left Great Britain a Mediterranean power, a position which, in spite of twice losing Minorca, she still holds. In the war of the Austrian Succession, ' France was forced to give up her conquests for want of a navy, and England saved her position by her sea-power, though she had failed to use it to the best advantage.'[1] This shows, as we shall find that a later war showed more plainly, that even the Government of a thoroughly maritime country is not always sure of conducting its naval affairs wisely. The Seven Years' war included some brilliant displays of the efficacy of sea-power. It was this which put the British in possession of Canada, decided which European race was to rule in India, and led to a British occupation of Havannah in one hemisphere and of Manila in the other. In the same war we learned how, by a feeble use of sea-power, a valuable possession like Minorca may be lost. At the same

[1] Mahan, *Inf. on Hist.* p. 280.

time our maritime trade and the general prosperity
of the kingdom increased enormously.   The result
of the conflict made plain to all the paramount
importance of having in the principal posts in the
Government men capable of understanding what
war is and how it ought to be conducted.

This lesson, as the sequel demonstrated, had not
been learned when Great Britain became involved
in a war with the insurgent colonies in North
America.   Mahan's comment is striking : ' The
magnificence of sea-power and its value had perhaps
been more clearly shown by the uncontrolled sway
and consequent exaltation of one belligerent ; but
the lesson thus given, if more striking, is less
vividly interesting than the spectacle of that
sea-power meeting a foe worthy of its steel, and
excited to exertion by a strife which endangered
not only its most valuable colonies, but even its
own shores.' [1]   We were, in fact, drawing too largely
on the *prestige* acquired during the Seven Years'
war ; and we were governed by men who did not
understand the first principles of naval warfare,
and would not listen to those who did.   They quite
ignored the teaching of the then comparatively recent
wars which has been alluded to already—that we
should look upon the enemy's coast as our frontier.
A century and a half earlier the Dutchman Grotius
had written—

> Quæ meta Britannis
> Litora sunt aliis.

[1] *Influence on Hist.* p. 338.

Though ordinary prudence would have suggested ample preparation, British ministers allowed their country to remain unprepared. Instead of concentrating their efforts on the main objective, they frittered away force in attempts to relieve two beleaguered garrisons under the pretext of yielding to popular pressure, which is the official term for acting on the advice of irresponsible and uninstructed busybodies. ' Depuis le début de la crise,' says Captain Chevalier, ' les ministres de la Grande Bretagne s'étaient montrés inférieurs à leur tâche.' An impressive result of this was the repeated appearance of powerful and indeed numerically superior hostile fleets in the English Channel. The war—notwithstanding that, perhaps because, land operations constituted an important part of it, and in the end settled the issue—was essentially oceanic. Captain Mahan says it was ' purely maritime.' It may be true that, whatever the belligerent result, the political result, as regards the *status* of the insurgent colonies, would have been the same. It is in the highest degree probable, indeed it closely approaches to certainty, that a proper use of the British sea-power would have prevented independence from being conquered, as it were, at the point of the bayonet. There can be no surprise in store for the student acquainted with the vagaries of strategists who are influenced in war by political in preference to military requirements. Still, it is difficult to repress an emotion of astonishment on finding that a British Government intentionally permitted De Grasse's fleet and the French army in its convoy to cross the Atlantic unmolested, for fear of postponing for a time the revictualling of the garrison beleaguered at Gibraltar. Washington's opinion as to the importance of the naval factor has been quoted already; and Mahan does not put the case too strongly when he declares that the success of the Americans was due to 'sea-power being in the hands of the French and its improper distribution by the English authorities.' Our navy, misdirected as it was, made a good fight of it, never allowed itself to be decisively beaten in a considerable battle, and won at least one great victory. At the point of contact with the enemy, however, it was not in general so conspicuously successful as it was in the Seven Years' war, or as it was to be in the great conflict with the French republic and empire. The truth is that its opponent, the French navy, was never so thoroughly a sea-going force as it was in the war of American Independence; and never so closely approached our own in real sea-experience as it did during that period. We met antagonists who were very nearly, but, fortunately for us, not quite as familiar with the sea as we were ourselves; and we never found it so hard to beat them, or even to avoid being beaten by them. An Englishman would, naturally enough, start at the conclusion confronting him, if he were to speculate as to the result of more than one battle had the great Suffren's captains and crews been quite up to the level of those commanded by stout old Sir Edward Hughes.

Suffren, it should be said, before going to the East
Indies, had ' thirty-eight years of almost uninterrupted sea-service.'[1] A glance at a chart of the
world, with the scenes of the general actions of the
war dotted on it, will show how notably oceanic
the campaigns were. The hostile fleets met over
and over again on the far side of the Atlantic and
in distant Indian seas. The French navy had
penetrated into the ocean as readily and as far as
we could do ourselves. Besides this, it should be
remembered that it was not until the 12th April 1782,
when Rodney in one hemisphere and Suffren in the
other showed them the way, that our officers were able
to escape from the fetters imposed on them by the
Fighting Instructions,—a fact worth remembering
in days in which it is sometimes proposed, by
establishing schools of naval tactics on shore, to
revive the pedantry which made a decisive success
in battle nearly impossible.

The mighty conflict which raged between Great
Britain on one side and France and her allies on
the other, with little intermission, for more than
twenty years, presents a different aspect from that
of the war last mentioned. The victories which the
British fleet was to gain were generally to be overwhelming ; if not, they were looked upon as almost
defeats. Whether the fleet opposed to ours was,
or was not, the more numerous, the result was
generally the same—our enemy was beaten. That
there was a reason for this which can be discovered

[1] Laughton, *Studies in Naval Hist.* p. 103.

is certain. A great deal has been made of the disorganisation in the French navy consequent on the confusion of the Revolution. That there was disorganisation is undoubted; that it did impair discipline and, consequently, general efficiency will not be disputed; but that it was considerable enough to account by itself for the French naval defeats is altogether inadmissible. Revolutionary disorder had invaded the land-forces to a greater degree than it had invaded the sea-forces. The supersession, flight, or guillotining of army officers had been beyond measure more frequent than was the case with the naval officers. In spite of all this the French armies were on the whole—even in the early days of the Revolution—extraordinarily successful. In 1792 'the most formidable invasion that ever threatened France,' as Alison calls it, was repelled, though the invaders were the highly disciplined and veteran armies of Prussia and Austria. It was nearly two years later that the French and English fleets came into serious conflict. The first great battle, which we call 'The Glorious First of June,' though a tactical victory for us, was a strategical defeat. Villaret-Joyeuse manœuvred so as to cover the arrival in France of a fleet of merchant vessels carrying sorely needed supplies of food, and in this he was completely successful. His plan involved the probability, almost the necessity, of fighting a general action which he was not at all sure of winning. He was beaten, it is true; but the French made so good a fight of it that their defeat was not nearly

so disastrous as the later defeats of the Nile or
Trafalgar, and—at the most—not more disastrous
than that of Dominica. Yet no one even alleges
that there was disorder or disorganisation in the
French fleet at the date of any one of those affairs.
Indeed, if the French navy was really disorganised
in 1794, it would have been better for France—
judging from the events of 1798 and 1805—if the
disorganisation had been allowed to continue. In
point of organisation the British Navy was inferior,
and in point of discipline not much superior to the
French at the earliest date; at the later dates,
and especially at the latest, owing to the all-pervading energy of Napoleon, the British was far behind
its rival in organisation, in ' science,' and in every
branch of training that can be imparted without
going to sea. We had the immense advantage
of counting amongst our officers some very able
men. Nelson, of course, stands so high that he
holds a place entirely by himself. The other British
chiefs, good as they were, were not conspicuously
superior to the Hawkes and Rodneys of an earlier
day. Howe was a great commander, but he did
little more than just appear on the scene in the war.
Almost the same may be said of Hood, of whom
Nelson wrote, ' He is the greatest sea-officer I ever
knew.'[1] There must have been something, therefore,
beyond the meritorious qualities of our principal
officers which helped us so consistently to victory.
The many triumphs won could not have been due

[1] Laughton, *Nelson's Lett. and Desp.* p. 71.

in every case to the individual superiority of the British admiral or captain to his opponent. There must have been bad as well as good amongst the hundreds on our lists ; and we cannot suppose that Providence had so arranged it that in every action in which a British officer of inferior ability commanded a still inferior French commander was opposed to him. The explanation of our nearly unbroken success is, that the British was a thoroughly sea-going navy, and became more and more so every month ; whilst the French, since the close of the American war, had lost to a great extent its sea-going character and, because we shut it up in its ports, became less and less sea-going as hostilities continued. The war had been for us, in the words of Mr. Theodore Roosevelt, ' a continuous course of victory won mainly by seamanship.' Our navy, as regards sea-experience, especially of the officers, was immensely superior to the French. This enabled the British Government to carry into execution sound strategic plans, in accordance with which the coasts of France and its dependent or allied countries were regarded as the English frontier to be watched or patrolled by our fleets.

Before the long European war had been brought to a formal ending we received some rude rebuffs from another opponent of unsuspected vigour. In the quarrel with the United States, the so-called ' War of 1812,' the great sea-power of the British in the end asserted its influence, and our antagonists suffered much more severely, even absolutely, than

ourselves. At the same time we might have learned,
for the Americans did their best to teach us, that
over-confidence in numerical strength and narrow
professional self-satisfaction are nearly sure to lead
to reverses in war, and not unlikely to end in grave
disasters. We had now to meet the *élite* of one
of the finest communities of seamen ever known.
Even in 1776 the Americans had a great maritime
commerce, which, as Mahan informs us, ' had come
to be the wonder of the statesmen of the mother
country.' In the six-and-thirty years which had
elapsed since then this commerce had further
increased. There was no finer nursery of seamen
than the then states of the American Union.
Roosevelt says that ' there was no better seaman
in the world ' than the American, who ' had been
bred to his work from infancy.' A large proportion
of the population ' was engaged in sea-going pursuits
of a nature strongly tending to develop a resolute
and hardy character in the men that followed them.' [1]
Having little or no naval protection, the American
seaman had to defend himself in many circumstances,
and was compelled to familiarise himself with the use
of arms. The men who passed through this practical,
and therefore supremely excellent, training school
were numerous. Very many had been trained in
English men-of-war, and some in French ships.
The state navy which they were called on to man was
small ; and therefore its *personnel*, though without
any regular or avowed selection, was virtually and

[1] *Naval War of* 1812, 3rd ed. pp. 29, 30.

in the highest sense a picked body. The lesson of the war of 1812 should be learned by Englishmen of the present day, when a long naval peace has generated a confidence in numerical superiority, in the mere possession of heavier *matériel*, and in the merits of a rigidly uniform system of training, which confidence, as experience has shown, is too often the forerunner of misfortune.   It is neither patriotic nor intelligent to minimise the American successes. Certainly they have been exaggerated by Americans and even by ourselves. To take the frigate actions alone, as being those which properly attracted most attention, we see that the captures in action amounted to three on each side, the proportionate loss to our opponents, considering the smallness of their fleet, being immensely greater than ours. We also see that no British frigate was taken after the first seven months of a war which lasted two and a half years, and that no British frigate succumbed except to admittedly superior force. Attempts have been made to spread a belief that our reverses were due to nothing but the greater size and heavier guns of our enemy's ships. It is now established that the superiority in these details, which the Americans certainly enjoyed, was not great, and not of itself enough to account for their victories. Of course, if superiority in mere *matériel*, beyond a certain well-understood amount, is possessed by one of two combatants, his antagonist can hardly escape defeat ; but it was never alleged that size of ship or calibre of guns—greater within reasonable limits than we had—necessarily led to the defeat of British ships by the French or Spaniards. In the words of Admiral Jurien de la Gravière, 'The ships of the United States constantly fought with the chances in their favour.' All this is indisputable. Nevertheless we ought to see to it that in any future war our sea-power, great as it may be, does not receive shocks like those that it unquestionably did receive in 1812.

Sea-power in Recent Times

We have now come to the end of the days of the naval wars of old time. The subsequent period has been illustrated repeatedly by manifestations of sea-power, often of great interest and importance, though rarely understood or even discerned by the nations which they more particularly concerned. The British sea-power, notwithstanding the first year of the war of 1812, had come out of the great European conflict unshaken and indeed more pre-eminent than ever. The words used, half a century before by a writer in the great French 'Encyclopédie,' seemed more exact than when first written. ' L'empire des mers,' he says, is, ' le plus avantageux de tous les empires ; les Phœniciens le possédoient autre fois et c'est aux Anglois que cette gloire appartient aujourd'hui sur toutes les puissances maritimes.'[1] Vast out-lying territories had been acquired or were more firmly held, and the

[1] *Encyclopédie*, 7th Jan. 1765, art. ' Thalassarchie.'

communications of all the over-sea dominions of the British Crown were secured against all possibility of serious menace for many years to come. Our sea-power was so ubiquitous and all-pervading that, like the atmosphere, we rarely thought of it and rarely remembered its necessity or its existence. It was not till recently that the greater part of the nation— for there were many, and still are some exceptions —perceived that it was the medium apart from which the British Empire could no more live than it could have grown up. Forty years after the fall of Napoleon we found ourselves again at war with a great power. We had as our ally the owner of the greatest navy in the world except our own. Our foe, as regards his naval forces, came the next in order. Yet so overwhelming was the strength of Great Britain and France on the sea that Russia never attempted to employ her navy against them. Not to mention other expeditions, considerable enough in themselves, military operations on the largest scale were undertaken, carried on for many months, and brought to a successful termination on a scene so remote that it was two thousand miles from the country of one, and three thousand from that of the other partner in the alliance. ' The stream of supplies and reinforcements, which in terms of modern war is called " communications," ' was kept free from even the threat of molestation, not by visible measures, but by the undisputed efficacy of a real, though imperceptible sea-power. At the close of the Russian war we encountered, and

unhappily for us in influential positions, men who,
undismayed by the consequences of mimicking in
free England the cast-iron methods of the Great
Frederick, began to measure British requirements
by standards borrowed from abroad and altogether
inapplicable to British conditions. Because other
countries wisely abstained from relying on that
which they did not possess, or had only imperfectly
and with elaborate art created, the mistress of the
seas was led to proclaim her disbelief in the very
force that had made and kept her dominion, and
urged to defend herself with fortifications by
advisers who, like Charles II and the Duke of York
two centuries before, were not ashamed of it.' It
was long before the peril into which this brought the
empire was perceived ; but at last, and in no small
degree owing to the teachings of Mahan, the people
themselves took the matter in hand and insisted that
a great maritime empire should have adequate
means of defending all that made its existence
possible.

In forms differing in appearance, but identical
in essentials, the efficacy of sea-power was proved
again in the American Secession war. If ever there
were hostilities in which, to the unobservant or short-
sighted, naval operations might at first glance seem
destined to count for little, they were these. The
sequel, however, made it clear that they constituted
one of the leading factors of the success of the
victorious side. The belligerents, the Northern or
Federal States and the Southern or Confederate

F

States, had a common land frontier of great length.
The capital of each section was within easy distance
of this frontier, and the two were not far apart.   In
wealth, population, and resources the Federals were
enormously superior.   They alone possessed a navy,
though at first it was a small one.   The one advantage on the Confederate side was the large proportion
of military officers which belonged to it and their
fine training as soldiers.   In *physique* as well as in
morale the army of one side differed little from
that of the other ; perhaps the Federal army was
slightly superior in the first, and the Confederate,
as being recruited from a dominant white race, in
the second.   Outnumbered, less well equipped, and
more scantily supplied, the Confederates nevertheless
kept up the war, with many brilliant successes on
land, for four years.   Had they been able to maintain their trade with neutral states they could have
carried on the war longer, and—not improbably—
have succeeded in the end.   The Federal navy,
which was largely increased, took away all chance
of this.   It established effective blockades of the
Confederate ports, and severed their communications
with the outside world.   Indispensable articles of
equipment could not be obtained, and the armies,
consequently, became less and less able to cope
with their abundantly furnished antagonists.   By
dominating the rivers the Federals cut the Con-
federacy asunder ; and by the power they possessed
of moving troops by sea at will, perplexed and
harassed the defence, and facilitated the occupation

of important points. Meanwhile the Confederates could make no reply on the water except by capturing merchant vessels, by which the contest was embittered, but the course of the war remained absolutely unaffected. The great numbers of men under arms on shore, the terrific slaughter in many battles of a war in which tactical ability, even in a moderate degree, was notably uncommon on both sides, and the varying fortunes of the belligerents, made the land campaigns far more interesting to the ordinary observer than the naval. It is not surprising, therefore, that peace had been re-established for several years before the American people could be made to see the great part taken by the navy in the restoration of the Union ; and what the Americans had not seen was hidden from the sight of other nations.

In several great wars in Europe waged since France and England made peace with Russia sea-power manifested itself but little. In the Russo-Turkish war the great naval superiority of the Turks in the Black Sea, where the Russians at the time had no fleet, governed the plans, if not the course, of the campaigns. The water being denied to them, the Russians were compelled to execute their plan of invading Turkey by land. An advance to the Bosphorus through the northern part of Asia Minor was impracticable without help from a navy on the right flank. Consequently the only route was a land one across the Danube and the Balkans. The advantages, though not fully utilised, which the enforcement of this line of advance put into the hands of the Turks, and the difficulties and losses which it caused the Russians, exhibited in a striking manner what sea-power can effect even when its operation is scarcely observable.

This was more conspicuous in a later series of hostilities. The civil war in Chili between Congressists and Balmacedists is specially interesting, because it throws into sharp relief the predominant influence, when a non-maritime enemy is to be attacked, of a navy followed up by an adequate land-force. At the beginning of the dispute the Balmacedists, or President's party, had practically all the army, and the Congressists, or Opposition party, nearly all the Chilian navy. Unable to remain in the principal province of the republic, and expelled from the waters of Valparaiso by the Balmacedist garrisons of the forts—the only and doubtful service which those works rendered to their own side—the Congressists went off with the ships to the northern provinces, where they counted many adherents. There they formed an army, and having money at command, and open sea communications, they were able to import equipment from abroad, and eventually to transport their land-force, secured from molestation on the voyage by the sea-power at their disposal, to the neighbourhood of Valparaiso, where it was landed and triumphantly ended the campaign.

It will have been noticed that, in its main outlines, this story repeated that of many earlier campaigns.

It was itself repeated, as regards its general features, by the story of the war between China and Japan in 1894-95. 'Every aspect of the war,' says Colomb, 'is interesting to this country, as Japan is to China in a position similar to that which the British Islands occupy to the European continent.'[1] It was additionally interesting because the sea-power of Japan was a novelty. Though a novelty, it was well known by English naval men to be superior in all essentials to that of China, a novelty itself. As is the rule when two belligerents are contending for something beyond a purely maritime object, the final decision was to be on land. Korea was the principal theatre of the land war; and, as far as access to it by sea was concerned, the chief bases of the two sides were about the same distance from it. It was possible for the Chinese to march there by land. The Japanese, coming from an island state, were obliged to cross the water. It will be seen at once that not only the success of the Japanese in the struggle, but also the possibility of its being carried on by them at all, depended on sea-power. The Japanese proved themselves decisively superior at sea. Their navy effectually cleared the way for one army which was landed in Korea, and for another which was landed in the Chinese province of Shantung. The Chinese land-forces were defeated. The navy of Japan, being superior on the sea, was able to keep its sister service supplied or reinforced as required. It was, however, not the navy, but

[1] *Naval Warfare*, 3rd ed. p. 436.

the army, which finally frustrated the Chinese efforts at defence, and really terminated the war. What the navy did was what, in accordance with the limitations of sea-power, may be expected of a navy. It made the transport of the army across the sea possible ; and enabled it to do what of itself the army could not have done, viz. overcome the last resistance of the enemy.

The issue of the Spanish-American war, at least as regards the mere defeat of Spain, was, perhaps, a foregone conclusion. That Spain, even without a serious insurrection on her hands, was unequal to the task of meeting so powerful an antagonist as the United States must have been evident even to Spaniards. Be that as it may, an early collapse of the Spanish defence was not anticipated, and however one-sided the war may have been seen to be, it furnished examples illustrating rules as old as naval warfare. Mahan says of it that, ' while possessing, as every war does, characteristics of its own differentiating it from others, nevertheless in its broad analogies it falls into line with its predecessors, evidencing that unity of teaching which pervades the art from its beginnings unto this day.'[1] The Spaniards were defeated by the superiority of the American sea-power. ' A million of the best soldiers,' says Mahan, ' would have been powerless in face of hostile control of the sea.' That control was obtained and kept by the United States navy, thus permitting the unobstructed

[1] *Lessons of the War with Spain*, p. 16.

despatch of troops—and their subsequent reinforcement and supply—to Spanish territory, which was
finally conquered, not by the navy, but by the army
on shore. That it was the navy which made this
final conquest possible happened, in this case, to be
made specially evident by the action of the United
States Government, which stopped a military
expedition on the point of starting for Cuba until
the sea was cleared of all Spanish naval force worth
attention.

The events of the long period which we have been
considering will have shown how sea-power operates,
and what it effects. What is in it will have appeared
from this narrative more clearly than would have
been possible from any mere definition. Like many
other things, sea-power is composed of several
elements. To reach the highest degree of efficacy
it should be based upon a population naturally
maritime, and on an ocean commerce naturally
developed rather than artificially enticed to extend
itself. Its outward and visible sign is a navy, strong
in the discipline, skill, and courage of a numerous
personnel habituated to the sea, in the number and
quality of its ships, in the excellence of its *matériel*,
and in the efficiency, scale, security, and geographical
position of its arsenals and bases. History has
demonstrated that sea-power thus conditioned can
gain any purely maritime object, can protect the
trade and the communications of a widely extended
empire, and whilst so doing can ward off from its
shores a formidable invader. There are, however,

limitations to be noted. Left to itself its operation is confined to the water, or at any rate to the inner edge of a narrow zone of coast. It prepares the way for the advance of an army, the work of which it is not intended, and is unable to perform. Behind it, in the territory of which it guards the shores, there must be a land-force adjusted in organisation, equipment, and numbers to the circumstances of the country. The possession of a navy does not permit a sea-surrounded state to dispense with all fixed defences or fortification; but it does render it unnecessary and indeed absurd that they should be abundant or gigantic. The danger which always impends over the sea-power of any country is that, after being long unused, it may lose touch of the sea. The revolution in the constructive arts during the last half-century, which has also been a period of but little-interrupted naval peace, and the universal adoption of mechanical appliances, both for ship-propulsion and for many minor services— mere *matériel* being thereby raised in the general estimation far above really more important matters —makes the danger mentioned more menacing in the present age than it has ever been before.

II

THE COMMAND OF THE SEA[1]

THIS phrase, a technical term of naval warfare, indicates a definite strategical condition. The term has been substituted occasionally, but less frequently of late years, for the much older ' Dominion of the sea ' or ' Sovereignty of the sea,' a legal term expressing a claim, if not a right. It has also been sometimes treated as though it were identical with the rhetorical expression ' Empire of the sea.' Mahan, instead of it, uses the term ' Control of the sea,' which has the merit of precision, and is not likely to be misunderstood or mixed up with a form of words meaning something different. The expression ' Command of the sea,' however, in its proper and strategic sense, is so firmly fixed in the language that it would be a hopeless task to try to expel it ; and as, no doubt, writers will continue to use it, it must be explained and illustrated. Not only does it differ in meaning from ' Dominion or Sovereignty of the sea,' it is not even truly derived therefrom, as can be briefly shown. ' It has become an uncontested principle of modern international law that the sea,

---

[1] Written in 1899. (*Encyclopædia Britannica.*)

73

as a general rule, cannot be subjected to appro-
priation.'[1]   This, however, is quite modern.   We
ourselves did not admit the principle till 1805 ;
the Russians did not admit it till 1824 ; and the
Americans, and then only tacitly, not till 1894.
Most European nations at some time or other have
claimed and have exercised rights over some part
of the sea, though far outside the now well-recog-
nised 'three miles' limit.'   Venice claimed the
Adriatic, and exacted a heavy toll from vessels
navigating its northern waters.   Genoa and France
each claimed portions of the western Mediterranean.
Denmark and Sweden claimed to share the Baltic
between them.   Spain claimed dominion over the
Pacific and the Gulf of Mexico, and Portugal over
the Indian Ocean and all the Atlantic south of
Morocco.[2]   The claim which has made the greatest
noise in the world is that once maintained by the
kings of England to the seas surrounding the British
Isles.   Like other institutions, the English sovereignty of the sea was, and was admitted to be,
beneficent for a long period.   Then came the time
when it ought to have been abandoned as obsolete ;
but it was not, and so it led to war.   The general
conviction of the maritime nations was that the Lord
of the Sea would provide for the police of the waters
over which he exercised dominion.   In rude ages
when men, like the ancients, readily ' turned them-

---

[1] W. E. Hall, *Treatise on International Law*, 4th ed. 1895,
p. 146.
[2] Hall, pp. 148, 149.

selves to piracy,' this was of immense importance to trade ; and, far from the right of dominion being disputed by foreigners, it was insisted upon by them and declared to carry with it certain duties. In 1299, not only English merchants, but also ' the maritime people of Genoa, Catalonia, Spain, Germany, Zealand, Holland, Frisia, Denmark, Norway, and several other places of the empire ' declared that the kings of England had from time immemorial been in ' peaceable possession of the sovereign lordship of the sea of England,' and had done what was ' needful for the maintenance of peace, right, and equity between people of all sorts, whether subjects of another kingdom or not, who pass through those seas.' [1] The English sovereignty was not exercised as giving authority to exact toll. All that was demanded in return for keeping the sea safe for peaceful traffic was a salute, enforced no doubt as a formal admission of the right which permitted the (on the whole, at any rate) effective police of the waters to be maintained. The Dutch in the seventeenth century objected to the demand for this salute. It was insisted upon. War ensued ; but in the end the Dutch acknowledged by solemn treaties their obligation to render the salute. The time for exacting it, however, was really past. S. R. Gardiner [2] maintains that though the ' question of the flag ' was the occasion, it was not the cause of the war. There was

[1] J. K. Laughton, ' Sovereignty of the Sea,' *Fortnightly Review*, August 1866.
[2] *The First Dutch War* (Navy Records Society), 1899.

not much, if any, piracy in the English Channel which the King of England was specially called upon to suppress, and if there had been the merchant vessels of the age were generally able to defend themselves, while if they were not their governments possessed force enough to give them the necessary protection. We gave up our claim to exact the salute in 1805.

The necessity of the foregoing short account of the ' Sovereignty or Dominion of the Seas ' will be apparent as soon as we come to the consideration of the first struggle, or rather series of struggles, for the command of the sea. Gaining this was the result of our wars with the Dutch in the seventeenth century. At the time of the first Dutch war, 1652-54, and probably of the later wars also, a great many people, and especially seamen, believed that the conflict was due to a determination on our part to retain, and on that of the Dutch to put an end to, the English sovereignty or dominion. The obstinacy of the Dutch in objecting to pay the old-established mark of respect to the English flag was quite reason enough in the eyes of most Englishmen, and probably of most Dutchmen also, to justify hostilities which other reasons may have rendered inevitable. The remarkable thing about the Dutch wars is that in reality what we gained was the possibility of securing an absolute command of the sea. We came out of the struggle a great, and in a fair way of becoming the greatest, naval power. It is this which prompted Vice-Admiral P. H. Colomb to hold that there are various kinds of command, such as 'absolute or assured,' 'temporary,' 'with definite ulterior purpose,' &c. An explanation that would make all these terms intelligible would be voluminous and is unnecessary here. It will be enough to say that the absolute command—of attempts to gain which, as Colomb tells us, the Anglo-Dutch wars were the most complete example—is nothing but an attribute of the nation whose power on the sea is paramount. It exists and may be visible in time of peace. The command which, as said above, expresses a definite strategical condition is existent only in time of war. It can easily be seen that the former is essential to an empire like the British, the parts of which are bound together by maritime communications. Inability to keep these communications open can have only one result, viz. the loss of the parts with which communication cannot be maintained. Experience of war as well as reason will have made it evident that inability to keep open sea-communications cannot be limited to any single line, because the inability must be due either to incapacity in the direction of hostilities or insufficiency of force. If we have not force enough to keep open all the communications of our widely extended empire, or if—having force enough—we are too foolish to employ it properly, we do not hold the command of the sea, and the empire must fall if seriously attacked.

The strategic command of the sea in a particular war or campaign has equal concern for all maritime belligerents. Before seeing what it is, it will be well to learn on high authority what it is not. Mahan says that command, or, to use his own term, ' control of the sea, however real, does not imply that an enemy's single ships or small squadrons cannot steal out of port, cannot cross more or less frequented tracts of ocean, make harassing descents upon unprotected points of a long coast-line, enter blockaded harbours. On the contrary, history has shown that such evasions are always possible, to some extent, to the weaker party, however great the inequality of naval strength.'[1] The Anglo-French command of the sea in 1854–56, complete as it was, did not enable the allies to intercept the Russian ships in the North-Western Pacific, nor did that held by the Federals in the American civil war put an early stop to the cruises of the Confederate vessels. What the term really does imply is the power possessed from the first, or gained during hostilities, by one belligerent of carrying out considerable over-sea expeditions at will. In the Russian war just mentioned the allies had such overwhelmingly superior sea-power that the Russians abandoned to them without a struggle the command of the sea ; and the more recent landing in South Africa, more than six thousand miles away, of a large British army without even a threat of interruption on the voyage is another instance of unchallenged command. In wars between great powers and also between secondary powers, if nearly equally matched, this absence of challenge is rare. The rule is that the command of the sea has to be won

[1] *Influence of Sea-power on History*, 1890, p. 14.

after hostilities begin.   To win it the enemy's naval force must be neutralised.   It must be driven into his ports and there blockaded or ' masked,' and thus rendered virtually innocuous ; or it must be defeated and destroyed.   The latter is the preferable, because the more effective, plan.   As was perceptible in the Spanish-American war of 1898, as long as one belligerent's fleet is intact or at large, the other is reluctant to carry out any considerable expedition over-sea. In fact, the command of the sea has not been secured whilst the enemy continues to have a ' fleet in being.' [1]

In 1782 a greatly superior Franco-Spanish fleet was covering the siege of Gibraltar.   Had this fleet succeeded in preventing the revictualling of the fortress the garrison would have been starved into surrender.   A British fleet under Lord Howe, though much weaker in numbers, had not been defeated and was still at large.   Howe, in spite of the odds against him, managed to get his supply-ships in to the anchorage and to fight a partial action, in which he did the allies as much damage as he received.   There has never been a display of higher tactical skill than this operation of Howe's, though, it may be said, he owes his fame much more to his less meritorious performance on the first of June.   The revictualling of Gibraltar surpassed even Suffren's feat of the capture of Trincomalee in the same year.   In 1798 the French, assuming that a temporary superiority in the Mediterranean had given them a free hand on the water, sent a great expedition to Egypt.   Though

[1] See *ante*, Sea-Power, p. 50.

the army which was carried succeeded in landing there, the covering fleet was destroyed by Nelson at the Nile, and the army itself was eventually forced to surrender. The French had not perceived that, except for a short time and for minor operations, you cannot separate the command of the Mediterranean or of any particular area of water from that of the sea in general. Local command of the sea may enable a belligerent to make a hasty raid, seize a relatively insignificant port, or cut out a vessel ; but it will not ensure his being able to effect anything requiring considerable time for its execution, or, in other words, anything likely to have an important influence on the course of the war. If Great Britain has not naval force enough to retain command of the Mediterranean, she will certainly not have force enough to retain command of the English Channel. It can be easily shown why it should be so. In war danger comes less from conditions of locality than from the enemy's power to hurt. Taking up a weak position when confronting an enemy may help him in the exercise of his power, but it does not constitute it.[1] A maritime enemy's power to hurt resides in his fleet. If that can be neutralised his power disappears. It is in the highest degree improbable that this end can be attained by splitting up our own fleet into

---

[1] In his *History of Scotland* (1873), J. H. M. Burton, speaking of the Orkney and Shetland Isles in the Viking times, says (vol. i. p. 320) : ' Those who occupied them were protected, not so much by their own strength of position, as by the complete command over the North Sea held by the fleets that found shelter in the fiords and firths.'

fragments so as to have a part of it in nearly every quarter in which the enemy may try to do us mischief. The most promising plan—as experience has often proved—is to meet the enemy, when he shows himself, with a force sufficiently strong to defeat him. The proper station of the British fleet in war should, accordingly, be the nearest possible point to the enemy's force. This was the fundamental principle of Nelson's strategy, and it is as valid now as ever it was. If we succeed in getting into close proximity to the hostile fleet with an adequate force of our own, our foe cannot obtain command of the sea, or of any part of it, whether that part be the Mediterranean or the English Channel, at any rate until he has defeated us. If he is strong enough to defeat our fleet he obtains the command of the sea in general ; and it is for him to decide whether he shall show the effectiveness of that command in the Mediterranean or in the Channel.

In the smaller operations of war temporary command of a particular area of water may suffice for the success of an expedition, or at least will permit the execution of the preliminary movements. When the main fleet of a country is at a distance— which it ought not to be except with the object of nearing the opposing fleet—a small hostile expedition may slip across, say the Channel, throw shells into a coast town or burn a fishing village, and get home again unmolested. Its action would have no sort of influence on the course of the campaign, and would, therefore, be useless. It would also most likely

G

lead to reprisals ; and, if this process were repeated, the war would probably degenerate into the anti-quated system of ' cross-raiding,' discarded centuries ago, not at all for reasons of humanity, but because it became certain that war could be more effectually waged in other ways. The nation in command of the sea may resort to raiding to expedite the formal submission of an already defeated enemy, as Russia did when at war with Sweden in 1719 ; but in such a case the other side cannot retaliate. Temporary command of local waters will also permit of operations rather more considerable than mere raiding attacks ; but the duration of these operations must be adjusted to the time available. If the duration of the temporary command is insufficient the operation must fail. It must fail even if the earlier steps have been taken successfully. Temporary command of the Baltic in war might enable a German force to occupy an Åland isle ; but unless the temporary could be converted into permanent command, Germany could make no use of the acquisition, which in the end would revert as a matter of course to its former possessors. The command of the English Channel, which Napoleon wished to obtain when maturing his invasion project, was only temporary. It is possible that a reminiscence of what had happened in Egypt caused him to falter at the last ; and that, quite independently of the proceedings of Villeneuve, he hesitated to risk a second battle of the Nile and the loss of a second army. It may have been this which justified his later statement that he did not really mean to invade England. In any case, the English practice of fixing the station of their fleet wherever that of the enemy's was, would have seriously shortened the duration of his command of the Channel, even if it had allowed it to be won at all. Moreover, attempts to carry out a great operation of war against time as well as against the efforts of the enemy to prevent it are in the highest degree perilous.

In war the British Navy has three prominent duties to discharge. It has to protect our maritime trade, to keep open the communications between the different parts of the empire, and to prevent invasion. If we command the sea these duties will be discharged effectually. As long as we command the sea the career of hostile cruisers sent to prey on our commerce will be precarious, because command of the sea carries with it the necessity of possessing an ample cruiser force. As long as the condition mentioned is satisfied our ocean communications will be kept open, because an inferior enemy, who cannot obtain the command required, will be too much occupied in seeing to his own safety to be able to interfere seriously with that of any part of our empire. This being so, it is evident that the greater operation of invasion cannot be attempted, much less carried to a successful termination, by the side which cannot make head against the opposing fleet. Command of the sea is the indispensable preliminary condition of a successful military expedition sent across the water. It enables the nation which possesses it to attack its foes where it pleases and where they seem to be most vulnerable. At the same time it gives to its possessor security against serious counter-attacks, and affords to his maritime commerce the most efficient protection that can be devised. It is, in fact, the main object of naval warfare.

III

WAR AND ITS CHIEF LESSONS [1]

HAD the expression ' real war ' been introduced into
the title of this chapter, its introduction would have
been justifiable. The sources—if not of our knowledge of combat, at least of the views which are
sure to prevail when we come to actual fighting—
are to be found in two well-defined, dissimilar, and
widely separated areas. Within one are included
the records of war ; within the other, remembrance
of the exercises and manœuvres of a time of peace.
The future belligerent will almost of a certainty
have taken a practical part in the latter, whilst it
is probable that he will have had no personal
experience of the former. The longer the time
elapsed since hostilities were in progress, the more
probable and more general does this absence of
experience become. The fighting man—that is
to say, the man set apart, paid, and trained so as
to be ready to fight when called upon—is of the
same nature as the rest of his species. This is a
truism ; but it is necessary to insist upon it, because
professional, and especially professorial, strategists

---

and tacticians almost invariably ignore it. That which we have seen and know has not only more, but very much more, influence upon the minds of nearly all of us than that of which we have only heard, and, most likely, heard but imperfectly. The result is that, when peace is interrupted and the fighting man—on both sea and land—is confronted with the problems of practical belligerency, he brings to his attempts at their solution an intellectual equipment drawn, not from knowledge of real war, but from the less trustworthy arsenal of the recollections of his peace training.

When peace, especially a long peace, ends, the methods which it has introduced are the first enemies which the organised defenders of a country have to overcome. There is plenty of evidence to prove that—except, of course, in unequal conflicts between highly organised, civilised states and savage or semi-barbarian tribes—success in war is directly proportionate to the extent of the preliminary victory over the predominance of impressions derived from the habits and exercises of an armed force during peace. That the cogency of this evidence is not invariably recognised is to be attributed to insufficient attention to history and to disinclination to apply its lessons properly. A primary object of the *Naval Annual* —indeed, the chief reason for its publication—being to assist in advancing the efficiency of the British Navy, its pages are eminently the place for a review of the historical examples of the often-recurring inability of systems established in peace to stand the test of war. Hostilities on land being more frequent, and much more frequently written about, than those by sea, the history of the former as well as of the latter must be examined. The two classes of warfare have much in common. The principles of their strategy are identical ; and, as regards some of their main features, so are those of the tactics followed in each. Consequently the history of land warfare has its lessons for those who desire to achieve success in warfare on the sea.

That this has often been lost sight of is largely due to a misapprehension of the meaning of terms. The two words ' military ' and ' army ' have been given, in English, a narrower signification than they ought, and than they used, to have. Both terms have been gradually restricted in their use, and made to apply only to the land service. This has been unfortunate ; because records of occurrences and discussions, capable of imparting much valuable instruction to naval officers, have been passed over by them as inapplicable to their own calling. It may have been noticed that Captain Mahan uses the word ' military ' in its right sense as indicating the members, and the most important class of operations, of both land- and sea-forces. The French, through whom the word has come to us from the Latin, use it in the same sense as Mahan. *Un militaire* is a member of either a land army or a navy. The ' Naval *and* Military Intelligence ' of the English press is given under the heading ' Nouvelles Militaires ' in the French. Our word ' army ' also came to us direct from the French, who still apply it equally to both services—*armée de terre, armée de mer*. It is a participle, and means ' armed,' the word ' force ' being understood. The kindred words *armada* in Spanish and Portuguese, and *armata* in Italian—equally derived from the Latin—are used to indicate a fleet or navy, another name being given to a land army. The word ' army ' was generally applied to a fleet in former days by the English, as will be seen on reference to the Navy Records Society's volumes on the defeat of the Spanish Armada.

This short etymological discussion is not inappropriate here, for it shows why we should not neglect authorities on the history and conduct of war merely because they do not state specially that they are dealing with the naval branch of it.

A very slight knowledge of history is quite enough to make us acquainted with the frequent recurrence of defeats and disasters inflicted on armed forces by antagonists whose power to do so had not been previously suspected. It has been the same on the sea as on the land, though—owing to more copious records—we may have a larger list of events on the latter. It will not be denied that it is of immense importance to us to inquire how this happened, and ascertain how—for the future—it may be rendered highly improbable in our own case. A brief enumeration of the more striking instances will make it plain that the events in question have been confined to no particular age and to no particular country.

It may be said that the more elaborately
organised and trained in peace time an armed force
happened to be, the more unexpected always, and
generally the more disastrous, was its downfall.
Examples of this are to be found in the earliest
campaigns of which we have anything like detailed
accounts, and they continue to reappear down to
very recent times. In the elaborate nature of its
organisation and training there probably never has
been an army surpassing that led by Xerxes into
Greece twenty-four centuries ago. Something like
eight years had been devoted to its preparation.
The minute account of its review by Xerxes on
the shores of the Hellespont proves that, however
inefficient the semi-civilised contingents accompany-
ing it may have been, the regular Persian army
appeared, in discipline, equipment, and drill, to
have come up to the highest standard of the most
intense 'pipeclay' epoch. In numbers alone its
superiority was considerable to the last, and down
to the very eve of Platæa its commander openly
displayed his contempt for his enemy. Yet no
defeat could be more complete than that suffered
by the Persians at the hands of their despised
antagonists.

As if to establish beyond dispute the identity of
governing conditions in both land and maritime wars,
the next very conspicuous disappointment of an
elaborately organised force was that of the Athenian
fleet at Syracuse. At the time Athens, without
question, stood at the head of the naval world : her

empire was in the truest sense the product of sea-power. Her navy, whilst unequalled in size, might claim, without excessive exaggeration, to be invincible. The great armament which the Athenians despatched to Sicily seemed, in numbers alone, capable of triumphing over all resistance. If the Athenian navy had already met with some explicable mishaps, it looked back with complacent confidence on the glorious achievements of more than half a century previously. It had enjoyed many years of what was so nearly a maritime peace that its principal exploits had been the subjection of states weak to insignificance on the sea as compared with imperial Athens. Profuse expenditure on its maintenance ; the ' continued practice ' of which Pericles boasted, the peace manœuvres of a remote past ; skilfully designed equipment ; and the memory of past glories ;—all these did not avail to save it from defeat at the hands of an enemy who only began to organise a fleet when the Athenians had invaded his coast waters.

Ideal perfection as a regular army has never been so nearly reached as by that of Sparta. The Spartan spent his life in the barrack and the mess-room ; his amusements were the exercises of the parade ground. For many generations a Spartan force had never been defeated in a pitched battle. We have had, in modern times, some instances of a hectoring soldiery arrogantly prancing amongst populations whose official defenders it had defeated in battle ; but none such could vie with the Spartans in the sublimity of their military self-esteem. Over-weening confidence in the prowess of her army led Sparta to trample with ruthless disdain on the rights of others. The iniquitous attack on Thebes, a state thought incapable of effectual resentment, was avenged by the defeat of Leuctra, which announced the end of the political supremacy and the military predominance of Sparta.

In the series of struggles with Carthage which resulted in putting Rome in a position enabling her eventually to win the dominion of the ancient world, the issue was to be decided on the water. Carthage was essentially a maritime state. The foundation of the city was effected by a maritime expedition ; its dominions lay on the neighbouring coast or in regions to which the Carthaginians could penetrate only by traversing the sea. To Carthage her fleet was ' all in all ' : her navy, supported by large revenues and continuously maintained, was more of a ' regular ' force than any modern navy before the second half of the seventeenth century. The Romans were almost without a fleet, and when they formed one the undertaking was ridiculed by the Carthaginians with an unconcealed assumption of superiority. The defeat of the latter off Mylæ, the first of several, came as a great surprise to them, and, as we can see now, indicated the eventual ruin of their city.

We are so familiar with stories of the luxury and corruption of the Romans during the decline of the empire that we are likely to forget that the decline went on for centuries, and that their armed forces, however recruited, presented over and over again abundant signs of physical courage and vigour. The victory of Stilicho over Alaric at Pollentia has been aptly paralleled with that of Marius over the Cimbri. This was by no means the only achievement of the Roman army of the decadence. A century and a quarter later—when the Empire of the West had fallen and the general decline had made further progress—Belisarius conducted successful campaigns in Persia, in North Africa, in Sicily, and in Italy. The mere list of countries shows that the mobility and endurance of the Roman forces during a period in which little creditable is generally looked for were not inferior to their discipline and courage. Yet they met with disastrous defeat after all, and at the hands of races which they had more than once proved themselves capable of withstanding. It could not have been because the later Roman equipment was inferior, the organisation less elaborate, or the training less careful than those of their barbarian enemies.

Though it is held by some in these days that the naval power of Spain in the latter part of the sixteenth century was not really formidable, that does not appear to have been the opinion of contemporaries, whether Spaniards or otherwise. Some English seamen of the time did, indeed, declare their conviction that Philip the Second's navy was not so much to be feared as many of their fellow-countrymen thought ; but, in the public opinion of the age,

Spain was the greatest, or indeed the one great, naval state. She possessed a more systematically organised navy than any other country having the ocean for a field of action had then, or till long afterwards. Even Genoa and Venice, whose operations, moreover, were restricted to Mediterranean waters, could not have been served by more finished specimens of the naval officer and the man-of-war's man of the time than a large proportion of the military *personnel* of the regular Spanish fleet. As Basques, Castilians, Catalans, or Aragonese, or all combined, the crews of Spanish fighting ships could look back upon a glorious past. It was no wonder that, by common consent of those who manned it, the title of ' Invincible ' was informally conferred upon the Armada which, in 1588, sailed for the English Channel. How it fared is a matter of common knowledge. No one could have been more surprised at the result than the gallant officers who led its squadrons.

Spain furnishes another instance of the unexpected overthrow of a military body to which long cohesion and precise organisation were believed to have secured invincibility. The Spanish was considered the ' most redoubtable infantry in Europe ' till its unexpected defeat at Rocroi. The effects of this defeat were far-reaching. Notwithstanding the bravery of her sons, which has never been open to question, and, in fact, has always been conspicuous, the military superiority of Spain was broken beyond repair.

In the history of other countries are to be found examples equally instructive. The defeats of Almansa, Brihuega, and Villaviciosa were nearly contemporary with the victories of Blenheim and Ramillies ; and the thousands of British troops compelled to lay down their arms at the first named belonged to the same service as their fellow-countrymen who so often marched to victory under Marlborough. A striking example of the disappointment which lies in wait for military self-satisfaction was furnished by the defeat of Soubise at Rossbach by Frederick the Great. Before the action the French had ostentatiously shown their contempt for their opponent.

The service which gloried in the exploits of Anson and of Hawke discerned the approach of the Seven Years' war without misgiving ; and the ferocity shown in the treatment of Byng enables us now to measure the surprise caused by the result of the action off Minorca. There were further surprises in store for the English Navy. At the end of the Seven Years' war its reputation for invincibility was generally established. Few, perhaps none, ventured to doubt that, if there were anything like equality between the opposing forces, a meeting between the French and the British fleets could have but one result—viz. the decisive victory of the latter. Experience in the English Channel, on the other side of the Atlantic, and in the Bay of Bengal—during the war of American Independence—roughly upset this flattering anticipation. Yet, in the end, the

British Navy came out the unquestioned victor in the struggle : which proves the excellence of its quality. After every allowance is made for the incapacity of the Government, we must suspect that there was something else which so often frustrated the efforts of such a formidable force as the British Navy of the day must essentially have been. On land the surprises were even more mortifying ; and it is no exaggeration to say that, a year before it occurred, such an event as the surrender of Burgoyne's army to an imperfectly organised and trained body of provincials would have seemed impossible.

The army which Frederick the Great bequeathed to Prussia was universally regarded as the model of efficiency. Its methods were copied in other countries, and foreign officers desiring to excel in their profession made pilgrimages to Berlin and Potsdam to drink of the stream of military knowledge at its source. When it came in contact with the tumultuous array of revolutionary France, the performances of the force that preserved the tradition of the great Frederick were disappointingly wanting in brilliancy. A few years later it suffered an overwhelming disaster. The Prussian defeat at Jena was serious as a military event ; its political effects were of the utmost importance. Yet many who were involved in that disaster took, later on, an effective part in the expulsion of the conquerors from their country, and in settling the history of Europe for nearly half a century at Waterloo.

The brilliancy of the exploits of Wellington and the British army in Portugal and Spain has thrown into comparative obscurity that part of the Peninsular war which was waged for years by the French against the Spaniards. Spain, distracted by palace intrigues and political faction, with the flower of her troops in a distant corner of Europe, and several of her most important fortresses in the hands of her assailant, seemed destined to fall an easy and a speedy prey to the foremost military power in the world. The attitude of the invaders made it evident that they believed themselves to be marching to certain victory. Even the British soldiers—of whom there were never many more than 50,000 in the Peninsula, and for some years not half that number— were disdained until they had been encountered. The French arms met with disappointment after disappointment. On one occasion a whole French army, over 18,000 strong, surrendered to a Spanish force, and became prisoners of war. Before the struggle closed there were six marshals of France with nearly 400,000 troops in the Peninsula. The great efforts which these figures indicate were unsuccessful, and the intruders were driven from the country. Yet they were the comrades of the victors of Austerlitz, of Jena, and of Wagram, and part of that mighty organisation which had planted its victorious standards in Berlin and Vienna, held down Prussia like a conquered province, and shattered into fragments the holy Roman Empire.

In 1812 the British Navy was at the zenith of its

glory. It had not only defeated all its opponents ; it had also swept the seas of the fleets of the historic maritime powers—of Spain, of France, which had absorbed the Italian maritime states, of the Netherlands, of Denmark. Warfare, nearly continuous for eighteen, and uninterrupted for nine years, had transformed the British Navy into an organisation more nearly resembling a permanently maintained force than it had been throughout its previous history. Its long employment in serious hostilities had saved it from some of the failings which the narrow spirit inherent in a close profession is only too sure to foster. It had, however, a confidence—not unjustified by its previous exploits —in its own invincibility. This confidence did not diminish, and was not less ostentatiously exhibited, as its great achievements receded more and more into the past. The new enemy who now appeared on the farther side of the Atlantic was not considered formidable. In the British Navy there were 145,000 men. In the United States Navy the number of officers, seamen, and marines available for ocean service was less than 4500—an insignificant numerical addition to the enemies with whom we were already contending. The subsequent and rapid increase in the American *personnel* to 18,000 shows the small extent to which it could be considered a ' regular ' force, its permanent nucleus being overwhelmingly outnumbered by the hastily enrolled additions. Our defeats in the war of 1812 have been greatly exaggerated ; but, all the same, they did constitute rebuffs to our naval self-esteem which were highly significant in themselves, and deserve deep attention. Rebuffs of the kind were not confined to the sea service, and at New Orleans our army, which numbered in its ranks soldiers of Busaco, Fuentes de Onoro, and Salamanca, met with a serious defeat.

When the Austro-Prussian war broke out in 1866, the Austrian commander-in-chief, General Benedek, published an order, probably still in the remembrance of many, which officially declared the contempt for the enemy felt in the Imperial army. Even those who perceived that the Prussian forces were not fit subjects of contempt counted with confidence on the victory of the Austrians. Yet the latter never gained a considerable success in their combats with the Prussians ; and within a few weeks from the beginning of hostilities the general who had assumed such a lofty tone of superiority in speaking of his foes had to implore his sovereign to make peace to avoid further disasters.

At the beginning of the Franco-German war of 1870, the widespread anticipation of French victories was clearly shown by the unanimity with which the journalists of various nationalities illustrated their papers with maps giving the country between the French frontier and Berlin, and omitting the part of France extending to Paris. In less than five weeks from the opening of hostilities events had made it certain that a map of the country to the eastward of Lorraine would be practically useless to a student of the campaign, unless it were to follow the route of the hundreds of thousands of French soldiers who were conveyed to Germany as prisoners of war.

It is to be specially noted that in the above enumeration only contests in which the result was unexpected—unexpected not only by the beaten side but also by impartial observers—have been specified. In all wars one side or the other is defeated ; and it has not been attempted to give a general *résumé* of the history of war. The object has been to show the frequency—in all ages and in all circumstances of systematic, as distinguished from savage, warfare —of the defeat of the force which by general consent was regarded as certain to win. Now it is obvious that a result so frequently reappearing must have a distinct cause, which is well worth trying to find out. Discovery of the cause may enable us to remove it in the future, and thus prevent results which are likely to be all the more disastrous because they have not been foreseen.

Professional military writers — an expression which, as before explained, includes naval—do not help us much in the prosecution of the search which is so eminently desirable. As a rule, they have contrived rather to hide than to bring to light the object sought for. It would be doing them injustice to assume that this has been done with deliberate intention. It is much more likely due to pro-fessional bias, which exercises over the minds of members of definitely limited professions incessant

and potent domination. When alluding to occurrences included in the enumeration given above,
they exhibit signs of a resolve to defend their profession against possible imputations of inefficiency,
much more than a desire to get to the root of the
matter. This explains the unremitting eagerness
of military writers to extol the special qualities
developed by long-continued service habits and
methods. They are always apprehensive of the
possibility of credit being given to fighting bodies
more loosely organised and less precisely trained
in peace time than the body to which they themselves belong.

This sensitiveness as to the merits of their
particular profession, and impatience of even indirect criticism, are unnecessary. There is nothing
in the history of war to show that an untrained force
is better than a trained force. On the contrary,
all historical evidence is on the other side. In quite
as many instances as are presented by the opposite,
the forces which put an unexpected end to the
military supremacy long possessed by their antagonists were themselves, in the strictest sense of the
word, ' regulars.' The Thebans whom Epaminondas
led to victory over the Spartans at Leuctra no more
resembled a hasty levy of armed peasants or men
imperfectly trained as soldiers than did Napoleon's
army which overthrew the Prussians at Jena, or
the Germans who defeated the French at Gravelotte
and Sedan. Nothing could have been less like an
' irregular ' force than the fleet with which La

Galissonnière beat Byng off Minorca, or the French
fleets which, in the war of American Independence,
so often disappointed the hopes of the British.
The records of war on land and by sea—especially the
extracts from them included in the enumeration
already given—lend no support to the silly suggestion that efficient defence can be provided for a
country by ' an untrained man with a rifle behind
a hedge.' The truth is that it was not the absence of
organisation or training on one side which enabled
it to defeat the other. If the beaten side had been
elaborately organised and carefully trained, there
must have been something bad in its organisation
or its methods.

Now this ' something bad,' this defect—wherever
it has disclosed itself—has been enough to neutralise
the most splendid courage and the most unselfish
devotion. It has been seen that armies and navies
the valour of which has never been questioned have
been defeated by antagonists sometimes as highly
organised as they were, and sometimes much less
so. This ought to put us on the track of the cause
which has produced an effect so little anticipated.
A ' regular ' permanently embodied or maintained
service of fighting men is always likely to develop
a spirit of intense professional self-satisfaction. The
more highly organised it is, and the more sharply
its official frontiers are defined, the more intense is
this spirit likely to become. A ' close ' service of
the kind grows restive at outside criticism, and yields
more and more to the conviction that no advance

in efficiency is possible unless it be the result of suggestions emanating from its own ranks.   Its view of
things becomes narrower and narrower, whereas
efficiency in war demands the very widest view.
Ignorant critics call the spirit thus engendered ' professional conservatism ' ; the fact being that change is
not objected to—is even welcomed, however frequent
it may be, provided only that it is suggested from
inside.   An immediate result is ' unreality and
formalism of peace training '—to quote a recent
thoughtful military critic.

As the formalism becomes more pronounced, so
the unreality increases.   The proposer or introducer
of a system of organisation of training or of exercises
is often, perhaps usually, capable of distinguishing
between the true and the false, the real and the
unreal.   His successors, the men who continue the
execution of his plans, can hardly bring to their work
the open mind possessed by the originator ; they
cannot escape from the influence of the methods
which have been provided for them ready made, and
which they are incessantly engaged in practising.
This is not a peculiarity of the military profession
in either branch—it extends to nearly every calling ;
but in the profession specified, which is a service
rather than a freely exercised profession, it is more
prominent.   Human thought always has a tendency
to run in grooves, and in military institutions the
grooves are purposely made deep, and departure
from them rigorously forbidden.   All exercises,
even those designed to have the widest scope, tend

to become mere drill.   Each performance produces,
and bequeaths for use on the next occasion, a set of
customary methods of execution which are readily
adopted by the subsequent performers.   There grows
up in time a kind of body of customary law governing
the execution of peace operations—the principles
being peace-operation principles wholly and solely—
which law few dare to disobey, and which eventually
obtains the sanction of official written regulations.
As Scharnhorst, quoted by Baron von der Goltz,
said, ' We have begun to place the art of war higher
than military virtues.'   The eminent authority who
thus expressed himself wrote the words before the
great catastrophe of Jena ; and, with prophetic
insight sharpened by his fear of the menacing
tendency of peace-training formalism and unreality,
added his conviction that ' this has been the ruin of
nations from time immemorial.'

Independently of the evidence of history already
adduced, it would be reasonable to conclude that
the tendency is strengthened and made more menacing when the service in which it prevails becomes
more highly specialised.   If custom and regulation
leave little freedom of action to the individual
members of an armed force, the difficulty—sure to
be experienced by them—of shaking themselves
clear of their fetters when the need for doing so
arises is increased.   To realise—when peace is
broken—the practical conditions of war demands
an effort of which the unfettered intelligence alone
seems capable.   The great majority of successful

leaders in war on both elements have not been considerably, or at all, superior in intellectual acuteness to numbers of their fellows ; but they have had strength of character, and their minds were not squeezed in a mould into a commonplace and uniform pattern.

The ' canker of a long peace,' during recent years at any rate, is not manifested in disuse of arms, but in mistaken methods. For a quarter of a century the civilised world has tended more and more to become a drill-ground, but the spirit dominating it has been that of the pedant. There has been more exercise and less reality. The training, especially of officers, becomes increasingly scholastic. This, and the deterioration consequent on it, are not merely modern phenomena. They appear in all ages. ' The Sword of the Saracens,' says Gibbon, ' became less formidable when their youth was drawn from the camp to the college.' The essence of pedantry is want of originality. It is nourished on imitation. For the pedant to imitate is enough of itself ; to him the suitability of the model is immaterial. Thus military bodies have been ruined by mimicry of foreign arrangements quite inapplicable to the conditions of the mimics' country. More than twenty years ago Sir Henry Maine, speaking of the war of American Independence, said, ' Next to their stubborn valour, the chief secret of the colonists' success was the incapacity of the English generals, trained in the stiff Prussian system soon to perish at Jena, to adapt themselves to new conditions of warfare.' He pointed out that the effect of this uncritical imitation of what was foreign was again experienced by men ' full of admiration of a newer German system.' We may not be able to explain what it is, but, all the same, there does exist something which we call national characteristics. The aim of all training should be to utilise these to the full, not to ignore them. The naval methods of a continental state with relatively small oceanic interests, or with but a brief experience of securing these, cannot be very applicable to a great maritime state whose chief interests have been on the seas for many years.

How is all this applicable to the ultimate efficiency of the British Navy ? It may be allowed that there is a good deal of truth in what has been written above ; but it may be said that considerations sententiously presented cannot claim to have much practical value so long as they are absolute and unapplied. The statement cannot be disputed. It is unquestionably necessary to make the application. The changes in naval *matériel*, so often spoken of, introduced within the last fifty years have been rivalled by the changes in the composition of the British Navy. The human element remains in original individual character exactly the same as it always was ; but there has been a great change in the opportunities and facilities offered for the development of the faculties most desired in men-of-war's men. All reform—using the word in its true sense of alteration, and not in its strained sense of improvement—has been in the direction of securing perfect uniformity. If we take the particular directly suggested by the word just used, we may remember, almost with astonishment, that there was no British naval uniform for any one below the rank of officer till after 1860. Now, at every inspection, much time is taken up in ascertaining if the narrow tape embroidery on a frock collar is of the regulation width, and if the rows of tape are the proper distance apart. The diameter of a cloth cap is officially defined ; and any departure from the regulation number of inches (and fractions of an inch) is as sure of involving punishment as insubordination.

It is the same in greater things. Till 1853—in which year the change came into force—there was no permanent British naval service except the commissioned and warrant officers. Not till several years later did the new ' continuous service ' men equal half of the bluejacket aggregate. Now, every bluejacket proper serves continuously, and has been in the navy since boyhood. The training of the boys is made uniform. No member of the ship's company—except a domestic—is now allowed to set foot on board a sea-going ship till he has been put through a training course which is exactly like that through which every other member of his class passes. Even during the comparatively brief period in which young officers entered the navy by joining the college at Portsmouth, it was only the minority who received the special academic training. Till the establishment of the *Illustrious* training school in

1855, the great majority of officers joined their first ship as individuals from a variety of different and quite independent quarters. Now, every one of them has, as a preliminary condition, to spend a certain time—the same for all—in a school. Till a much later period, every engineer entered separately. Now, passing through a training establishment is obligatory for engineers also.

Within the service there has been repeated formation of distinct branches or 'schools,' such as the further specialised specialist gunnery and torpedo sections. It was not till 1860 that uniform watch bills, quarter bills, and station bills were introduced, and not till later that their general adoption was made compulsory. Up to that time the internal organisation and discipline of a ship depended on her own officers, it being supposed that capacity to command a ship implied, at least, capacity to distribute and train her crew. The result was a larger scope than is now thought permissible for individual capability. However short-lived some particular drill or exercise may be, however soon it is superseded by another, as long as it lasts the strictest conformity to it is rigorously enforced. Even the number of times that an exercise has to be performed, difference in class of ship or in the nature of the service on which she is employed notwithstanding, is authoritatively laid down. Still more noteworthy, though much less often spoken of than the change in *matériel*, has been the progress of the navy towards centralisation.

Naval duties are now formulated at a desk on shore, and the mode of carrying them out notified to the service in print. All this would have been quite as astonishing to the contemporaries of Nelson or of Exmouth and Codrington as the aspect of a battle-ship or of a 12-inch breech-loading gun.

Let it be clearly understood that none of these things has been mentioned with the intention of criticising them either favourably or unfavourably. They have been cited in order that it may be seen that the change in naval affairs is by no means one in *matériel* only, and that the transformation in other matters has been stupendous and revolutionary beyond all previous experience. It follows inevitably from this that we shall wage war in future under conditions dissimilar from any hitherto known. In this very fact there lies the making of a great surprise. It will have appeared from the historical statement given above how serious a surprise sometimes turns out to be. Its consequences, always significant, are not unfrequently far-reaching. The question of practical moment is : How are we to guard ourselves against such a surprise ? To this a satisfactory answer can be given. It might be summarised in the admonitions : abolish over-centralisation ; give proper scope to individual capacity and initiative ; avoid professional self-sufficiency.

When closely looked at, it is one of the strangest manifestations of the spirit of modern navies that, though the issues of land warfare are rarely thought instructive, the peace methods of land forces are extensively and eagerly copied by the sea-service. The exercises of the parade ground and the barrack square are taken over readily, and so are the parade ground and the barrack square themselves. This may be right. The point is that it is novel, and that a navy into the training of which the innovation has entered must differ considerably from one that was without it and found no need of it during a long course of serious wars. At any rate, no one will deny that parade-ground evolutions and barrack-square drill expressly aim at the elimination of individuality, or just the quality to the possession of which we owe the phenomenon called, in vulgar speech, the ' handy man.' Habits and sentiments based on a great tradition, and the faculties developed by them, are not killed all at once ; but innovation in the end annihilates them, and their not having yet entirely disappeared gives no ground for doubting their eventual, and even near, extinction. The aptitudes still universally most prized in the seaman were produced and nourished by practices and under conditions no longer allowed to prevail. Should we lose those aptitudes, are we likely to reach the position in war gained by our predecessors ?

For the British Empire the matter is vital : success in maritime war, decisive and overwhelming, is indispensable to our existence. We have to consider the desirability of ' taking stock ' of our moral, as well as of our material, naval equipment : to ascertain where the accumulated effect of repeated innovations has carried us. The mere fact of completing the investigation will help us to rate at their true value the changes which have been introduced ; will show us what to retain, what to reject, and what to substitute. There is no essential vagueness in these allusions. If they seem vague, it is because the moment for particularising has not yet come. The public opinion of the navy must first be turned in the right direction. It must be led to question the soundness of the basis on which many present methods rest. Having once begun to do this, we shall find no difficulty in settling, in detail and with precision, what the true elements of naval efficiency are.

THE HISTORICAL RELATIONS BETWEEN THE NAVY AND THE MERCHANT SERVICE

THE regret, often expressed, that the crews of British merchant ships now include a large proportion of foreigners, is founded chiefly on the apprehension that a well-tested and hitherto secure recruiting ground for the navy is likely to be closed. It has been stated repeatedly, and the statement has been generally accepted without question, that in former days, when a great expansion of our fleet was forced on us by the near approach of danger, we relied upon the ample resources of our merchant service to complete the manning of our ships of war, even in a short time, and that the demands of the navy upon the former were always satisfied. It is assumed that compliance with those demands was as a rule not voluntary, but was enforced by the press-gang. The resources, it is said, existed and were within reach, and the method employed in drawing upon them was a detail of comparatively minor importance ; our merchant ships were manned by native-born British seamen, of whom tens of thousands were always at hand, so that if volunteers were not forthcoming the number wanted could be ' pressed ' into the Royal service. It is lamented that at the present day the condition of affairs is different, that the presence in it of a large number of foreigners forbids us to regard with any confidence the merchant service as an adequate naval recruiting ground in the event of war, even though we are ready to substitute for the system of ' impressment '—which is now considered both undesirable and impossible— rewards likely to attract volunteers. The importance of the subject need not be dwelt upon. The necessity to a maritime state of a powerful navy, including abundant resources for manning it, is now no more disputed than the law of gravitation.   If the proportion of foreigners in our merchant service is too high it is certainly deplorable ; and if, being already too high, that proportion is rising, an early remedy is urgently needed.   I do not propose to speak here of that matter, which is grave enough to require separate treatment.

My object is to present the results of an inquiry into the history of the relations between the navy and the merchant service, from which will appear to what extent the latter helped in bringing the former up to a war footing, how far its assistance was affected by the presence in it of any foreign element, and in what way impressment ensured or expedited the rendering of the assistance.   The inquiry has

necessarily been largely statistical; consequently
the results will often be given in a statistical form.
This has the great advantage of removing the
conclusions arrived at from the domain of mere
opinion into that of admitted fact. The statistics
used are those which have not been, and are not
likely to be, questioned. It is desirable that this
should be understood, because official figures have
not always commanded universal assent. Lord
Brougham, speaking in the House of Lords in
1849 of tables issued by the Board of Trade, said
that a lively impression prevailed ' that they could
prove anything and everything'; and in connection
with them he adopted some unnamed person's
remark, 'Give me half an hour and the run of the
multiplication table and I'll engage to pay off the
National Debt.' In this inquiry there has been no
occasion to use figures relating to the time of Lord
Brougham's observations. We will take the last
three great maritime wars in which our country
has been engaged. These were: the war of
American Independence, the war with Revolutionary France to the Peace of Amiens, and the war
with Napoleon. The period covered by these three
contests roughly corresponds to the last quarter
of the eighteenth and the first fifteen years of the
nineteenth century. In each of the three wars
there was a sudden and large addition to the number
of seamen in the navy; and in each there were
considerable annual increases as the struggle continued. It must be understood that we shall deal

with the case of seamen only ; the figures, which also were large, relating to the marines not being included in our survey because it has never been contended that their corps looked to the merchant service for any appreciable proportion of its recruits. In taking note of the increase of seamen voted for any year it will be necessary to make allowance also for the ' waste ' of the previous year. The waste, even in the latter part of the last century, was large. Commander Robinson, in his valuable work, ' The British Fleet,' gives details showing that the waste during the Seven Years' war was so great as to be truly shocking. In 1895 Lord Brassey (*Naval Annual*) allowed for the *personnel* of the navy, even in these days of peace and advanced sanitary science, a yearly waste of 5 per cent., a percentage which is, I expect, rather lower than that officially accepted. We may take it as certain that, during the three serious wars above named, the annual waste was never less than 6 per cent. This is, perhaps, to put it too low ; but it is better to understate the case than to appear to exaggerate it. The recruiting demand, therefore, for a year of increased armament will be the sum of the increase in men *plus* the waste on the previous year's numbers.

The capacity of the British merchant service to supply what was demanded would, of course, be all the greater the smaller the number of foreigners it contained in its ranks. This is not only generally admitted at the present day ; it is also frequently pointed out when it is asserted that the conditions

now are less favourable than they were owing to a
recent influx of foreign seamen. The fact, however,
is that there were foreigners on board British
merchant ships, and, it would seem, in considerable
numbers, long before even the war of American
Independence. By 13 George II, c. 3, foreigners,
not exceeding three-fourths of the crew, were
permitted in British vessels, ' and in two years to
be naturalised.' By 13 George II, c. 17, exemption from impressment was granted to ' every
person, being a foreigner, who shall serve in any
merchant ship, or other trading vessel or privateer
belonging to a subject of the Crown of Great Britain.'
The Acts quoted were passed about the time of the
' Jenkins' Ear War ' and the war of the Austrian
Succession ; but the fact that foreigners were
allowed to form the majority of a British vessel's
crew is worthy of notice. The effect and, probably,
the object of this legislation were not so much to
permit foreign seamen to enter our merchant
service as to permit the number of those already
there to be increased. It was in 1759 that Lord,
then Commander, Duncan reported that the crew of
the hired merchant ship *Royal Exchange* consisted
' to a large extent of boys and foreigners, many
of whom could not speak English.' In 1770 by
11 George III, c. 3, merchant ships were allowed
to have three-fourths of their crews foreigners till
the 1st February 1772. Acts permitting the same
proportion of foreign seamen and extending the time
were passed in 1776, 1778, 1779, 1780, 1781, and

1782. A similar Act was passed in 1792. It was in contemplation to reduce the foreign proportion, after the war, to one-fourth. In 1794 it was enacted (34 George III, c. 68), ' for the encouragement of British seamen,' that after the expiration of six months from the conclusion of the war, vessels in the foreign, as distinguished from the coasting, trade were to have their commanders and three-fourths of their crews British subjects. From the wording of the Act it seems to have been taken for granted that the proportion of three-fourths *bona fide* British-born seamen was not likely to be generally exceeded. It will have been observed that in all the legislation mentioned, from the time of George II down-wards, it was assumed as a matter of course that there were foreign seamen on board our merchant vessels. The United States citizens in the British Navy, about whom there was so much discussion on the eve of the war of 1812, came principally from our own merchant service, and not direct from the American. It is remarkable that, until a recent date, the presence of foreigners in British vessels, even in time of peace, was not loudly or generally complained of. Mr. W. S. Lindsay, writing in 1876, stated that the throwing open the coasting trade in 1855 had ' neither increased on the average the number of foreigners we had hitherto been allowed to employ in our ships, nor deteriorated the number and quality of British seamen.' I have brought forward enough evidence to show that, as far as the merchant service was the proper recruiting ground for the British Navy, it was not one which was devoid of a considerable foreign element.

We may, nevertheless, feel certain that that element never amounted to, and indeed never nearly approached, three-fourths of the whole number of men employed in our 'foreign-going' vessels. For this, between 50,000 and 60,000 men would have been required, at least in the last of the three wars above mentioned. If all the foreign mercantile marines at the present day, when nearly all have been so largely increased, were to combine, they could not furnish the number required after their own wants had been satisfied. During the period under review some of the leading commercial nations were at war with us ; so that few, if any, seamen could have come to us from them. Our custom-house statistics indicate an increase in the shipping trade of the neutral nations sufficient to have rendered it impossible for them to spare us any much larger number of seamen. Therefore, it is extremely difficult to resist the conclusion that during the wars the composition of our merchant service remained nearly what it was during peace. It contained a far from insignificant proportion of foreigners ; and that proportion was augmented, though by no means enormously, whilst war was going on. This leads us to the further conclusion that, if our merchant service supplied the navy with many men, it could recover only a small part of the number from foreign countries. In fact, any that it could give it had to replace from our own population almost exclusively.

The question now to be considered is, What was the capacity of the merchant service for supplying the demands of the navy ?   In the year 1770 the number of seamen voted for the navy was 11,713. Owing to a fear of a difficulty with Spain about the Falkland Islands, the number for the following year was suddenly raised to 31,927.   Consequently, the increase was 20,214, which, added to the ' waste ' on the previous year, made the whole naval demand about 21,000.   We have not got statistics of the seamen of the whole British Empire for this period, but we have figures which will enable us to compute the number with sufficient accuracy for the purpose in hand.   In England and Wales there were some 59,000 seamen, and those of the rest of the empire amounted to about 21,000.   Large as the ' waste ' was in the Royal Navy, it was, and still is, much larger in the merchant service.   We may safely put it at 8 per cent. at least.   Therefore, simply to keep up   its   numbers—80,000—the   merchant   service would   have had to engage fully 6400 fresh hands. In view of these figures, it is difficult to believe that it could have furnished the navy with 21,000 men, or, indeed, with any number approximating thereto. It could not possibly have done so without restricting its operations, if only for a time.   So far were its operations from shrinking that they were positively extended.   The English tonnage ' cleared outwards ' from our ports was for the years mentioned as follows: 1770, 703,495 ; 1771, 773,390 ; 1772, 818,108.

Owing to the generally slow rate of sailing when on voyages and to the great length of time taken in unloading and reloading abroad—both being often effected ' in the stream ' and with the ship's own boats—the figures for clearances outward much more nearly represented the amount of our ' foreign-going ' tonnage a century ago than similar figures would now in these days of rapid movement. After 1771 the navy was reduced and kept at a relatively low standard till 1775. In that year the state of affairs in America rendered an increase of our naval forces neces-sary. In 1778 we were at war with France ; in 1779 with Spain as well ; and in December 1780 we had the Dutch for enemies in addition. In September 1783 we were again at peace. The way in which we had to increase the navy will be seen in the following table :—

Year.	Seamen voted for the navy.	Increase.	' Waste.'	Total addi-tional num-ber required.
1774	15,646	—	—	—
1775	18,000	2,354	936	3,290
1776	21,335	3,335	1,080	4,415
1777	34,871	13,536	1,278	14,184
1778	48,171	13,300	2,088	15,388
1779	52,611	4,440	2,886	7,326
1780	66,221	13,610	3,156	16,766
1781	69,683	3,462	3,972	7,434
1782	78,695	9,012	4,176	13,188
1783	84,709	6,014	4,722	10,736

It cannot be believed that the merchant service, with its then dimensions, could have possibly satisfied these great and repeated demands, besides making up its own ' waste,' unless its size were much reduced.   After 1777, indeed, there was a considerable fall in the figures of English tonnage ' outwards.' I give these figures down to the first year of peace.

1777..736,234 tons ' outwards.'	1781..547,953 tons ' outwards.'
1778..657,238 ,, ,,	1782..552,851 ,, ,,
1779..590,911 ,, ,,	1783..795,669 ,, ,,
1780..619,462 ,, ,,	1784..846,355 ,, ,,

At first sight it would seem as if there had, indeed, been a shrinkage.   We find, however, on further examination that in reality there had been none. ' During the [American] war the ship-yards in every port of Britain were full of employment ;   and consequently new ship-yards were set up in places where ships had never been built before.'   Even the diminution in the statistics of outward clearances indicated no diminution in the number of merchant ships or their crews.   The missing tonnage was merely employed elsewhere.   ' At this time there were about 1000 vessels of private property employed by the Government as transports and in other branches of the public service.'   Of course there had been some diminution due to the transfer of what had been British-American shipping to a new independent flag.   This would not have set free any men to join the navy.

When we come to the Revolutionary war we find ourselves confronted with similar conditions.   The case of this war has often been quoted as proving that in former days the navy had to rely practically exclusively on the merchant service when expansion

was necessary. In giving evidence before a Parlia-
mentary committee about fifty years ago, Admiral
Sir T. Byam Martin, referring to the great increase
of the fleet in 1793, said, ' It was the merchant
service that enabled us to man some sixty ships of
the line and double that number of frigates and
smaller vessels.' He added that we had been able
to bring promptly together ' about 35,000 or 40,000
men of the mercantile marine.' The requirements
of the navy amounted, as stated by the admiral,
to about 40,000 men ; to be exact, 39,045. The
number of seamen in the British Empire in 1793
was 118,952. In the next year the number showed
no diminution ; in fact it increased, though but
slightly, to 119,629. How our merchant service
could have satisfied the above-mentioned immense
demand on it in addition to making good its waste
and then have even increased is a thing that baffles
comprehension. No such example of elasticity is
presented by any other institution. Admiral Byam
Martin spoke so positively, and, indeed, with such
justly admitted authority, that we should have to
give up the problem as insoluble were it not for
other passages in the admiral's own evidence. It
may be mentioned that all the witnesses did not hold
his views. Sir James Stirling, an officer of nearly
if not quite equal authority, differed from him.
In continuation of his evidence Sir T. Byam Martin
stated that afterwards the merchant service could
give only a small and occasional supply, as ships
arrived from foreign ports or as apprentices grew out

of their time. Now, during the remaining years of this war and throughout the Napoleonic war, great as were the demands of the navy, they only in one year, that of the rupture of the Peace of Amiens, equalled the demand at the beginning of the Revolutionary war. From the beginning of hostilities till the final close of the conflict in 1815 the number of merchant seamen fell only once—viz. in 1795, the fall being 3200. In 1795, however, the demand for men for the navy was less than half that of 1794. The utmost, therefore, that Sir T. Byam Martin desired to establish was that, on a single occasion in an unusually protracted continuance of war, the strength of our merchant service enabled it to reinforce the navy up to the latter's requirements; but its doing so prevented it from giving much help afterwards. All the same, men in large numbers had to be found for the navy yearly for a long time. This will appear from the tables which follow :—

REVOLUTIONARY WAR

—	Seamen voted for the navy.	Increase.	' Waste.'	Total number required.
1794	72,885	36,885	2,160	39,045
1795	85,000	12,115	4,368	16,483
1796	92,000	7,000	5,100	12,100
1797	100,000	8,000	5,520	13,520
1798	100,000	—	6,000	6,000
1799	100,000	—	6,000	6,000
1800	97,300	—	—	—
1801	105,000	7,700	Absorbed by previous reduction.	7,700

NAPOLEONIC WAR

—	Seamen voted for the navy.	Increase.	'Waste.'	Total number required.
1803	{ 38,000 } { 77,600 }	39,600	—	39,600
1804	78,000	400	3,492 (for nine months)	3,892
1805	90,000	12,000	4,680	16,680
1806	91,000	1,000	5,400	6,400
1807	98,600	7,600	5,460	13,060
1808	98,600	—	5,460	5,460
1809	98,600	—	5,460	5,460
1810	113,600	15,000	5,460	20,460
1811	113,600	—	6,816	6,816
1812	113,600	—	6,816	6,816
1813	108,600	Reduction	—	—
1814	{ 86,000 } { 74,000 }	Do.	—	—

(No ' waste ' is allowed for when there has been
a reduction.)

It is a reasonable presumption that, except
perhaps on a single occasion, the merchant service
did not furnish the men required—not from any
want of patriotism or of public spirit, but simply
because it was impossible. Even as regards the
single exception the evidence is not uncontested ;
and by itself, though undoubtedly strong, it is
not convincing, in view of the well-grounded
presumptions the other way. The question then
that naturally arises is—If the navy did not fill
up its complements from the merchant service,
how did it fill them up ? The answer is easy.

Our naval complements were filled up largely with boys, largely with landsmen, largely with fishermen, whose numbers permitted this without inconvenience to their trade in general, and, to a small extent, with merchant seamen. It may be suggested that the men wanted by the navy could have been passed on to it from our merchant vessels, which could then complete their own crews with boys, landsmen, and fishermen. It was the age in which Dr. Price was a great authority on public finance, the age of Mr. Pitt's sinking fund, when borrowed money was repaid with further borrowings; so that a corresponding roundabout method for manning the navy may have had attractions for some people. A conclusive reason why it was not adopted is that its adoption would have been possible only at the cost of disorganising such a great industrial undertaking as our maritime trade. That this disorganisation did not arise is proved by the fact that our merchant service flourished and expanded.

It is widely supposed that, wherever the men wanted for the navy may have come from, they were forced into it by the system of ' impressment.' The popular idea of a man-of-war's ' lower deck ' of a century ago is that it was inhabited by a ship's company which had been captured by the press-gang and was restrained from revolting by the presence of a detachment of marines. The prevalence of the belief that seamen were ' raised '—' recruited ' is not a naval term—for the navy by forcible means can be accounted for without difficulty. The supposed ubiquity of the press-gang and its violent procedure added much picturesque detail, and even romance, to stories of naval life. Stories connected with it, if authentic, though rare, would, indeed, make a deep impression on the public; and what was really the exception would be taken for the rule. There is no evidence to show that even from the middle of the seventeenth century any considerable number of men was raised by forcible impressment. I am not acquainted with a single story of the press-gang which, even when much embellished, professes to narrate the seizure of more than an insignificant body. The allusions to forcible impressment made by naval historians are, with few exceptions, complaints of the utter inefficiency of the plan. In Mr. David Hannay's excellent 'Short History of the Royal Navy' will be found more than one illustration of its inefficient working in the seventeenth century. Confirmation, if confirmation is needed, can be adduced on the high authority of Mr. M. Oppenheim. We wanted tens of thousands, and forcible impressment was giving us half-dozens, or, at the best, scores. Even of those it provided, but a small proportion was really forced to serve. Mr. Oppenheim tells us of an Act of Parliament (17 Charles I) legalising forcible impressment, which seems to have been passed to satisfy the sailors. If anyone should think this absurd, he may be referred to the remarkable expression of opinion by some of the older seamen of Sunderland and Shields when the Russian war broke out in 1854. The married sailors, they said, naturally waited for the impressment, for ' we know that has always been and always will be preceded by the proclamation of bounty.'

The most fruitful source of error as to the procedure of the press-gang has been a deficient knowledge of etymology. The word has, properly, no relation to the use of force, and has no etymological connection with ' press ' and its compounds, ' compress,' ' depress,' ' express,' ' oppress,' &c. ' Prest money is so-called from the French word *prest*—that is, readie money, for that it bindeth all those that have received it to be ready at all times appointed.' Professor Laughton tells us that ' A prest or imprest was an earnest or advance paid on account. A prest man was really a man who received the prest of 12*d.*, as a soldier when enlisted.' Writers, and some in an age when precision in spelling is thought important, have frequently spelled *prest* pressed, and *imprest* impressed. The natural result has been that the thousands who had received ' prest money ' were classed as ' pressed ' into the service by force.

The foregoing may be summed up as follows :—

For 170 years at least there never has been a time when the British merchant service did not contain an appreciable percentage of foreigners.

During the last three (and greatest) maritime wars in which this country has been involved only a small proportion of the immense number of men required by the navy came, or could have come, from the merchant service.

The number of men raised for the navy by forcible impressment in war time has been enormously exaggerated owing to a confusion of terms. As a matter of fact the number so raised, for quite two centuries, was only an insignificant fraction of the whole.

V

FACTS AND FANCIES ABOUT THE PRESS-GANG[1]

OF late years great attention has been paid to our naval history, and many even of its obscure byways have been explored. A general result of the investigation is that we are enabled to form a high estimate of the merits of our naval administration in former centuries. We find that for a long time the navy has possessed an efficient organisation; that its right position as an element of the national defences was understood ages ago; and that English naval officers of a period which is now very remote showed by their actions that they exactly appreciated and—when necessary—were able to apply the true principles of maritime warfare. If anyone still believes that the country has been saved more than once merely by lucky chances of weather, and that the England of Elizabeth has been converted into the great oceanic and colonial British Empire of Victoria in ' a fit of absence of mind,' it will not be for want of materials with which to form a correct judgment on these points.

It has been accepted generally that the principal

[1] Written in 1900. (*National Review.*)

method of manning our fleet in the past—especially
when war threatened to arise—was to seize and
put men on board the ships by force. This has
been taken for granted by many, and it seems to
have been assumed that, in any case, there is no
way of either proving it or disproving it. The
truth, however, is that it is possible and—at least as
regards the period of our last great naval war—not
difficult to make sure if it is true or not. Records
covering a long succession of years still exist, and
in these can be found the name of nearly every
seaman in the navy and a statement of the conditions on which he joined it. The exceptions would
not amount to more than a few hundreds out of
many tens of thousands of names, and would be
due to the disappearance—in itself very infrequent
—of some of the documents and to occasional, but
also very rare, inaccuracies in the entries.

The historical evidence on which the belief
in the prevalence of impressment as a method of
recruiting the navy for more than a hundred years
is based, is limited to contemporary statements
in the English newspapers, and especially in the
issues of the periodical called *The Naval Chronicle*,
published in 1803, the first year of the war following
the rupture of the Peace of Amiens. Readers of
Captain Mahan's works on Sea-Power will remember
the picture he draws of the activity of the press-gang
in that year, his authority being *The Naval Chronicle*.
This evidence will be submitted directly to close
examination, and we shall see what importance

K

ought to be attached to it. In the great majority of cases, however, the belief above mentioned has no historical foundation, but is to be traced to the frequency with which the supposed operations of the press-gang were used by the authors of naval stories and dramas, and by artists who took scenes of naval life for their subject. Violent seizure and abduction lend themselves to effective treatment in literature and in art, and writers and painters did not neglect what was so plainly suggested.

A fruitful source of the widespread belief that our navy in the old days was chiefly manned by recourse to compulsion, is a confusion between two words of independent origin and different meaning, which, in ages when exact spelling was not thought indispensable, came to be written and pronounced alike. During our later great maritime wars, the official term applied to anyone recruited by impressment was 'prest-man.' In the sixteenth and seventeenth centuries, and part of the eighteenth century, this term meant the exact opposite. It meant a man who had voluntarily engaged to serve, and who had received a sum in advance called 'prest-money.' 'A prest-man,' we are told by that high authority, Professor Sir J. K. Laughton, 'was really a man who received the prest of 12*d*., as a soldier when enlisted.' In the 'Encyclopædia Metropolitana' (1845), we find:—'Impressing, or, more correctly, impresting, i.e. paying earnest-money to seamen by the King's Commission to the Admiralty, is a right of very ancient date, and

established by prescription, though not by statute.
Many statutes, however, imply its existence—one as
far back as 2 Richard II, cap. 4.' An old dictionary
of James I's time (1617), called 'The Guide into
the Tongues, by the Industrie, Studie, Labour, and
at the Charges of John Minshew,' gives the following
definition :—' Imprest-money. G. [Gallic or French],
Imprest-ànce ; *Imprestanza,* from *in* and *prestare,*
to lend or give beforehand. . . . Presse-money.
T. [Teutonic or German], Soldt, from salz, *salt.*
For anciently agreement or compact between the
General and the soldier was signified by salt.'
Minshew also defines the expression ' to presse
souldiers ' by the German *soldatenwerben,* and explains that here the word *werben* means prepare
(*parare*). ' Prest-money,' he says, ' is so-called of
the French word *prest,* i.e. readie, for that it bindeth
those that have received it to be ready at all times
appointed.' In the posthumous work of Stephen
Skinner, ' Etymologia Linguæ Anglicanæ ' (1671),
the author joins together ' press or imprest ' as
though they were the same, and gives two definitions,
viz. : (1) recruiting by force (*milites cogere*) ; (2)
paying soldiers a sum of money and keeping them
ready to serve. Dr. Murray's ' New English
Dictionary,' now in course of publication, gives
instances of the confusion between imprest and
impress. A consequence of this confusion has
been that many thousands of seamen who had
received an advance of money have been regarded
as carried off to the navy by force. If to this

misunderstanding we add the effect on the popular mind of cleverly written stories in which the press-gang figured prominently, we can easily see how the belief in an almost universal adoption of compulsory recruiting for the navy became general. It should, therefore, be no matter of surprise when we find that the sensational reports published in the English newspapers in 1803 were accepted without question.

Impressment of seamen for the navy has been called ' lawless,' and sometimes it has been asserted that it was directly contrary to law. There is, however, no doubt that it was perfectly legal, though its legality was not based upon any direct statutory authority. Indirect confirmations of it by statute are numerous. These appear in the form of exemptions. The law of the land relating to this subject was that all ' sea-faring ' men were liable to impressment unless specially protected by custom or statute. A consideration of the long list of exemptions tends to make one believe that in reality very few people were liable to be impressed. Some were ' protected ' by local custom, some by statute, and some by administrative order. The number of the last must have been very great. The ' Protection Books ' preserved in the Public Record Office form no inconsiderable section of the Admiralty records. For the period specially under notice, viz. that beginning with the year 1803, there are no less than five volumes of ' protections.' Exemptions by custom probably originated at a very remote date : ferrymen, for example, being everywhere privileged from impressment. The crews of colliers seem to have enjoyed the privilege by custom before it was confirmed by Act of Parliament. The naval historian, Burchett, writing of 1691, cites a ' Proclamation forbidding pressing men from colliers.'

Every ship in the coal trade had the following persons protected, viz. two A.B.'s for every ship of 100 tons, and one for every 50 tons in larger ships. When we come to consider the sensational statements in *The Naval Chronicle* of 1803, it will be well to remember what the penalty for infringing the colliers' privilege was. By the Act 6 & 7 William III, c. 18, sect. 19, ' Any officer who presumes to impress any of the above shall forfeit to the master or owner of such vessel £10 for every man so impressed ; and such officer shall be incapable of holding any place, office, or employment in any of His Majesty's ships of war.' It is not likely that the least scrupulous naval officer would make himself liable to professional ruin as well as to a heavy fine. No parish apprentice could be impressed for the sea service of the Crown until he arrived at the age of eighteen (2 & 3 Anne, c. 6, sect. 4). Persons voluntarily binding themselves apprentices to sea service could not be impressed for three years from the date of their indentures. Besides sect. 15 of the Act of Anne just quoted, exemptions were granted, before 1803, by 4 Anne, c. 19 ; and 13 George II, c. 17. By the Act last mentioned all persons fifty-five years of age and under eighteen were exempted, and every foreigner serving in a ship belonging to a British subject, and also all persons ' of what age soever who shall use the sea ' for two years, to be computed from the time of their first using it. A customary exemption was extended to the proportion of the crew of any ship necessary for her safe navigation. In practice this must have reduced the numbers liable to impressment to small dimensions.

Even when the Admiralty decided to suspend all administrative exemptions—or, as the phrase was, ' to press from all protections '—many persons were still exempted. The customary and statutory exemptions, of course, were unaffected. On the 5th November 1803 their Lordships informed officers in charge of rendezvous that it was ' necessary for the speedy manning of H.M. ships to impress all persons of the denominations exprest in the press-warrant which you have received from us, without regard to any protections, excepting, however, all such persons as are protected pursuant to Acts of Parliament, and all others who by the printed instructions which accompanied the said warrant are forbidden to be imprest.' In addition to these a long list of further exemptions was sent. The last in the list included the crews of ' ships and vessels bound to foreign parts which are laden and cleared outwards by the proper officers of H.M. Customs.' It would seem that there was next to no one left liable to impressment ; and it is not astonishing that the Admiralty, as shown by its action very shortly afterwards, felt that pressing seamen was a poor way of manning the fleet.

Though the war which broke out in 1803 was not formally declared until May, active preparations were begun earlier.   The navy had been greatly reduced since the Peace of Amiens, and as late as the 2nd December 1802 the House of Commons had voted that '50,000 seamen be employed for the service of the year 1803, including 12,000 marines.' On the 14th March an additional number was voted. It amounted to 10,000 men, of whom 2400 were to be marines.   Much larger additions were voted a few weeks later.   The total increase was 50,000 men ; viz. 39,600 seamen and 10,400 marines.   It never occurred to anyone that forcible recruiting would be necessary in the case of the marines, though the establishment of the corps was to be nearly doubled, as it had to be brought up to 22,400 from 12,000.   Attention may be specially directed to this point.   The marine formed an integral part of a man-of-war's crew just as the seamen did.   He received no better treatment than the latter ; and as regards pecuniary remuneration, prospects of advancement, and hope of attaining to the position of warrant officer, was, on the whole, in a less favourable position.   It seems to have been universally accepted that voluntary enlistment would prove—as, in fact, it did prove—sufficient in the case of the marines.   What we have got to see is how far it failed in the case of the seamen, and how far its deficiencies were made up by compulsion.

On the 12th March the Admiralty notified the Board of Ordnance that twenty-two ships of the line —the names of which were stated—were 'coming forward' for sea. Many of these ships are mentioned in *The Naval Chronicle* as requiring men, and that journal gives the names of several others of various classes in the same state. The number altogether is thirty-one. The aggregate complements, including marines and boys, of these ships amounted to 17,234. The number of 'seamen' was 11,861, though this included some of the officers who were borne on the same muster-list. The total number of seamen actually required exceeded 11,500. *The Naval Chronicle* contains a vivid, not to say sensational, account of the steps taken to raise them. The report from Plymouth, dated 10th March, is as follows : 'Several bodies of Royal Marines in parties of twelve and fourteen each, with their officers and naval officers armed, proceeded towards the quays. So secret were the orders kept that they did not know the nature of the business on which they were going until they boarded the tier of colliers at the New Quay, and other gangs the ships in the Catwater and the Pool, and the gin-shops. A great number of prime seamen were taken out and sent on board the Admiral's ship. They also pressed landsmen of all descriptions ; and the town looked as if in a state of siege. At Stonehouse, Mutton Cove, Morris Town, and in all the receiving and gin-shops at Dock [the present Devonport] several hundreds of seamen and landsmen were picked up and sent directly aboard the flag-ship. By the returns last night it appears that upwards of 400 useful hands were pressed last night in the Three Towns. . . . One press-gang entered the Dock [Devonport] Theatre and cleared the whole gallery except the women.' The reporter remarks : ' It is said that near 600 men have been impressed in this neighbourhood.' The number—if obtained— would not have been sufficient to complete the seamen in the complements of a couple of line-of-battle ships. Naval officers who remember the methods of manning ships which lasted well into the middle of the nineteenth century, and of course long after recourse to impressment had been given up, will probably notice the remarkable fact that the reporter makes no mention of any of the parties whose proceedings he described being engaged in picking up men who had voluntarily joined ships fitting out, but had not returned on board on the expiration of the leave granted them. The description in *The Naval Chronicle* might be applied to events which—when impressment had ceased for half a century—occurred over and over again at Portsmouth, Devonport, and other ports when two or three ships happened to be put in commission about the same time.

We shall find that the 600 reported as impressed had to be considerably reduced before long. The reporter afterwards wisely kept himself from giving figures, except in a single instance when he states that ' about forty ' were taken out of the flotilla of Plymouth trawlers. Reporting on 11th March he says that 'Last Thursday and yesterday'—the day of the sensational report above given—'several useful hands were picked up, mostly seamen, who were concealed in the different lodgings and were discovered by their girls.' He adds, 'Several prime seamen were yesterday taken disguised as labourers in the different marble quarries round the town.' On 14th October the report is that 'the different press-gangs, with their officers, literally scoured the country on the eastern roads and picked up several fine young fellows.' Here, again, no distinction is drawn between men really impressed and men who were arrested for being absent beyond the duration of their leave. We are told next that 'upon a survey of all impressed men before three captains and three surgeons of the Royal Navy, such as were deemed unfit for His Majesty's service, as well as all apprentices, were immediately discharged,' which, no doubt, greatly diminished the above-mentioned 600.

The reporter at Portsmouth begins his account of the 'press' at that place by saying, 'They indiscriminately took every man on board the colliers.' In view of what we know of the heavy penalties to which officers who pressed more than a certain proportion of a collier's crew were liable, we may take it that this statement was made in error. On 14th March it was reported that 'the constables and gangs from the ships continue very alert in obtaining seamen, many of whom have

been sent on board different ships in the harbour
this day.' We do not hear again from Portsmouth
till May, on the 7th of which month it was reported
that ' about 700 men were obtained.' On the 8th
the report was that ' on Saturday afternoon the
gates of the town were shut and soldiers placed
at every avenue. Tradesmen were taken from their
shops and sent on board the ships in the harbour
or placed in the guard-house for the night, till they
could be examined. If fit for His Majesty's service
they were kept, if in trade set at liberty.' The
' tradesmen,' then, if really taken, were taken
simply to be set free again. As far as the reports
first quoted convey any trustworthy information,
it appears that at Portsmouth and Plymouth during
March, April, and the first week of May, 1340 men
were ' picked up,' and that of these many were
immediately discharged. How many of the 1340
were not really impressed, but were what in the
navy are called ' stragglers,' i.e. men over-staying
their leave of absence, is not indicated.

The Times of the 11th March 1803, and 9th May
1803, also contained reports of the impressment
operations. It says : ' The returns to the Admiralty
of the seamen impressed (apparently at the Thames
ports) on Tuesday night amounted to 1080, of whom
no less than two-thirds are considered prime hands.
At Portsmouth, Portsea, Gosport, and Cowes a
general press took place the same night. . . . Upwards of 600 seamen were collected in consequence
of the promptitude of the measures adopted.'

It was added that the Government ' relied upon increasing our naval forces with 10,000 seamen, either volunteers or impressed men, in less than a fortnight.' The figures show us how small a proportion of the 10,000 was even alleged to be made up of impressed men. A later *Times* report is that : ' The impress on Saturday, both above and below the bridge, was the hottest that has been for some time. The boats belonging to the ships at Deptford were particularly active, and it is supposed they obtained upwards of 200 men.' *The Times* reports thus account for 1280 men over and above the 1340 stated to have been impressed at Plymouth and Portsmouth, thus making a grand total of 2620. It will be proved by official figures directly that the last number was an over-estimate.

Before going farther, attention may be called to one or two points in connection with the above reports. The increase in the number of seamen voted by Parliament in March was 7600. The reports of the impressment operations only came down to May. It was not till the 11th June that Parliament voted a further addition to the navy of 32,000 seamen. Yet whilst the latter great increase was being obtained—for obtained it was—the reporters are virtually silent as to the action of the press-gang. We must ask ourselves, if we could get 32,000 additional seamen with so little recourse to impressment that the operations called for no special notice, how was it that compulsion was necessary when only 7600 men were wanted ? The

question is all the more pertinent when we recall
the state of affairs in the early part of 1803.
The navy had been greatly reduced in the year
before, the men voted having diminished from 100,000
to 56,000. What became of the 44,000 men not
required, of whom about 35,000 must have been
of the seaman class and have been discharged
from the service ?   There was a further reduction of
6000, to take effect in the beginning of 1803. Sir
Sydney Smith, at that time a Member of Parliament,
in the debate of the 2nd December 1802, ' expressed
considerable regret at the great reductions which
were suddenly made, both in the King's dockyards
and in the navy in general. A prodigious number
of men,' he said, ' had been thus reduced to the
utmost poverty and distress.' He stated that he
' knew, from his own experience, that what was
called an ordinary seaman could hardly find employment at present, either in the King's or in the
merchants' service.' The increase of the fleet in
March must have seemed a godsend to thousands
of men-of-war's men. If there was any holding
back on their part, it was due, no doubt, to an
expectation—which the sequel showed to be well
founded—that a bounty would be given to men
joining the navy.

The muster-book of a man-of-war is the official
list of her crew. It contains the name of every
officer and man in the complement. Primarily it
was an account-book, as it contains entries of the
payments made to each person whose name appears

in it. At the beginning of the nineteenth century it
was usual to make out a fresh muster-book every two
months, though that period was not always exactly
adhered to. Each new book was a copy of the preceding one, with the addition of the names of persons
who had joined the ship since the closing of the latter.
Until the ship was paid off and thus put out of commission—or, in the case of a very long commission,
until ' new books ' were ordered to be opened so as
to escape the inconveniences due to the repetition
of large numbers of entries—the name of every man
that had belonged to her remained on the list, his
disposal—if no longer in the ship—being noted in the
proper column. One column was headed ' Whence,
and whether prest or not ? ' In this was noted his
former ship, or the fact of his being entered direct
from the shore, which answered to the question
' Whence ? ' There is reason to believe that the
muster-book being, as above said, primarily an
account-book, the words ' whether prest or not '
were originally placed at the head of the column so
that it might be noted against each man entered
whether he had been paid ' prest-money ' or not.
However this may be, the column at the beginning
of the nineteenth century was used for a record of the
circumstances of the man's entering the ship, whether
he had been transferred from another, had joined as
a volunteer from the shore, or had been impressed.

I have examined the muster-book of every ship
mentioned in the Admiralty letter to the Board of
Ordnance above referred to, and also of the ships

mentioned in *The Naval Chronicle* as fitting out in
the early part of 1803. There are altogether thirty-
three ships ; but two of them, the *Utrecht* and the
Gelykheid, were used as temporary receiving ships for
newly raised men.[1] The names on their lists are,
therefore, merely those of men who were passed
on to other ships, in whose muster-books they
appeared again. There remained thirty-one ships
which, as far as could be ascertained, account for
the additional force which the Government had
decided to put in commission, more than two-thirds
of them being ships of the line. As already stated,
their total complements amounted to 17,234, and the
number of the ' blue-jackets ' of full age to at least
11,500. The muster-books appear to have been
kept with great care. The only exception seems to
be that of the *Victory*, in which there is some reason
to think the number of men noted as ' prest ' has
been over-stated owing to an error in copying the
earlier book. Ships in 1803 did not get their full
crews at once, any more than they did half a century
later. I have, therefore, thought it necessary to
take the muster-books for the months in which the
crews had been brought up to completion.

An examination of the books would be likely to
dispel many misconceptions about the old navy.
Not only is it noted against each man's name whether
he was ' pressed ' or a volunteer, it is also noted if he

[1] The words ' recruit ' and ' enlist,' except as regards marines,
are unknown in the navy, in which they are replaced by ' raise '
and ' enter.'

was put on board ship as an alternative to imprison-
ment on shore, this being indicated by the words
'civil power,' an expression still used in the navy,
but with a different meaning. The percentage of
men thus 'raised' was small. Sometimes there is
a note stating that the man had been allowed to
enter from the '——shire Militia.' A rare note is
'Brought on board by soldiers,' which most likely
indicated that the man had been recaptured when
attempting to desert. It is sometimes asserted
that many men who volunteered did so only to
escape impressment. This may be so; but it
should be said that there are frequent notations
against the names of 'prest' men that they afterwards volunteered. This shows the care that was
taken to ascertain the real conditions on which a man
entered the service. For the purposes of this
inquiry all these men have been considered as impressed, and they have not been counted amongst
the volunteers. It is, perhaps, permissible to set
off against such men the number of those who
allowed themselves to be impressed to escape inconveniences likely to be encountered if they remained
at home. Of two John Westlakes, ordinary seamen
of the *Boadicea*, one—John (I.)—was 'prest,' but
was afterwards 'taken out of the ship for a debt of
twenty pounds'; which shows that he had preferred to trust himself to the press-gang rather than
to his creditors. Without being unduly imaginative,
we may suppose that in 1803 there were heroes who
preferred being 'carried off' to defend their country

afloat to meeting the liabilities of putative paternity in their native villages.

The muster-books examined cover several months, during which many ' prest ' men were discharged and some managed to desert, so that the total was never present at any one time. That total amounts to 1782. It is certain that even this is larger than the reality, because it has been found impossible— without an excessive expenditure of time and labour —to trace the cases of men being sent from one ship to another, and thus appearing twice over, or oftener, as ' prest ' men. As an example of this the *Minotaur* may be cited. Out of twenty names on one page of her muster-book thirteen are those of ' prest ' men discharged to other ships. The discharges from the *Victory* were numerous ; and the *Ardent*, which was employed in keeping up communication with the ships off Brest, passed men on to the latter when required. I have, however, made no deductions from the ' prest ' total to meet these cases. We can see that not more than 1782 men, and probably considerably fewer, were impressed to meet the increase of the navy during the greater part of 1803. Admitting that there were cases of impressment from merchant vessels abroad to complete the crews of our men-of-war in distant waters, the total number impressed—including these latter—could not have exceeded greatly the figures first given. We know that owing to the reduction of 1802, as stated by Sir Sydney Smith, the seamen were looking for ships rather than the ships for seamen. It seems justifiable

L

to infer that the whole number of impressed men on any particular day did not exceed, almost certainly did not amount to, 2000. If they had been spread over the whole navy they would not have made 2 per cent. of the united complements of the ships ; and, as it was, did not equal one-nineteenth of the 39,600 seamen (' blue-jackets ') raised to complete the navy to the establishment sanctioned by Parliament. A system under which more than 37,000 volunteers come forward to serve and less than 2000 men are obtained by compulsion cannot be properly called compulsory.

The Plymouth reporter of *The Naval Chronicle* does not give many details of the volunteering for the navy in 1803, though he alludes to it in fluent terms more than once. On the 11th October, however, he reports that, ' So many volunteer seamen have arrived here this last week that upwards of £4000 bounty is to be paid them afloat by the Paying Commissioner, Rear-Admiral Dacres.' At the time the bounty was £2 10s. for an A.B., £1 10s. for an ordinary seaman, and £1 for a landsman. Taking only £4000 as the full amount paid, and assuming that the three classes were equally represented, three men were obtained for every £5, or 2400 in all, a number raised in about a week, that may be compared with that given as resulting from impressment. In reality, the number of volunteers must have been larger, because the A.B.'s were fewer than the other classes.

Some people may be astonished because the

practice of impressment, which had proved to be so utterly inefficient, was not at once and formally given up. No astonishment will be felt by those who are conversant with the habits of Government Departments. In every country public officials evince great and, indeed, almost invincible reluctance to give up anything, whether it be a material object or an administrative process, which they have once possessed or conducted. One has only to stroll through the arsenals of the world, or glance at the mooring-grounds of the maritime states, to see to what an extent the passion for retaining the obsolete and useless holds dominion over the official mind. A thing may be known to be valueless—its retention may be proved to be mischievous—yet proposals to abandon it will be opposed and defeated. It is doubtful if any male human being over forty was ever converted to a new faith of any kind. The public has to wait until the generation of administrative Conservatives has either passed away or been outnumbered by those acquainted only with newer methods. Then the change is made ; the certainty, nevertheless, being that the new men in their turn will resist improvements as obstinately and in exactly the same way as their predecessors.

To be just to the Board of Admiralty of 1803, it must be admitted that some of its members seem to have lost faith in the efficacy of impressment as a system of manning the navy. The Lords Commissioners of that date could hardly—all of them, at any rate — have been so thoroughly destitute of humour as not to suspect that seizing a few score of men here and a few there when tens of thousands were needed, was a very insufficient compensation for the large correspondence necessitated by adherence to the system (and still in existence). Their Lordships actively bombarded the Home Office with letters pointing out, for example, that a number of British seamen at Guernsey 'appeared to have repaired to that island with a view to avoid being pressed'; that they were 'of opinion that it would be highly proper that the sea-faring men (in Jersey as well as Guernsey), not natives nor settled inhabitants, should be impressed'; that when the captain of H.M.S. *Aigle* had landed at Portland 'for the purpose of raising men' some resistance had 'been made by the sailors'; and dealing with other subjects connected with the system. A complaint sent to the War Department was that 'amongst a number of men lately impressed (at Leith) there were eight or ten shipwrights who were sea-faring men, and had been claimed as belonging to a Volunteer Artillery Corps.'

We may suspect that there was some discussion at Whitehall as to the wisdom of retaining a plan which caused so much inconvenience and had such poor results. The conclusion seems to have been to submit it to a searching test. The coasts of the United Kingdom were studded with stations—thirty-seven generally, but the number varied—for the entry of seamen. The ordinary official description of these— as shown by entries in the muster-books—was

' rendezvous ' ; but other terms were used.   It has
often been thought that they were simply impressment offices.   The fact is that many more men were
raised at these places by volunteering than by
impressment.   The rendezvous, as a rule, were in
charge of captains or commanders, some few being
entrusted to lieutenants.   The men attached to each
were styled its ' gang,' a word which conveys no
discredit in nautical language.   On 5th November
1803 the Admiralty sent to the officers in charge of
rendezvous the communication already mentioned—
to press men ' without regard to any protections,'
—the exceptions, indeed, being so many that the
officers must have wondered who could legitimately
be taken.

The order at first sight appeared sweeping enough.
It contained the following words : ' Whereas we
think fit that a general press from all protections
as above mentioned shall commence at London and
in the neighbourhood thereof on the night of Monday
next, the 7th instant, you are therefore (after taking
the proper preparatory measures with all possible
secrecy) hereby required to impress and to give orders
to the lieutenants under your command to impress
all persons of the above-mentioned denominations
(except as before excepted) and continue to do so
until you receive orders from us to the contrary.'
As it was addressed to officers in all parts of the
United Kingdom, the ' general press ' was not confined to London and its neighbourhood, though it
was to begin in the capital.

Though returns of the numbers impressed have not been discovered, we have strong evidence that this 'general press,' notwithstanding the secrecy with which it had been arranged, was a failure. On the 6th December 1803, just a month after it had been tried, the Admiralty formulated the following conclusion : ' On a consideration of the expense attending the service of raising men on shore for His Majesty's Fleet comparatively with the number procured, as well as from other circumstances, there is reason to believe that either proper exertions have not been made by some of the officers employed on that service, or that there have been great abuses and mismanagement in the expenditure of the public money.' This means that it was now seen that impressment, though of little use in obtaining men for the navy, was a very costly arrangement. The Lords of the Admiralty accordingly ordered that ' the several places of rendezvous should be visited and the conduct of the officers employed in carrying out the above-mentioned service should be inquired into on the spot.' Rear-Admiral Arthur Phillip, the celebrated first Governor of New South Wales, was ordered to make the inquiry. This was the last duty in which that distinguished officer was employed, and his having been selected for it appears to have been unknown to all his biographers.

It is not surprising that after this the proceedings of the press-gang occupy scarcely any space in our naval history. Such references to them as there are will be found in the writings of the novelist and the

dramatist.   Probably individual cases of impressment occurred till nearly the end of the Great War ;
but they could not have been many.   Compulsory
service most unnecessarily caused — not much,
but still some — unjustifiable personal hardship.
It tended to stir up a feeling hostile to the navy.   It
required to work it machinery costly out of all proportion to the results obtained.   Indeed, it failed
completely to effect what had been expected of it.
In the great days of old our fleet, after all, was
manned, not by impressed men, but by volunteers.
It was largely due to that that we became masters
of the sea.

VI

PROJECTED INVASIONS OF THE BRITISH ISLES [1]

THE practice to which we have become accustomed of late, of publishing original documents relating to naval and military history, has been amply justified by the results. These meet the requirements of two classes of readers. The publications satisfy, or at any rate go far towards satisfying, the wishes of those who want to be entertained, and also of those whose higher motive is a desire to discover the truth about notable historical occurrences. Putting the public in possession of the materials, previously hidden in more or less inaccessible muniment-rooms and record offices, with which the narratives of professed historians have been constructed, has had advantages likely to become more and more apparent as time goes on. It acts as a check upon the imaginative tendencies which even eminent writers have not always been able, by themselves, to keep under proper control. The certainty, nay the mere probability, that you will be confronted with the witnesses on whose evidence

[1] Written in 1900. (*The Times.*)

you profess to have relied—the 'sources' from which your story is derived — will suggest the necessity of sobriety of statement and the advisability of subordinating rhetoric to veracity. Had the contemporary documents been available for an immediate appeal to them by the reading public, we should long ago have rid ourselves of some dangerous superstitions. We should have abandoned our belief in the fictions that the Armada of 1588 was defeated by the weather, and that the great Herbert of Torrington was a lubber, a traitor, and a coward. It is not easy to calculate the benefit that we should have secured, had the presentation of some important events in the history of our national defence been as accurate as it was effective. Enormous sums of money have been wasted in trying to make our defensive arrangements square with a conception of history based upon misunderstanding or misinterpretation of facts. Pecuniary extravagance is bad enough; but there is a greater evil still. We have been taught to cherish, and we have been reluctant to abandon, a false standard of defence, though adherence to such a standard can be shown to have brought the country within measurable distance of grievous peril. Captain Duro, of the Spanish Navy, in his 'Armada Invencible,' placed within our reach contemporary evidence from the side of the assailants, thereby assisting us to form a judgment on a momentous episode in naval history. The evidence was completed; some being adduced from the other side, by our fellow-countryman Sir J. K. Laughton, in his 'Defeat of the Spanish Armada,' published by the Navy Records Society. Others have worked on similar lines; and a healthier view of our strategic conditions and needs is more widely held than it was; though it cannot be said to be, even yet, universally prevalent. Superstition, even the grossest, dies hard.

Something deeper than mere literary interest, therefore, is to be attributed to a work which has recently appeared in Paris.[1] To speak strictly, it should be said that only the first volume of three which will complete it has been published. It is, however, in the nature of a work of the kind that its separate parts should be virtually independent of each other. Consequently the volume which we now have may be treated properly as a book by itself. When completed the work is to contain all the documents relating to the French preparations during the period 1793–1805, for taking the offensive against England (*tous les documents se rapportant à la préparation de l'offensive contre l'Angleterre*). The search for, the critical examination and the methodical classification of, the papers were begun in October 1898. The book is compiled by Captain Desbrière, of the French Cuirassiers, who was specially authorised to continue his editorial labours

---

[1] *1793–1805. Projets et Tentatives de Débarquement aux Iles Britanniques*, par Édouard Desbrière, Capitaine breveté aux Ier Cuirassiers. Paris, Chapelot et Cie. 1900. (Publié sous la direction de la section historique de l'État-Major de l'Armée.)

even after he had resumed his ordinary military
duties. It bears the *imprimatur* of the staff of the
army ; and its preface is written by an officer who
was—and so signs himself—chief of the historical
section of that department. There is no necessity to
criticise the literary execution of the work. What
is wanted is to explain the nature of its contents and
to indicate the lessons which may be drawn from
them. Nevertheless, attention may be called to a
curious misreading of history contained in the
preface. In stating the periods which the different
volumes of the book are to cover, the writer alludes
to the Peace of Amiens, which, he affirms, England
was compelled to accept by exhaustion, want of
means of defence, and fear of the menaces of the
great First Consul then disposing of the resources
of France, aggrandised, pacified, and reinforced by
alliances. The book being what it is and coming
whence it does, such a statement ought not to be
passed over. ' The desire for peace,' says an
author so easily accessible as J. R. Green, ' sprang
from no sense of national exhaustion. On the contrary, wealth had never increased so fast. . . . Nor
was there any ground for despondency in the aspect
of the war itself.' This was written in 1875 by an
author so singularly free from all taint of Chauvinism
that he expressly resolved that his work ' should
never sink into a drum and trumpet history.' A
few figures will be interesting and, it may be added,
conclusive. Between 1793 when the war began
and 1802 when the Peace of Amiens interrupted it,

the public income of Great Britain increased from
£16,382,000 to £28,000,000, the war taxes not being
included in the latter sum.   The revenue of France,
notwithstanding her territorial acquisitions, sank
from £18,800,000 to £18,000,000.   The French
exports and imports by sea were annihilated;
whilst the British exports were doubled and the
imports increased more than 50 per cent.   The
French Navy had at the beginning 73, at the
end of the war 39, ships of the line; the British
began the contest with 135 and ended it with
202.   Even as regards the army, the British force
at the end of the war was not greatly inferior
numerically to the French.   It was, however, much
scattered, being distributed over the whole British
Empire.   In view of the question under discussion,
no excuse need be given for adducing these facts.

Captain Desbrière in the present volume carries
his collection of documents down to the date at which
the then General Bonaparte gave up his connection
with the flotilla that was being equipped in the
French Channel ports, and prepared to take
command of the expedition to Egypt.   The volume
therefore, in addition to accounts of many projected,
but never really attempted, descents on the British
Isles, gives a very complete history of Hoche's
expedition to Ireland; of the less important, but
curious, descent in Cardigan Bay known as the
Fishguard, or Fishgard, expedition; and of the
formation of the first 'Army of England,' a designation destined to attain greater celebrity in the

subsequent war, when France was ruled by the great soldier whom we know as the Emperor Napoleon. The various documents are connected by Captain Desbrière with an explanatory commentary, and here and there are illustrated with notes. He has not rested content with the publication of MSS. selected from the French archives. In preparing his book he visited England and examined our records ; and, besides, he has inserted in their proper place passages from Captain Mahan's works and also from those of English authors. The reader's interest in the book is likely to be almost exclusively concentrated on the detailed, and, where Captain Desbrière's commentary appears, lucid, account of Hoche's expedition. Of course, the part devoted to the creation of the ' Army of England ' is not uninteresting ; but it is distinctly less so than the part relating to the proceedings of Hoche. Several of the many plans submitted by private persons, who here describe them in their own words, are worth examination ; and some, it may be mentioned, are amusing in the *naïveté* of their Anglophobia and in their obvious indifference to the elementary principles of naval strategy. In this indifference they have some distinguished companions.

We are informed by Captain Desbrière that the idea of a hostile descent on England was during a long time much favoured in France. The national archives and those of the Ministries of War and of Marine are filled with proposals for carrying it out, some dating back to 1710. Whether emanating from private persons or formulated in obedience to official direction, there are certain features in all the proposals so marked that we are able to classify the various schemes by grouping together those of a similar character. In one class may be placed all those which aimed at mere annoyance, to be effected by landing small bodies of men, not always soldiers, to do as much damage as possible. The appearance of these at many different points, it was believed, would so harass the English that they would end the war, or at least so divide their forces that their subjection might be looked for with confidence. In another class might be placed proposals to seize outlying, but not distant, British territory—the Channel Islands or the Isle of Wight, for example. A third class might comprise attempts on a greater scale, necessitating the employment of a considerable body of troops and meriting the designation 'Invasion.' Some of these attempts were to be made in Great Britain, some in Ireland. In every proposal for an attempt of this class, whether it was to be made in Great Britain or in Ireland, it was assumed that the invaders would receive assistance from the people of the country invaded. Indeed, generally the bulk of the force to be employed was ultimately to be composed of native sympathisers, who were also to provide—at least at the beginning —all the supplies and transport, both vehicles and animals, required. Every plan, no matter to which class it might belong, was based upon the assumption that the British naval force could be avoided. Until we come to the time when General Bonaparte, as he then was, dissociated himself from the first 'Army of England,' there is no trace, in any of the documents now printed, of a belief in the necessity of obtaining command of the sea before sending across it a considerable military expedition. That there was such a thing as the command of the sea is rarely alluded to ; and when it is, it is merely to accentuate the possibility of neutralising it by evading the force holding it. There is something which almost deserves to be styled comical in the absolutely unvarying confidence, alike of amateurs and highly placed military officers, with which it was held that a superior naval force was a thing that might be disregarded. Generals who would have laughed to scorn any one maintaining that, though there was a powerful Prussian army on the road to one city and an Austrian army on the road to the other, a French army might force its way to either Berlin or Vienna without either fighting or even being prepared to fight, such generals never hesitated to approve expeditions obliged to traverse a region in the occupation of a greatly superior force, the region being pelagic and the force naval. We had seized the little islands of St. Marcoff, a short distance from the coast of Normandy, and held them for years. It was expressly admitted that their recapture was impossible, ' à raison de la supériorité des forces navales Anglaises ' ; but it was not even suspected that a much more difficult operation, requiring longer time and a longer voyage, was likely to be impracticable. We shall see by and by how far this remarkable attitude of mind was supported by the experience of Hoche's expedition to Ireland.

Hoche himself was the inventor of a plan of harassing the English enemy which long remained in favour. He proposed to organise what was called a *Chouannerie* in England. As that country had no *Chouans* of her own, the want was to be supplied by sending over an expedition composed of convicts. Hoche's ideas were approved and adopted by the eminent Carnot. The plan, to which the former devoted great attention, was to land on the coast of Wales from 1000 to 1200 *forçats*, to be commanded by a certain Mascheret, of whom Hoche wrote that he was ' le plus mauvais sujet dont on puisse purger la France.' In a plan accepted and forwarded by Hoche, it was laid down that the band, on reaching the enemy's country, was, if possible, not to fight, but to pillage ; each man was to understand that he was sent to England to steal 100,000*f.*, ' pour ensuite finir sa carrière tranquillement dans l'aisance,' and was to be informed that he would receive a formal pardon from the French Government. The plan, extraordinary as it was, was one of the few put into execution. The famous Fishguard Invasion was carried out by some fourteen hundred convicts commanded by an American adventurer named Tate. The direction to avoid fighting was exactly obeyed by Colonel Tate and the armed criminals under his orders. He landed in Cardigan Bay from a small squadron of French men-of-war at sunset on the 22nd February 1797 ; and, on the appearance of Lord Cawdor with the local Yeomanry and Militia, asked to be allowed to surrender on the 24th. At a subsequent exchange of prisoners the French authorities refused to receive any of the worthies who had accompanied Tate. At length 512 were allowed to land ; but were imprisoned in the forts of Cherbourg. The French records contain many expressions of the dread experienced by the inhabitants of the coast lest the English should put on shore in France the malefactors whom they had captured at Fishguard.

A more promising enterprise was that in which it was decided to obtain the assistance of the Dutch, at the time in possession of a considerable fleet. The Dutch fleet was to put to sea with the object of engaging the English. An army of 15,000 was then to be embarked in the ports of Holland, and was to effect a diversion in favour of another and larger body, which, starting from France, was to land in Ireland, repeating the attempt of Hoche in December 1796, which will be dealt with later on. The enterprise was frustrated by the action of Admiral Duncan, who decisively defeated the Dutch fleet off Camperdown in October. It might have been supposed that this would have driven home the lesson that no considerable military expedition across the water has any chance of success till the country sending it has obtained

M

command of the sea ; but it did not. To Bonaparte
the event was full of meaning ; but no other French
soldier seems to have learned it—if we may take
Captain Desbrière's views as representative—even
down to the present day. On the 23rd February
1798 Bonaparte wrote : ' Opérer une descente en
Angleterre sans être maître de la mer est l'opération
la plus hardie et la plus difficile qui ait été faite.'
There has been much speculation as to the reasons
which induced Bonaparte to quit the command
of the 'Army of England' after holding it but a
short time, and after having devoted great attention to its organisation and proposed methods of
transport across the Channel. The question is less
difficult than it has appeared to be to many. One
of the foremost men in France, Bonaparte was
ready to take the lead in any undertaking which
seemed likely to have a satisfactory ending—an
ending which would redound to the glory of the
chief who conducted it. The most important
operation contemplated was the invasion of England;
and—now that Hoche was no more—Bonaparte
might well claim to lead it. His penetrating
insight soon enabled him to see its impractica-
bility until the French had won the command of
the Channel. Of that there was not much likeli-
hood ; and at the first favourable moment he
dissociated himself from all connection with an
enterprise which offered so little promise of a
successful termination that it was all but certain
not to be begun. An essential condition, as already

pointed out, of all the projected invasions was the receipt of assistance from sympathisers in the enemy's country. Hoche himself expected this even in Tate's case; but experience proved the expectation to be baseless. When the prisoners taken with Tate were being conducted to their place of confinement, the difficulty was to protect them, ' car la population furieuse contre les Français voulait les lyncher.' Captain Desbrière dwells at some length on the mutinies in the British fleet in 1797, and asks regretfully, ' Qu'avait-on fait pour profiter de cette chance unique ? ' He remarks on the undoubted and really lamentable fact that English historians have usually paid insufficient attention to these occurrences. One, and perhaps the principal reason of their silence, was the difficulty, at all events till quite lately, of getting materials with which to compose a narrative. The result is that the real character of the great mutinies has been altogether misunderstood. Lord Camperdown's recently published life of his great ancestor, Lord Duncan, has done something to put them in their right light. As regards defence against the enemy, the mutinies affected the security of the country very little. The seamen always expressed their determination to do their duty if the enemy put to sea. Even at the Nore they conspicuously displayed their general loyalty ; and, as a matter of fact, discipline had regained its sway some time before the expedition preparing in Holland was ready. How effectively the crews of the ships not long before involved in the mutiny could fight, was proved at Camperdown.

Though earlier in date than the events just discussed, the celebrated first expedition to Ireland has been intentionally left out of consideration till now. As to the general features of the undertaking, and even some of its more important details, the documents now published add little to our knowledge. The literature of the expedition is large, and Captain Chevalier had given us an admirable account of it in his ' Histoire de la Marine Française sous la première République.' The late Vice-Admiral Colomb submitted it to a most instructive examination in the *Journal of the Royal United Service Institution* for January 1892. We can, however, learn something from Captain Desbrière's collection. The perusal suggests, or indeed compels, the conclusion that the expedition was doomed to failure from the start. It had no money, stores, or means of transport. There was no hope of finding these in a country like the south-western corner of Ireland. Grouchy's decision not to land the troops who had reached Bantry Bay was no doubt dictated in reality by a perception of this ; and by the discovery that, even if he got on shore, sympathisers with him would be practically non-existent. On reading the letters now made public, one is convinced of Hoche's unfitness for the leadership of such an enterprise. The adoration of mediocrities is confined to no one cult and to no one age. Hoche's canonisation, for he is a prominent saint in the

Republican calendar, was due not so much to what he did as to what he did not do. He did not hold the supreme command in La Vendée till the most trying period of the war was past. He did not continue the cruelties of the Jacobin emissaries in the disturbed districts ; but then his pacificatory measures were taken when the spirit of ferocity which caused the horrors of the *noyades* and of the Terror had, even amongst the mob of Paris, burnt itself out. He did not overthrow a constitutional Government and enslave his country as Bonaparte did ; and, therefore, he is favourably compared with the latter, whose opportunities he did not have. His letters show him to have been an adept in the art of traducing colleagues behind their backs. In writing he called Admiral Villaret-Joyeuse ' perfide,' and spoke of his ' mauvaise foi.' He had a low opinion of General Humbert, whom he bracketed with Mascheret. Grouchy, he said, was ' un inconséquent paperassier,' and General Vaillant ' un misérable ivrogne.' He was placed in supreme command of the naval as well as of the military forces, and was allowed to select the commander of the former. Yet he and his nominee were amongst the small fraction of the expeditionary body which never reached a place where disembarkation was possible.

Notwithstanding all this, the greater part of the fleet, and of the troops conveyed by it, did anchor in Bantry Bay without encountering an English man-of-war ; and a large proportion continued in the Bay, unmolested by our navy, for more than a fortnight. Is not this, it may be asked, a sufficient refutation of those who hold that command of the sea gives security against invasion ? As a matter of fact, command of the sea—even in the case in question—did prevent invasion from being undertaken, still more from being carried through, on a scale likely to be very formidable. The total number of troops embarked was under 14,000, of whom 633 were lost, owing to steps taken to avoid the hostile navy, before the expedition had got fully under way. It is not necessary to rate Hoche's capacity very highly in order to understand that he, who had seen something of war on a grand scale, would not have committed himself to the command of so small a body, without cavalry, without means of transport on land, without supplies, with but an insignificant artillery and that not furnished with horses, and, as was avowed, without hope of subsequent reinforcement or of open communications with its base—that he would not have staked his reputation on the fate of a body so conditioned, if he had been permitted by the naval conditions of the case to lead a larger, more effectually organised, and better supplied army. The commentary supplied by Captain Desbrière to the volume under notice discloses his opinion that the failure of the expedition to Ireland was due to the inefficiency of the French Navy. He endeavours to be scrupulously fair to his naval fellow-countrymen ; but his conviction is apparent. It hardly admits of doubt that this view has generally been, and still is, prevalent in the French Army. Foreign soldiers of talent and experience generalise from this as follows : Let them but have the direction of the naval as well as of the military part of an expedition, and the invasion of England must be successful. The complete direction which they would like is exactly what Hoche did have. He chose the commander of the fleet, and also chose or regulated the choice of the junior flag officers and several of the captains. Admiral Morard de Galles was not, and did not consider himself, equal to the task for which Hoche's favour had selected him. His letter pointing out his own disqualifications has a striking resemblance to the one written by Medina Sidonia in deprecation of his appointment in place of Santa Cruz. Nevertheless, the French naval officers did succeed in conveying the greater part of the expeditionary army to a point at which disembarkation was practicable.

Now we have some lessons to learn from this. The advantages conferred by command of the sea must be utilised intelligently ; and it was bad management which permitted an important anchorage to remain for more than a fortnight in the hands of an invading force. We need not impute to our neighbours a burning desire to invade us ; but it is a becoming exercise of ordinary strategic precaution to contemplate preparations for repelling what, as a mere military problem, they consider still feasible. No amount of naval superiority will ever ensure every part of our coast against incursions like that of Tate and his gaol-birds. Naval superiority, however, will put in our hands the power of preventing the arrival of an army strong enough to carry out a real invasion. The strength of such an army will largely depend upon the amount of mobile land force of which we can dispose. Consequently, defence against invasion, even of an island, is the duty of a land army as well as of a fleet. The more important part may, in our case, be that of the latter ; but the services of the former cannot be dispensed with. The best method of utilising those services calls for much thought. In 1798, when the ' First Army of England ' menaced us from the southern coast of the Channel, it was reported to our Government that an examination of the plans formerly adopted for frustrating intended invasions showed the advantage of troubling the enemy in his own home and not waiting till he had come to injure us in ours.

VII

OVER-SEA RAIDS AND RAIDS ON LAND [1]

It has been contended that raids by 'armaments with 1000, 20,000, and 50,000 men on board respectively' have succeeded in evading 'our watching and chasing fleets,' and that consequently invasion of the British Isles on a great scale is not only possible but fairly practicable, British naval predominance notwithstanding. I dispute the accuracy of the history involved in the allusions to the above-stated figures. The number of men comprised in a raiding or invading expedition is the number that is or can be put on shore. The crews of the transports are not included in it. In the cases alluded to, Humbert's expedition was to have numbered 82 officers and 1017 other ranks, and 984 were put on shore in Killala Bay. Though the round number, 1000, represents this figure fairly enough, there was a 10 per cent. shrinkage from the original embarkation strength. In Hoche's expedition the total number of troops embarked

---

[1] Written in 1906. (*The Morning Post.*)

169

was under 14,000, of whom 633 were lost before the
expedition had got clear of its port of starting, and
of the remainder only a portion reached Ireland.
General Bonaparte landed in Egypt not 50,000 men,
but about 36,000.   In the expeditions of Hoche and
Humbert it was not expected that the force to be
landed would suffice of itself, the belief being that
it would be joined in each case by a large body of
adherents in the raided country. Outside the
ranks of the ' extremists of the dinghy school '—
whose number is unknown and is almost certainly
quite insignificant — no one asserts or ever has
asserted that raids in moderate strength are not
possible even in the face of a strong defending navy.
It is a fact that the whole of our defence policy for
many generations has been based upon an admission
of their possibility. Captain Mahan's statement
of the case has never been questioned by anyone of
importance.   It is as follows : ' The control of the
sea, however real, does not imply that an enemy's
single ships or small squadrons cannot steal out of
port, cannot cross more or less frequented tracts of
ocean, make harassing descents upon unprotected
points of a long coast-line, enter blockaded harbours.'
It is extraordinary that everyone does not perceive
that if this were not true the ' dinghy school '
would be right. Students of Clausewitz may be
expected to remember that the art of war does not
consist in making raids that are unsuccessful ; that
war is waged to gain certain great objects ; and
that the course of hostilities between two powerful

antagonists is affected little one way or the other by raids even on a considerable scale.

The Egyptian expedition of 1798 deserves fuller treatment than it has generally received. The preparations at Toulon and some Italian ports were known to the British Government. It being impossible for even a Moltke or—comparative resources being taken into account—the greater strategist Kodama to know everything in the mind of an opponent, the sensible proceeding is to guard against his doing what would be likely to do you most harm. The British Government had reason to believe that the Toulon expedition was intended to reinforce at an Atlantic port another expedition to be directed against the British Isles, or to effect a landing in Spain with a view to marching into Portugal and depriving our navy of the use of Lisbon. Either if effected would probably cause us serious mischief, and arrangements were made to prevent them. A landing in Egypt was, as the event showed, of little importance. The threat conveyed by it against our Indian possessions proved to be an empty one. Upwards of 30,000 hostile troops were locked up in a country from which they could exercise no influence on the general course of the war, and in which in the end they had to capitulate. Suppose that an expedition crossing the North Sea with the object of invading this country had to content itself with a landing in Iceland, having eventual capitulation before it, should we not consider ourselves very fortunate, though it may have temporarily occupied one of the Shetland Isles *en route*? The truth of the matter is that the Egyptian expedition was one of the gravest of strategical mistakes, and but for the marvellous subsequent achievements of Napoleon it would have been the typical example of bad strategy adduced by lecturers and writers on the art of war for the warning of students.

The supposition that over-sea raids, even when successful in part, in any way demonstrate the inefficiency of naval defence would never be admitted if only land and sea warfare were regarded as branches of one whole and not as quite distinct things. To be consistent, those that admit the supposition should also admit that the practicability of raids demonstrates still more conclusively the insufficiency of defence by an army. An eminent military writer has told us that ' a raiding party of 1000 French landed in Ireland without opposition, after sixteen days of navigation, unobserved by the British Navy ; defeated and drove back the British troops opposing them on four separate occasions . . . entirely occupied the attention of all the available troops of a garrison of Ireland 100,000 strong ; penetrated almost to the centre of the island, and compelled the Lord-Lieutenant to send an urgent requisition for "as great a reinforcement as possible." ' If an inference is to be drawn from this in the same way as one has been drawn from the circumstances on the sea, it would follow that one hundred thousand troops are not sufficient to prevent a raid by one thousand, and consequently that one million troops

would not be sufficient to prevent one by ten thousand
enemies. On this there would arise the question, If
an army a million strong gives no security against a
raid by ten thousand men, is an army worth having?
And this question, be it noted, would come, not
from disciples of the Blue Water School, 'extremist'
or other, but from students of military narrative.

The truth is that raids are far more common on
land than on the ocean. For every one of the latter
it would be possible to adduce several of the former.
Indeed, accounts of raids are amongst the common-
places of military history. There are few campaigns
since the time of that smart cavalry leader Mago,
the younger brother of Hannibal, in which raids
on land did not occur or in which they exercised
any decisive influence on the issue of hostilities.
It is only the failure to see the connection between
warfare on land and naval warfare that prevents
these land raids being given the same significance
and importance that is usually given to those
carried out across the sea.

In the year 1809, the year of Wagram, Napoleon's
military influence in Central Germany was, to say
the least, not at its lowest. Yet Colonel Schill, of
the Prussian cavalry, with 1200 men, subsequently
increased to 2000 infantry and 12 squadrons,
proceeded to Wittenberg, thence to Magdeburg, and
next to Stralsund, which he occupied and where
he met his death in opposing an assault made by
6000 French troops. He had defied for a month
all the efforts of a large army to suppress him. In

the same year the Duke of Brunswick-Oels and Colonel Dornberg, notwithstanding the smallness of the force under them, by their action positively induced Napoleon, only a few weeks before Wagram, to detach the whole corps of Kellerman, 30,000 strong, which otherwise would have been called up to the support of the Grande Armée, to the region in which these enterprising raiders were operating. The mileage covered by Schill was nearly as great as that covered by the part of Hoche's expedition which under Grouchy did reach an Irish port, though it was not landed. Instances of cavalry raids were frequent in the War of Secession in America. The Federal Colonel B. H. Grierson, of the 6th Illinois Cavalry, with another Illinois and an Iowa cavalry regiment, in April 1863 made a raid which lasted sixteen days, and in which he covered 600 miles of hostile country, finally reaching Baton Rouge, where a friendly force was stationed. The Confederate officers, John H. Morgan, John S. Mosby, and especially N. B. Forrest, were famous for the extent and daring of their raids. Of all the leaders of important raids in the War of Secession none surpassed the great Confederate cavalry General, J. E. B. Stuart, whose riding right round the imposing Federal army is well known. Yet not one of the raids above mentioned had any effect on the main course of the war in which they occurred or on the result of the great conflict.

In the last war the case was the same. In January 1905, General Mischenko with 10,000 sabres and three batteries of artillery marched right round the flank of Marshal Oyama's great Japanese army, and occupied Niu-chwang—not the treaty port so-called, but a place not very far from it. For several days he was unmolested, and in about a week he got back to his friends with a loss which was moderate in proportion to his numbers. In the following May Mischenko made another raid, this time round General Nogi's flank. He had with him fifty squadrons, a horse artillery battery, and a battery of machine guns. Starting on the 17th, he was discovered on the 18th, came in contact with his enemy on the 19th, but met with no considerable hostile force till the 20th, when the Japanese cavalry arrived just in time to collide with the Russian rearguard of two squadrons. On this General Mischenko 'retired at his ease for some thirty miles along the Japanese flank and perhaps fifteen miles away from it.' These Russians' raids did not alter the course of the war nor bring ultimate victory to their standards.

It would be considered by every military authority as a flagrant absurdity to deduce from the history of these many raids on land that a strong army is not a sufficient defence for a continental country against invasion. What other efficient defence against that can a continental country have ? Apply the reasoning to the case of an insular country, and reliance on naval defence will be abundantly justified.

To maintain that Canada, India, and Egypt respectively could be invaded by the United States,

Russia, and Turkey, backed by Germany, notwithstanding any action that our navy could take, would be equivalent to maintaining that one part of our empire cannot or need not reinforce another. Suppose that we had a military force numerically equal to or exceeding the Russian, how could any of it be sent to defend Canada, India, and Egypt, or to reinforce the defenders of those countries, unless our sea communications were kept open ? Can these be kept open except by the action of our navy ?   It is plain that they cannot.

VIII

QUEEN ELIZABETH AND HER SEAMEN [1]

An eminent writer has recently repeated the accusations made within the last forty years, and apparently only within that period, against Queen Elizabeth of having starved the seamen of her fleet by giving them food insufficient in quantity and bad in quality, and of having robbed them by keeping them out of the pay due to them. He also accuses the Queen, though somewhat less plainly, of having deliberately acquiesced in a wholesale slaughter of her seamen by remaining still, though no adequate provision had been made for the care of the sick and wounded. There are further charges of obstinately objecting, out of mere stinginess, to take proper measures for the naval defence of the country, and of withholding a sufficient supply of ammunition from her ships when about to meet the enemy. Lest it should be supposed that this is an exaggerated statement of the case against Elizabeth as formulated by the writer in question, his own words are given. He says : 'Instead of strengthening her armaments to the utmost, and throwing herself upon her

---

[1] Written in 1900. (*Nineteenth Century and After*, 1901.)

Parliament for aid, she clung to her moneybags, actually reduced her fleet, withheld ammunition and the more necessary stores, cut off the sailor's food, did, in short, everything in her power to expose the country defenceless to the enemy. The pursuit of the Armada was stopped by the failure of the ammunition, which, apparently, had the fighting continued longer, would have been fatal to the English fleet.'

The writer makes on this the rather mild comment that ' treason itself could scarcely have done worse.' Why ' scarcely ' ? Surely the very blackest treason could not have done worse. He goes on to ask : ' How were the glorious seamen, whose memory will be for ever honoured by England and the world, rewarded after their victory ? '

This is his answer : ' Their wages were left unpaid, they were docked of their food, and served with poisonous drink, while for the sick and wounded no hospitals were provided. More of them were killed by the Queen's meanness than by the enemy.'

It is safe to challenge the students of history throughout the world to produce any parallel to conduct so infamous as that which has thus been imputed to an English queen. If the charges are true, there is no limit to the horror and loathing with which we ought to regard Elizabeth. Are they true ? That is the question. I respectfully invite the attention of those who wish to know the truth and to retain their reverence for a great historical character, to the following examination of the accusations and of the foundations on which they rest. It will not, I hope, be considered presumptuous if I say that—in making this examination —personal experience of life in the navy sufficiently extensive to embrace both the present day and the time before the introduction of the great modern changes in system and naval *matériel* will be of great help. Many things which have appeared so extraordinary to landsmen that they could account for their occurrence only by assuming that this must have been due to extreme culpability or extreme folly will be quite familiar to naval officers whose experience of the service goes back forty years or more, and can be satisfactorily explained by them.

There is little reason to doubt that the above-mentioned charges against the great Queen are based exclusively on statements in Froude's History. It is remarkable how closely Froude has been followed by writers treating of Elizabeth and her reign. He was known to have gone to original documents for the sources of his narrative ; and it seems to have been taken for granted, not only that his fidelity was above suspicion—an assumption with which I do not deal now—but also that his interpretation of the meaning of those who wrote the papers consulted must be correct. Motley, in his ' History of the United Netherlands,' published in 1860, had dwelt upon the shortness of ammunition and provisions in the Channel Fleet commanded

by Lord Howard of Effingham ; but he attributed
this to bad management on the part of officials,
and not to downright baseness on that of
Elizabeth.

Froude has placed beyond doubt his determination to make the Queen responsible for all short-
comings.

'The Queen,' he says, 'has taken upon herself
the detailed arrangement of everything. She and
she alone was responsible. She had extended to
the dockyards the same hard thrift with which
she had pared down her expenses everywhere. She
tied the ships to harbour by supplying the stores
in driblets. She allowed rations but for a month,
and permitted no reserves to be provided in the
victualling offices. The ships at Plymouth, furnished
from a distance, and with small quantities at a
time, were often for many days without food of
any kind. Even at Plymouth, short food and
poisonous drink had brought dysentery among
them. They had to meet the enemy, as it were,
with one arm bandaged by their own sovereign.
The greatest service ever done by an English fleet
had been thus successfully accomplished by men
whose wages had not been paid from the time of
their engagement, half-starved, with their clothes
in rags, and so ill-found in the necessaries of war
that they had eked out their ammunition by
what they could take in action from the enemy
himself. The men expected that at least after such
a service they would be paid their wages in full.

The Queen was cavilling over the accounts, and would give no orders for money till she had demanded the meaning of every penny that she was charged. . . . Their legitimate food had been stolen from them by the Queen's own neglect.'

We thus see that Froude has made Elizabeth personally responsible for the short rations, the undue delay in paying wages earned, and the fearful sickness which produced a heavy mortality amongst the crews of her Channel Fleet ; and also for insufficiently supplying her ships with ammunition.

The quotations from the book previously referred to make it clear that it is possible to outdo Froude in his denunciations, even where it is on his statements that the accusers found their charges. In his ' History of England '—which is widely read, especially by the younger generation of Englishmen —the Rev. J. Franck Bright tells us, with regard to the defensive campaign against the Armada : ' The Queen's avarice went near to ruin the country. The miserable supplies which Elizabeth had alone allowed to be sent them (the ships in the Channel) had produced all sorts of disease, and thousands of the crews came from their great victory only to die. In the midst of privations, and wanting in all the necessaries of life, the sailors had fought with unflagging energy, with their wages unpaid, with ammunition supplied to them with so stingy a hand that each shot sent on board was registered and accounted for ; with provisions withheld, so that the food of four men had habitually to be divided among six, and that food so bad as to be really poisonous.'

J. R. Green, in his 'History of the English People,' states that : 'While England was thrilling with the triumph over the Armada, its Queen was coolly grumbling over the cost and making her profit out of the spoiled provisions she had ordered for the fleet that had saved her.'

The object of each subsequent historian was to surpass the originator of the calumnies against Elizabeth.   In his sketch of her life in the 'Dictionary of National Biography,' Dr. Augustus Jessopp asserts that the Queen's ships 'were notoriously and scandalously ill-furnished with stores and provisions for the sailors, and it is impossible to lay the blame on anyone but the Queen.' He had previously remarked that the merchant vessels which came to the assistance of the men-of-war from London and the smaller ports 'were as a rule far better furnished than the Queen's ships,' which were 'without the barest necessaries.' After these extracts one from Dr. S. R. Gardiner's 'Student's History of England' will appear moderate.   Here it is : 'Elizabeth having with her usual economy kept the ships short of powder, they were forced to come back' from the chase of the Armada.

The above allegations constitute a heavy indictment of the Queen. No heavier could well be brought against any sovereign or government.

Probably the first thing that occurs to anyone who, knowing what Elizabeth's position was, reads the tremendous charges made against her will be, that —if they are true—she must have been without a rival in stupidity as well as in turpitude. There was no person in the world who had as much cause to desire the defeat of the Armada as she had. If the Duke of Medina Sidonia's expedition had been successful she would have lost both her throne and her life. She herself and her father had shown that there could be a short way with Queens— consort or regnant—whom you had in your power, and whose existence might be inconvenient to you. Yet, if we are to believe her accusers, she did her best to ensure her own dethronement and decapitation. 'The country saved itself and its cause in spite of its Queen.'

How did this extraordinary view of Elizabeth's conduct arise ? What had Froude to go upon when he came forward as her accuser ? These questions can be answered with ease. Every Government that comes near going to war, or that has gone to war, is sure to incur one of two charges, made according to circumstances. If the Government prepares for war and yet peace is preserved, it is accused of unpardonable extravagance in making preparations. Whether it makes these on a sufficient scale or not, it is accused, if war does break out—at least in the earlier period of the contest— of not having done enough. Political opponents and the ' man in the street ' agree in charging the administration with panic profusion in one case, and with criminal niggardliness in the other. Elizabeth hoped to preserve peace. She had succeeded in keeping out of an 'official' war for a long time, and she had much justification for the belief that she could do so still longer. 'She could not be thoroughly persuaded,' says Mr. David Hannay,[1] 'that it was hopeless to expect to avert the Spanish invasion by artful diplomacy.' Whilst reasonable precautions were not neglected, she was determined that no one should be able to say with truth that she had needlessly thrown away money in a fright. For the general naval policy of England at the time, Elizabeth, as both the nominal and the real head of the Government, is properly held responsible. The event showed the perfect efficiency of that policy.

The war having really come, it was inevitable that the Government, and Elizabeth as its head, should be blamed sooner or later for not having made adequate provision for it. No one is better entitled to speak on the naval policy of the Armada epoch than Mr. Julian Corbett,[2] who is not disposed to assume that the Queen's action was above criticism. He says that 'Elizabeth has usually been regarded as guilty of complete and unpardonable inaction.' He explains that 'the event at least justified the Queen's policy. There is no trace of her having been blamed for it at the time

---

[1] *A Short History of the Royal Navy*, pp. 96, 97.
[2] *Drake and the Tudor Navy*, 1898, vol. ii. p. 117.

at home ; nor is there any reason to doubt it was adopted sagaciously and deliberately on the advice of her most capable officers.' Mr. David Hannay, who, as an historian, rightly takes into consideration the conditions of the age, points out that ' Elizabeth was a very poor sovereign, and the maintenance of a great fleet was a heavy drain upon her resources.' He adds : ' There is no reason to suppose that Elizabeth and her Lord Treasurer were careless of their duty ; but the Government of the time had very little experience in the maintenance of great military forces.'

If we take the charges against her in detail, we shall find that each is as ill-founded as that of criminal neglect of naval preparations generally. The most serious accusation is that with regard to the victuals. It will most likely be a surprise to many people to find that the seamen of Elizabeth were victualled on a more abundant and much more costly scale than the seamen of Victoria. Nevertheless, such is the fact. In 1565 the contract allowance for victualling was 4½d. a day for each man in harbour, and 5d. a day at sea. There was also an allowance of 4d. a man per month at sea and 8d. in harbour for ' purser's necessaries.' Mr. Oppenheim, in whose valuable work [1] on naval administration the details as to the Elizabethan victualling system are to be found, tells us that in 1586 the rate was raised to 6d. a day in harbour

---

[1] *The Administration of the Royal Navy, 1509–1660.* London, 1896.

and 6½d. at sea; and that in 1587 it was again raised, this time to 6½d. in harbour and 7d. at sea. These sums were intended to cover both the cost of the food and storage, custody, conveyance, &c., the present-day 'establishment charges.' The repeated raising of the money allowance is convincing proof that the victualling arrangements had not been neglected, and that there was no refusal to sanction increased expenditure to improve them. It is a great thing to have Mr. Oppenheim's high authority for this, because he is not generally favourable to the Queen, though even he admits that it 'is a moot point' how far she was herself responsible.

If necessary, detailed arguments could be adduced to show that to get the present value of the sums allowed in 1588 we ought to multiply them by six.[1] The sum allowed for each man's daily food and the 'establishment charges'— increased as they had been in 1586—did little more than cover the expenditure; and, though it does not appear that the contractor lost money, he nevertheless died a poor man. It will be hardly imputed to Elizabeth for iniquity that she did not consider that the end of government was the enrichment of contractors. The fact that she increased the money payment again in 1587 may be accepted as proof that she did not object to a fair bargain. As has been just said, the Elizabethan

---

[1] See Mr. Hubert Hall's *Society in the Elizabethan Age*, and Thorold Rogers's *History of Agriculture and Prices*, vols. v. and vi. Froude himself puts the ratio at six to one.

scale of victualling was more abundant than the early Victorian, and not less abundant than that given in the earlier years of King Edward VII.[1] As shown by Mr. Hubert Hall and Thorold Rogers, in the price-lists which they publish, the cost of a week's allowance of food for a man-of-war's man in 1588, in the money of the time, amounted to about 1s. 11½d., which, multiplied by six, would be about 11s. 9d. of our present money. The so-called 'savings price' of the early twentieth century

[1] It will be convenient to compare the 'two scales in a footnote, observing that—as I hope will not be thought impertinent—I draw on my own personal experience for the more recent, which was in force for some years after I went to sea.

WEEKLY

	Elizabethan scale.	Early Victorian scale.
Beef	8 lbs.	7 lbs.
Biscuit	7 ,,	7 ,,
Salted fish	9 ,,	none
Cheese	¾ lb.	,,
Butter	,,	,,
Beer	7 gallons	,,
Vegetables	none	3½ lbs.
Spirits	,,	⅞ pint
Tea	,,	1¾ oz.
Sugar	,,	14 ,,
Cocoa	,,	7 ,,

There is now a small allowance of oatmeal, pepper, mustard, and vinegar, against which we may set the 'purser's necessaries' of Elizabeth's day. In that day but little sugar was used, and tea and cocoa were unknown even in palaces. It is just a question if seven gallons of beer did not make up for the weekly allowance of these and for the seven-eighths of a pint of spirits. Tea was only allowed in 1850, and was not an additional article. It replaced part of the spirits. The biscuit allowance is now 8¾ lbs. weekly.

allowance was about $9\frac{1}{2}d$. a day, or $5s$. $6\frac{1}{2}d$. weekly. The 'savings price' is the amount of money which a man received if he did not take up his victuals, each article having a price attached to it for that purpose. It may be interesting to know that the full allowance was rarely, perhaps never, taken up, and that some part of the savings was till the last, and for many years had been, almost invariably paid.

The Victorian dietary is more varied and wholesome than the Elizabethan ; but, as we have seen, it is less abundant and can be obtained for much less money, even if we grant that the 'savings price'—purposely kept low to avoid all suggestion that the men are being bribed into stinting themselves—is less than the real cost. The excess of this latter, however, is not likely to be more than 30 per cent., so that Elizabeth's expenditure in this department was more liberal than the present. Such defects as were to be found in the Elizabethan naval dietary were common to it with that of the English people generally. If there was plenty, there was but little variety in the food of our ancestors of all ranks three centuries ago. As far as was possible in the conditions of the time, Elizabeth's Government did make provision for victualling the fleet on a sufficient and even liberal scale ; and, notwithstanding slender pecuniary resources, repeatedly increased the money assigned to it, on cause being shown. In his eagerness to make Queen Elizabeth a monster of treacherous rapacity, Froude has completely overreached himself. He says that 'she permitted some miserable scoundrel to lay a plan before her for saving expense, by cutting down the seamen's diet.' The 'miserable scoundrel' had submitted a proposal for diminishing the expenses which the administration was certainly ill able to bear. The candid reader will draw his own conclusions when he finds that the Queen did not approve the plan submitted ; and yet that not one of her assailants has let this appear.[1]

It is, of course, possible to concede that adequate arrangements had been made for the general victualling of the fleet ; and still to maintain that, after all, the sailors afloat actually did run short of food. In his striking 'Introduction to the Armada Despatches' published by the Navy Records Society, Professor Sir John Laughton declares that : 'To any one examining the evidence, there can be no question as to victualling being conducted on a fairly liberal scale, as far as the money was concerned. It was in providing the victuals that the difficulty lay. . . . When a fleet of unprecedented magnitude was collected, when a sudden and unwonted demand was made on the victualling officers, it would have been strange indeed if things had gone quite smoothly.'

There are plenty of naval officers who have had

---

[1] It may be stated here that the word ' rations ' is unknown in the navy. The official term is ' victuals.' The term in common use is ' provisions.'

experience, and within the last ten years of the nine-teenth century, of the difficulty, and sometimes of the impossibility, of getting sufficient supplies for a large number of ships in rather out-of-the-way places. In 1588 the comparative thinness of population and insufficiency of communications and means of trans-port must have constituted obstacles, far greater than any encountered in our own day, to the collection of supplies locally and to their timely importation from a distance. 'You would not believe,' says Lord Howard of Effingham himself, 'what a wonderful thing it is to victual such an army as this is in such a narrow corner of the earth, where a man would think that neither victuals were to be had nor a cask to put it in.' No more effective defence of Elizabeth and her Ministers could well be advanced than that which Mr. Oppenheim puts forward as a corrobora-tion of the accusation against them. He says that the victualling officials 'found no difficulty in arranging for 13,000 men in 1596 and 9200 in 1597 after timely notice.' This is really a high compli-ment, as it proves that the authorities were quite ready to, and in fact did, learn from experience. Mr. Oppenheim, however, is not an undiscriminating assailant of the Queen ; for he remarks, as has been already said, that, 'how far Elizabeth was herself answerable is a moot point.' He tells us that there ' is no direct evidence against her ' ; and the charge levelled at her rests not on proof, but on ' strong probability.' One would like to have another instance out of all history, of probability, however strong, being deemed sufficient to convict a person of unsurpassed treachery and stupidity combined, when the direct evidence, which is not scanty, fails to support the charge and indeed points the other way.

The Lord Admiral himself and other officers have been quoted to show how badly off the fleet was for food. Yet at the close of the active operations against the Armada, Sir J. Hawkins wrote : ' Here is victual sufficient, and I know not why any should be provided after September, but for those which my Lord doth mean to leave in the narrow seas.' On the same day Howard himself wrote from Dover : ' I have caused all the remains of victuals to be laid here and at Sandwich, for the maintaining of them that shall remain in the Narrow Seas.' Any naval officer with experience of command who reads Howard's representations on the subject of the victuals will at once perceive that what the Admiral was anxious about was not the quantity on board the ships, but the stock in reserve. Howard thought that the latter ought to be a supply for six weeks. The Council thought a month's stock would be enough ; and—as shown by the extracts from Howard's and Hawkins's letters just given—the Council was right in its estimate. Anyone who has had to write or to read official letters about stocks of stores and provisions will find something especially modern in Howard's representations.

Though the crews of the fleet did certainly come near the end of their victuals afloat, there is no case of their having actually run out of them. The complement of an ordinary man-of-war in the latter part of the sixteenth century, judged by our modern standard, was very large in proportion to her size. It was impossible for her to carry provisions enough to last her men for a long time. Any unexpected prolongation of a cruise threatened a reduction to short commons. A great deal has been made of the fact that Howard had to oblige six men to put up with the allowance of four. ' When a large force,' says Mr. D. Hannay, ' was collected for service during any length of time, it was the common rule to divide four men's allowance among six.' There must be still many officers and men to whom the plan would seem quite familiar. It is indicated by a recognised form of words, ' six upon four.' I have myself been ' six upon four ' several times, mostly in the Pacific, but also, on at least one occasion, in the East Indies. As far as I could see, no one appeared to regard it as an intolerable hardship. The Government, it should be known, made no profit out of the process, because money was substituted for the food not issued. Howard's recourse to it was not due to immediate insufficiency. Speaking of the merchant vessels which came to reinforce him, he says : ' We are fain to help them with victuals to bring them thither. There is not any of them that hath one day's victuals.' These merchant vessels were supplied by private owners ; and it is worth noting that, in the teeth of this statement by Howard, Dr. Jessopp, in his eagerness to blacken Elizabeth, says that they ' were, as a rule, far better furnished than the Queen's ships.' The Lord Admiral on another occasion, before the fight off Gravelines, said of the ships he hoped would join him from Portsmouth : ' Though they have not two days' victuals, let that not be the cause of their stay, for they shall have victuals out of our fleet,' a conclusive proof that his ships were not very short.

As to the accusation of deliberately issuing food of bad quality, that is effectually disposed of by the explanation already given of the method employed in victualling the navy. A sum was paid for each man's daily allowance to a contractor, who was expressly bound to furnish ' good and seasonable victuals.' [1] Professor Laughton, whose competence in the matter is universally allowed, informs us that complaints of bad provisions are by no means confined to the Armada epoch, and were due, not to intentional dishonesty and neglect, but to insufficient knowledge of the way to preserve provisions for use on rather long cruises. Mr. Hannay says that the fleet sent to the coast of Spain, in the year after the defeat of the Armada, suffered much from want of food and sickness. ' Yet it was organised, not by the Queen, but by a committee of adventurers who had every motive to fit it out well.' It is the fashion with English historians to paint the condition of the navy in the time of the Commonwealth in glowing colours, yet Mr. Oppenheim cites many

[1] See ' The Mariners of England before the Armada,' by Mr. H. Halliday Sparling, in the *English Illustrated Magazine*, July 1, 1891.

occasions of well-founded complaints of the victuals. He says : ' The quality of the food supplied to the men and the honesty of the victualling agents both steadily deteriorated during the Commonwealth.' Lord Howard's principal difficulty was with the beer, which would go sour. The beer was the most frequent subject of protest in the Commonwealth times. Also, in 1759, Lord (then Sir Edward) Hawke reported : ' Our daily employment is condemning the beer from Plymouth.' The difficulty of brewing beer that would stand a sea voyage seemed to be insuperable. The authorities, however, did not soon abandon attempts to get the right article. Complaints continued to pour in ; but they went on with their brewing till 1835, and then gave it up as hopeless.

One must have had personal experience of the change to enable one to recognise the advance that has been made in the art of preserving articles of food within the last half-century. In the first Drury Lane pantomime that I can remember—about a year before I went to sea—a practical illustration of the quality of some of the food supplied to the navy was offered during the harlequinade by the clown, who satisfied his curiosity as to the contents of a large tin of ' preserved meat ' by pulling out a dead cat. On joining the service I soon learned that, owing to the badness of the ' preserved ' food that had been supplied, the idea of issuing tinned meat had been abandoned. It was not resumed till some years later. It is often made a joke against naval officers of a certain age that, before eating a biscuit, they

have a trick of rapping the table with it. We con-
tracted the habit as midshipmen when it was necessary to get rid of the weevils in the biscuit before it
could be eaten, and a fairly long experience taught
us that rapping the table with it was an effectual
plan for expelling them.

There is no more justification for accusing Queen
Elizabeth of failure to provide well-preserved food
to her sailors than there is for accusing her of not
having sent supplies to Plymouth by railway.
Steam transport and efficient food preservation were
equally unknown in her reign and for long after.
It has been intimated above that, even had she
wished to, she could not possibly have made any
money out of bad provisions. The victualling
system did not permit of her doing so. The austere
republican virtue of the Commonwealth authorities
enabled them to do what was out of Elizabeth's
power. In 1653, ' beer and other provisions " de-
cayed and unfit for use " were licensed for export
free of Customs.' Mr. Oppenheim, who reports this
fact, makes the remarkable comment that this was
done ' perhaps in the hope that such stores would go
to Holland,' with whose people we were at war.
As the heavy mortality in the navy had always been
ascribed to the use of bad provisions, we cannot
refuse to give to the sturdy Republicans who
governed England in the seventeenth century the
credit of contemplating a more insidious and more
effective method of damaging their enemy than
poisoning his wells. One would like to have it from

some jurist if the sale of poisonously bad food to your enemy is disallowed by international law.

That there was much sickness in the fleet and that many seamen died is, unfortunately, true. If Howard's evidence is to be accepted—as it always is when it seems to tell against the Queen—it is impossible to attribute this to the bad quality of the food then supplied. The Lord Admiral's official report is ' that the ships of themselves be so infectious and corrupted as it is thought to be a very plague ; and we find that the fresh men that we draw into our ships are infected one day and die the next.' The least restrained assertor of the ' poisonous ' food theory does not contend that it killed men within twenty-four hours. The Armada reached the Channel on the 20th of July (30th, New Style). A month earlier Howard had reported that ' several men have fallen sick and by thousands fain to be discharged ' ; and, after the fighting was over, he said of the *Elizabeth Jonas*, she ' hath had a great infection in her from the beginning.' Lord Henry Seymour, who commanded the division of the fleet stationed in the Straits of Dover, noted that the sickness was a repetition of that of the year before, and attributed it not to bad food, but to the weather. ' Our men,' he wrote, ' fall sick by reason of the cold nights and cold mornings we find ; and I fear me they will drop away faster than they did last year with Sir Henry Palmer, which was thick enough.'

' The sickness,' says Professor Laughton, ' was primarily and chiefly due to infection from the shore and ignorance or neglect of what we now know as sanitary laws. . . . Similar infections continued occasionally to scourge our ships' companies, and still more frequently French and Spanish ships' companies, till near the close of the eighteenth century.' It is not likely that any evidence would suffice to divert from their object writers eager to hurl calumny at a great sovereign ; but a little knowledge of naval and of military history also would have saved their readers from a belief in their accusations. In 1727 the fleet in the West Indies commanded by Admiral Hosier, commemorated in Glover's ballad, lost ten flag officers and captains, fifty lieutenants, and 4000 seamen. In the Seven Years' war the total number belonging to the fleet killed in action was 1512 ; whilst the number that died of disease and were missing was 133,708. From 1778 to 1783, out of 515,000 men voted by Parliament for the navy, 132,623 were ' sent sick.' In the summer, 1779, the French fleet cruising at the mouth of the English Channel, after landing 500, had still about 2000 men sick. At the beginning of autumn the number of sick had become so great that many ships had not enough men to work them. The *Ville de Paris* had 560 sick, and lost 61. The *Auguste* had 500 sick, and lost 44. On board the *Intrépide* 70 died out of 529 sick. These were the worst cases ; but other ships also suffered heavily.

It is, perhaps, not generally remembered till what a very late date armies and navies were more than decimated by disease. In 1810 the House of

Commons affirmed by a resolution, concerning the Walcheren Expedition: 'That on the 19th of August a malignant disorder showed itself amongst H.M. troops; and that on the 8th of September the number of sick amounted to upwards of 10,948 men. That of the army which embarked for service in the Scheldt sixty officers and 3900 men, exclusive of those killed by the enemy, had died before the 1st of February last.'

In a volume of 'Military, Medical, and Surgical Essays'[1] prepared for the United States' Sanitary Commission, and edited by Dr. Wm. A. Hammond, Surgeon-General of the U.S. Army, it is stated that, in our Peninsular army, averaging a strength of 64,227 officers and men, the annual rate of mortality from the 25th of December 1810 to the 25th of May 1813 was 10 per cent. of the officers and 16 per cent. of the men. We may calculate from this that some 25,000 officers and men died. There were $22\frac{1}{2}$ per cent., or over 14,000, 'constantly sick.' Out of 309,268 French soldiers sent to the Crimea in 1855-6, the number of killed and those who died of wounds was 7500, the number who died of disease was 61,700. At the same date navies also suffered. Dr. Stilon Mends, in his life of his father,[2] Admiral Sir William Mends, prints a letter in which the Admiral, speaking of the cholera in the fleets at Varna, says: 'The mortality on board the *Montebello, Ville de Paris, Valmy* (French ships), and *Britannia* (British) has been terrible; the first lost 152 in three days, the

[1] Philadelphia, 1864.   [2] London, 1899.

second 120 in thrée days, the third 80 in ten days, but the last lost 50 in one night and 10 the subsequent day.' Kinglake tells us that in the end the *Britannia's* loss went up to 105. With the above facts before us, we are compelled to adopt one of two alternatives. We must either maintain that sanitary science made no advance between 1588 and 1855, or admit that the mortality in Elizabeth's fleet became what it was owing to ignorance of sanitary laws and not to intentional bad management. As regards care of the sick, it is to be remembered that the establishment of naval and military hospitals for the reception of sick soldiers and sailors is of recent date. For instance, the two great English military hospitals, Netley and the Herbert, are only about sixty years old.

So far from our fleet in 1588 having been ill-supplied with ammunition, it was in reality astonishingly well equipped, considering the age. We learn from Mr. Julian Corbett,[1] that ' during the few years immediately preceding the outbreak of the war, the Queen's navy had been entirely re-armed with brass guns, and in the process of re-armament a great advance in simplicity had been secured.' Froude, without seeing where the admission would land him, admits that our fleet was more plentifully supplied than the Armada, in which, he says, ' the supply of cartridges was singularly small. The King [Philip the Second] probably considered that a single action

[1] *The Spanish War, 1585–87* (Navy Records Society), 1898, p. 323.

would decide the struggle ; and it amounted to but fifty rounds for each gun.' Our own supply therefore exceeded fifty rounds. In his life of Vice-Admiral Lord Lyons,[1] Sir S. Eardley Wilmot tells us that the British ships which attacked the Sebastopol forts in October 1854 ' could only afford to expend seventy rounds per gun.' At the close of the nineteenth century, the regulated allowance for guns mounted on the broadside was eighty-five rounds each. Consequently, the Elizabethan allowance was nearly, if not quite, as much as that which our authorities, after an experience of naval warfare during three centuries, thought sufficient. ' The full explanation,' says Professor Laughton, ' of the want [of ammunition] seems to lie in the rapidity of fire which has already been mentioned. The ships had the usual quantity on board ; but the expenditure was more, very many times more, than anyone could have conceived.' Mr. Julian Corbett considers it doubtful if the ammunition, in at least one division of the fleet, was nearly exhausted.

Exhaustion of the supply of ammunition in a single action is a common naval occurrence. The not very decisive character of the battle of Malaga between Sir George Rooke and the Count of Toulouse in 1704 was attributed to insufficiency of ammunition, the supply in our ships having been depleted by what ' Mediterranean ' Byng, afterwards Lord Torrington, calls the ' furious fire ' opened on Gibraltar. The Rev. Thomas Pocock, Chaplain of

[1] London, 1898, p. 236.

the *Ranelagh*, Byng's flag-ship at Malaga, says : [1]
'Many of our ships went out of the line for want of
ammunition.' Byng's own opinion, as stated by the
compiler of his memoirs, was, that 'it may without
great vanity be said that the English had gained a
greater victory if they had been supplied with ammunition as they ought to have been.' I myself
heard the late Lord Alcester speak of the anxiety
that had been caused him by the state of his ships'
magazines after the attack on the Alexandria forts
in 1882. At a still later date, Admiral Dewey in
Manila Bay interrupted his attack on the Spanish
squadron to ascertain how much ammunition his
ships had left. The carrying capacity of ships being
limited, rapid gun-fire in battle invariably brings
with it the risk of running short of ammunition. It
did this in the nineteenth century just as much as,
probably even more than, it did in the sixteenth.

To charge Elizabeth with criminal parsimony
because she insisted on every shot being 'registered
and accounted for' will be received with ridicule by
naval officers. Of course every shot, and for the
matter of that every other article expended, has to
be accounted for. One of the most important duties
of the gunner of a man-of-war is to keep a strict
account of the expenditure of all gunnery stores.
This was more exactly done under Queen Victoria
than it was under Queen Elizabeth. Naval officers
are more hostile to 'red tape' than most men, and

[1] In his journal (p. 197), printed as an Appendix to *Memoirs
relating to the Lord Torrington*, edited by J. K. Laughton for
the Camden Society, 1889.

they may lament the vast amount of bookkeeping that modern auditors and committees of public accounts insist upon, but they are convinced that a reasonable check on expenditure of stores is indispensable to efficient organisation. So far from blaming Elizabeth for demanding this, they believe that both she and Burleigh, her Lord Treasurer, were very much in advance of their age.

Another charge against her is that she defrauded her seamen of their wages. The following is Froude's statement :—

' Want of the relief, which, if they had been paid their wages, they might have provided for themselves had aggravated the tendencies to disease, and a frightful mortality now set in through the entire fleet.' The word ' now ' is interesting, Froude having had before him Howard's and Seymour's letters, already quoted, showing that the appearance of the sickness was by no means recent. Elizabeth's illiberality towards her seamen may be judged from the fact that in her reign their pay was certainly increased once and perhaps twice.[1] In 1585 the sailor's pay was raised from 6s. 8d. to 10s. a month. A rise of pay of 50 per cent. all at once is, I venture to say, entirely without parallel in the navy since, and cannot well be called illiberal. The Elizabethan 10s. would be equal to £3 in our present accounts ; and, as the naval month at the earlier date was the lunar, a sailor's yearly wages would be equal to £39

[1] Mr. Halliday Sparling, in the article already referred to (p. 651), says twice ; but Mr. Oppenheim seems to think that the first increase was before Elizabeth's accession.

now. The year's pay of an A.B., ' non-continuous service,' as Elizabeth's sailors were, is at the present time £24 6s. 8d. It is true that the sailor now can receive additional pay for good-conduct badges, gunnery-training, &c., and also can look forward to that immense boon—a pension—nearly, but thanks to Sir J. Hawkins and Drake's establishment of the ' Chatham Chest,' not quite unknown in the sixteenth century. Compared with the rate of wages ruling on shore, Elizabeth's seamen were paid highly. Mr. Hubert Hall states that for labourers ' the usual rate was 2d. or 3d. a day.' Ploughmen received a shilling a week. In these cases ' board ' was also given. The sailor's pay was 5s. a week with board. Even compared with skilled labour on shore the sailor of the Armada epoch was well paid. Thorold Rogers gives, for 1588, the wages, without board, of carpenters and masons at 10d. and 1s. a day. A plumber's wages varied from 10½d. to 1s. ; but there is one case of a plumber receiving as much as 1s. 4d., which was probably for a single day.

Delay in the payment of wages was not peculiar to the Elizabethan system. It lasted very much longer, down to our own times in fact. In 1588 the seamen of the fleet were kept without their pay for several months. In the great majority of cases, and most likely in all, the number of these months was less than six. Even within the nineteenth century men-of-war's men had to wait for their pay for years. Commander C. N. Robinson, in his ' British Fleet,'[1] a

---

[1] London, 1894.

book that ought to be in every Englishman's library, remarks : ' All through the seventeenth and eighteenth centuries it was the rule not to pay anybody until the end of the commission, and to a certain degree the practice obtained until some fifty years ago.' As to the nineteenth century, Lord Dundonald, speaking in Parliament, may be quoted. He said that of the ships on the East Indies station, the *Centurion's* men had been unpaid for eleven years ; the *Rattlesnake's* for fourteen ; the *Fox's* for fifteen. The Elizabethan practice compared with this will look almost precipitate instead of dilatory. To draw again on my personal experience, I may say that I have been kept without pay for a longer time than most of the people in Lord Howard's fleet, as, for the first two years that I was at sea, young officers were paid only once in six months ; and then never in cash, but always in bills. The reader may be left to imagine what happened when a naval cadet tried to get a bill for some £7 or £8 cashed at a small Spanish-American port.

A great deal has been made of the strict audit of the accounts of Howard's fleet. The Queen, says Froude, ' would give no orders for money till she had demanded the meaning of every penny that she was charged.' Why she alone should be held up to obloquy for this is not clear. Until a very recent period, well within the last reign, no commanding officer, on a ship being paid off, could receive the residue of his pay, or get any half-pay at all, until his ' accounts had been passed.'[1] The same rule applied

[1] This happened to me in 1904.

to officers in charge of money or stores. It has been made a further charge against Elizabeth that her officers had to meet certain expenditure out of their own pockets. That certainly is not a peculiarity of the sixteenth-century navy. Till less than fifty years ago the captain of a British man-of-war had to provide one of the three chronometers used in the navigation of his ship. Even later than that the articles necessary for cleaning the ship and everything required for decorating her were paid for by the officers, almost invariably by the first lieutenant, or second in command. There must be many officers still serving who have spent sums, considerable in the aggregate, of their own money on public objects. Though pressure in this respect has been much relieved of late, there are doubtless many who do so still. It is, in fact, a traditional practice in the British Navy and is not in the least distinctly Elizabethan.

Some acquaintance with present conditions and accurate knowledge of the naval methods prevailing in the great Queen's reign—a knowledge which the publication of the original documents puts within the reach of anyone who really cares to know the truth — will convince the candid inquirer that Elizabeth's administration of the navy compares favourably with that of any of her successors ; and that, for it, she deserves the admiration and un-alloyed gratitude of the nation.

IX[1]

NELSON : THE CENTENARY OF TRAFALGAR

[The following article was read as an address, in compliance
with the request of its Council, at the annual meeting of the
Navy Records Society in July 1905. It was, and indeed is
still, my opinion, as stated to the meeting in some prefatory
remarks, that the address would have come better from a
professed historian, several members of the Society being
well known as entitled to that designation. The Council,
however, considered that, as Nelson's tactical principles and
achievements should be dealt with, it would be better for the
address to be delivered by a naval officer—one, moreover, who
had personal experience of the manœuvres of fleets under sail.
Space would not suffice for treating of Nelson's merits as a
strategist, though they are as great as those which he possessed
as a tactician.]

CENTENARY commemorations are common enough ;
but the commemoration of Nelson has a characteristic
which distinguishes it from most, if not from all,
others.   In these days we forget soon.   What place
is still kept in our memories by even the most
illustrious of those who have but recently left us ?
It is not only that we do not remember their wishes
and injunctions ; their existence has almost faded
from our recollection.   It is not difficult to persuade
people to commemorate a departed worthy ; but
in most cases industry has to take the place of

enthusiasm, and moribund or extinct remembrances have to be galvanised by assiduity into a semblance of life. In the case of Nelson the conditions are very different. He may have been misunderstood ; even by his professional descendants his acts and doctrines may have been misinterpreted ; but he has never been forgotten.

The time has now come when we can specially do honour to Nelson's memory without wounding the feelings of other nations. There is no need to exult over or even to expatiate on the defeats of others. In recalling the past it is more dignified as regards ourselves, and more considerate of the honour of our great admiral, to think of the valour and self-devotion rather than the misfortunes of those against whom he fought. We can do full justice to Nelson's memory without reopening old wounds.

The first thing to be noted concerning him is that he is the only man who has ever lived who by universal consent is without a peer. This is said in full view of the new constellation rising above the Eastern horizon ; for that constellation, brilliant as it is, has not yet reached the meridian. In every walk of life, except that which Nelson chose as his own, you will find several competitors for the first place, each one of whom will have many supporters. Alexander of Macedon, Hannibal, Cæsar, Marlborough, Frederick the Great, and Napoleon have been severally put forward for the palm of generalship. To those who would acclaim Richelieu as the first of statesmen, others would oppose Chatham, or William Pitt, or Cavour, or Bismarck, or Marquis Ito. Who was the first of sculptors? who the first of painters? who the first of poets? In every case there is a great difference of opinion. Ask, however, who was the first of admirals, and the unanimous reply will still be—' Nelson,' tried as he was by many years of high command in war. It is not only amongst his fellow-countrymen that his pre-eminence is acknowledged. Foreigners admit it as readily as we proclaim it ourselves.

We may consider what it was that gave Nelson this unique position among men. The early conditions of his naval career were certainly not favourable to him. It is true that he was promoted when young; but so were many other officers. Nelson was made a commander only a few months after the outbreak of war between Great Britain and France, and was made a post-captain within a few days of the declaration of war by Spain. An officer holding a rank qualifying him for command at the outset of a great war might well have looked forward confidently to exceptional opportunities of distinguishing himself. Even in our own days, when some trifling campaign is about to be carried on, the officers who are employed where they can take no part in it vehemently lament their ill-fortune. How much more disheartening must it have been to be excluded from active participation in a great and long-continued conflict! This was Nelson's case. As far as his hopes of gaining distinction were concerned, fate seemed to persecute him pertinaciously. He was a captain of more than four years' seniority when the treaty of Versailles put an end to the war of American Independence. Yet, with the exception of the brief Nicaragua expedition—which by the side of the important occurrences of grand naval campaigns must have seemed insignificant—his services during all those years of hostilities were uneventful, and even humdrum. He seemed to miss every important operation ; and when the war ended—we may almost say—he had never seen a ship fire a broadside in anger.

There then came what promised to be, and in fact turned out to be, a long period of peace. With no distinguished war service to point to, and with the prospect before him of only uneventful employment, or no employment afloat at all, Nelson might well have been disheartened to the verge of despondency. That he was not disheartened, but, instead thereof, made a name for himself in such unfavourable circumstances, must be accepted as one of the most convincing proofs of his rare force of character. To have attracted the notice, and to have secured the confidence, of so great a sea-officer as Lord Hood constituted a distinction which could have been won only by merit so considerable that it could not long remain unrecognised. The war of American Independence had still seven months to run when Lord Hood pointed to Nelson as an officer to be consulted on ' questions relative to naval tactics.' Professor Laughton tells us that at that time Nelson had

P

never served with a fleet. Lord Hood was one of
the last men in the world to go out of his way to pay
to a youthful subordinate an empty compliment,
and we may confidently base our estimate of an
officer's merits on Lord Hood's belief in them.

He, no doubt, gave a wide signification to the
term ' tactics,' and used it as embracing all that is
included in the phrase ' conduct of war.' He must
have found out, from conversations with, and from
the remarks of, the young captain, whom he treated
as intimately as if he was his son, that the latter was
already, what he continued to be till the end, viz.
a student of naval warfare. This point deserves
particular attention. The officers of the navy of
the present day, period of peace though it be, can
imitate Nelson at least in this. He had to wait
a long time before he could translate into brilliant
action the result of his tactical studies. Fourteen
years after Lord Hood spoke of him as above
related, by a ' spontaneous and sudden act, for
which he had no authority by signal or otherwise,
except his own judgment and quick perceptions,'
Nelson entirely defeated the movement of the
enemy's fleet, contributed to the winning of a great
victory, and, as Captain Mahan tells us, ' emerged
from merely personal distinction to national renown.'
The justification of dwelling on this is to be found in
the necessity, even at this day, of preventing the
repetition of mistakes concerning Nelson's qualities
and disposition. His recent biographers, Captain
Mahan and Professor Laughton, feel constrained to

tell us over and over again that Nelson's predominant characteristic was not mere ' headlong valour and instinct for fighting ' ; that he was not the man ' to run needless and useless risks ' in battle. ' The breadth and acuteness of Nelson's intellect,' says Mahan, ' have been too much overlooked in the admiration excited by his unusually grand moral endowments of resolution, dash, and fearlessness of responsibility ! '

In forming a true conception of what Nelson was, the publications of the Navy Records Society will help us greatly. There is something very remarkable in the way in which Mr. Gutteridge's volume[1] not only confirms Captain Mahan's refutation of the aspersions on Nelson's honour and humanity, but also establishes Professor Laughton's conclusions, reached many years ago, that it was the orders given to him, and not his amour, which detained him at Naples at a well-known epoch. The last volume issued by the Society, that of Mr. Julian Corbett,[2] is, I venture to affirm, the most useful to naval officers that has yet appeared among the Society's publications. It will provide them with an admirable historical introduction to the study of tactics, and greatly help them in ascertaining the importance of Nelson's achievements as a tactician. For my own part, I may say with gratitude that but for Mr. Corbett's valuable work I could not have completed this appreciation.

[1] *Nelson and the Neapolitan Jacobins.*
[2] *Fighting Instructions, 1530–1816.*

The most renowned of Nelson's achievements was that performed in his final battle and victory. Strange as it may seem, that celebrated performance has been the subject of much controversy, and, brilliant as it was, the tactics adopted in it have been freely, and indeed unfavourably, criticised. There is still much difference of opinion as to the preliminary movements, and as to the exact method by which Nelson's attack was made. It has been often asserted that the method really followed was not that which Nelson had expressly declared his intention of adopting. The question raised concerning this is a difficult one, and, until the appearance of Mr. Julian Corbett's recent work and the interesting volume on Trafalgar lately published by Mr. H. Newbolt, had not been fully discussed. The late Vice-Admiral P. H. Colomb contributed to the *United Service Magazine* of September 1899 a very striking article on the subject of Nelson's tactics in his last battle, and those who propose to study the case should certainly peruse what he wrote.

The criticism of Nelson's procedure at Trafalgar in its strongest form may be summarised as follows. It is affirmed that he drew up and communicated to the officers under his orders a certain plan of attack ; that just before the battle he changed his plan without warning ; that he hurried on his attack unnecessarily ; that he exposed his fleet to excessive peril ; and, because of all this, that the British loss was much heavier and much less evenly distributed among the ships of the fleet than it need have been. The most formidable arraignment of the mode of Nelson's last attack is, undoubtedly, to be found in the paper published by Sir Charles Ekins in his book on ' Naval Battles,' and vouched for by him as the work of an eye-witness—almost certainly, as Mr. Julian Corbett holds, an officer on board the *Conqueror* in the battle. It is a remarkable document. Being critical rather than instructive, it is not to be classed with the essay of Clerk of Eldin ; but it is one of the most important contributions to the investigation of tactical questions ever published in the English tongue. On it are based nearly, or quite, all the unfavourable views expressed concerning the British tactics at Trafalgar. As it contains a respectfully stated, but still sharp, criticism of Nelson's action, it will not be thought presumptuous if we criticise it in its turn.

Notwithstanding the fact that the author of the paper actually took part in the battle, and that he was gifted with no mean tactical insight, it is permissible to say that his remarks have an academic tinge. In fact, they are very much of the kind that a clever professor of tactics, who had not felt the responsibilities inseparable from the command of a fleet, would put before a class of students. Between a professor of tactics, however clever, and a commanding genius like Nelson the difference is great indeed. The writer of the paper in question perhaps expressed the more general opinion of his day. He has certainly suggested opinions to later generations of naval officers. The captains who shared in Nelson's last great victory did not agree among themselves as to the mode in which the attack was introduced. It was believed by some of them, and, thanks largely to the *Conqueror* officer's paper, it is generally believed now, that, whereas Nelson had announced his intention of advancing to the attack in lines-abreast or lines-of-bearing, he really did so in lines-ahead. Following up the path of investigation to which, in his article above mentioned, Admiral Colomb had already pointed, we can, I think, arrive only at the conclusion that the announced intention was adhered to.

Before the reasons for this conclusion are given it will be convenient to deal with the suggestions, or allegations, that Nelson exposed his fleet at Trafalgar to unduly heavy loss, putting it in the power of the enemy—to use the words of the *Conqueror's* officer—to ' have annihilated the ships one after another in detail '; and that ' the brunt of the action would have been more equally felt ' had a different mode of advance from that actually chosen been adopted. Now, Trafalgar was a battle in which an inferior fleet of twenty-six ships gained a victory over a superior fleet of thirty-three. The victory was so decisive that more than half of the enemy's capital ships were captured or destroyed on the spot, and the remainder were so battered that some fell an easy prey to the victor's side soon after the battle, the rest having limped painfully to the shelter of a fortified port near at hand. To gain such a victory over a

superior force of seamen justly celebrated for their
spirit and gallantry, very hard fighting was necessary.
The only actions of the Napoleonic period that can
be compared with it are those of Camperdown,
the Nile, and Copenhagen.   The proportionate loss
at Trafalgar was the least in all the four battles.[1]
The allegation that, had Nelson followed a different
method at Trafalgar, the ' brunt of the action
would have been more equally felt ' can be disposed
of easily.   In nearly all sea-fights, whether Nelsonic
in character or not, half of the loss of the victors
has fallen on considerably less than half the fleet.
That this has been the rule, whatever tactical
method may have been adopted, will appear from
the following statement.   In Rodney's victory (12th
April 1782) half the loss fell upon nine ships out
of thirty-six, or one-fourth ; at ' The First of June '
it fell upon five ships out of twenty-five, or one-fifth ;
at St. Vincent it fell upon three ships out of fifteen,
also one-fifth ; at Trafalgar half the loss fell on five
ships out of twenty-seven, or very little less than an
exact fifth.   It has, therefore, been conclusively
shown that, faulty or not faulty, long-announced
or hastily adopted, the plan on which the battle of
Trafalgar was fought did not occasion excessive
loss to the victors or confine the loss, such as it was,
to an unduly small portion of their fleet.   As bearing
on this question of the relative severity of the

[1] Camperdown   .   825 loss out of 8,221 : 10   per cent.
The Nile .   .   896 ,,   ,,   7,401 : 12·1   ,,
Copenhagen   .   941 ,,   ,,   6,892 : 13·75   ,,
Trafalgar   . 1,690 ,,   ,,   17,256 : 9·73   ,,

British loss at Trafalgar, it may be remarked that in that battle there were several British ships which had been in other great sea-fights. Their losses in these latter were in nearly every case heavier than their Trafalgar losses.[1] Authoritative and undisputed figures show how baseless are the suggestions that Nelson's tactical procedure at Trafalgar caused his fleet to suffer needlessly heavy loss.

It is now necessary to investigate the statement that Nelson, hastily and without warning, changed his plan for fighting the battle. This investigation is much more difficult than that into the losses of the British fleet, because, whilst the latter can be settled by arithmetic, the former must proceed largely upon conjecture. How desirable it is to make the investigation of the statement mentioned will be manifest when we reflect on the curious fact

[1]

Ship	Action	Killed	Wounded	Total	Trafalgar		
					Killed	Wounded	Total
Ajax . .	Rodney's (Ap. 12, 1782)	9	10	19	2	9	11
Agamemnon.	,,	15	22	37	2	8	10
Conqueror .	,,	7	22	29	3	9	12
Defence . .	1st June	17	36	53	7	29	36
Bellerophon .	The Nile	49	148	197	27	123	150
Swiftsure .	,,	7	22	29	9	8	17
Defiance .	Copenhagen	24	21	45	17	53	70
Polyphemus.	,,	6	25	31	2	4	6

In only one case was the Trafalgar total loss greater than the total loss of the same ship in an earlier fight ; and in this case (the *Defiance*) the number of killed at Trafalgar was only about two-thirds of the number killed in the other action.

that the very completeness of Nelson's success at Trafalgar checked, or, indeed, virtually destroyed, the study of tactics in the British Navy for more than three-quarters of a century. His action was so misunderstood, or, at any rate, so variously represented, that it generally passed for gospel in our service that Nelson's method consisted merely in rushing at his enemy as soon as he saw him. Against this conception his biographers, one after another, have protested in vain.

At the outset of this investigation it will be well to call to mind two or three things, simple enough, but not always remembered. One of these is that advancing to the attack and the attack itself are not the same operations. Another is, that, in the order of sailing in two or more columns, if the ships were ' by the wind ' or close-hauled— the column-leaders were not abeam of each other, but bore from one another in the direction of the wind. Also, it may be mentioned that by simple alterations of course a line-abreast may be converted into a line-of-bearing and a line-of-bearing into a line-ahead, and that the reverse can be effected by the same operation. Again, adherence to a plan which presupposes the enemy's fleet to be in a particular formation after he is found to be in another is not to be expected of a consummate tactician. This remark is introduced here with full knowledge of the probability that it will be quoted as an admission that Nelson did change his plan without warning. No admission of the kind is intended. ' In all cases of anticipated battle,' says Mahan, ' Nelson was careful to put his subordinates in possession both of his general plans and, as far as possible, of the underlying ideas.' The same biographer tells us, what is well worth remembering, that ' No man was ever better served than Nelson by the inspiration of the moment ; no man ever counted on it less.'

The plan announced in the celebrated memorandum of 9th October 1805 indicated, for the attack from to windward, that the British fleet, in what would be called on shore an echelon of two main divisions and an ' advance squadron,' would move against an enemy assumed to be in single line-ahead. The ' advance squadron,' it should be noted, was not to be ahead of the two main divisions, but in such a position that it could be moved to strengthen either. The name seems to have been due to the mode in which the ships composing the squadron were employed in, so to speak, ' feeling for ' the enemy. On 19th October six ships were ordered ' to go ahead during the night ' ; and, besides the frigates, two more ships were so stationed as to keep up the communication between the six and the commander-in-chief's flag-ship. Thus eight ships in effect composed an ' advance squadron,' and did not join either of the main divisions at first.

When it was expected that the British fleet would comprise forty sail-of-the-line and the enemy's fleet forty-six, each British main division was to be made up of sixteen ships ; and eight

two-deckers added to either division would increase
the strength of the latter to twenty-four ships.
It is interesting to note that, omitting the *Africa*,
which ship came up late, each British main division
on the morning of 21st October 1805 had nine ships—
a number which, by the addition of the eight already
mentioned as distinct from the divisions, could have
been increased to seventeen, thus, except for a
fraction, exactly maintaining the original proportion
as regards the hostile fleet, which was now found to
be composed of thirty-three ships.

During the night of 20th–21st October the Franco-
Spanish fleet, which had been sailing in three divisions
and a ' squadron of observation,' formed line and
stood to the southward, heading a little to the
eastward of south. The ' squadron of observation '
was parallel to the main body and to windward (in
this case to the westward) of it, with the leading
ships rather more advanced.

The British main divisions steered WSW. till
1 A.M. After that they steered SW. till 4 A.M.
There are great difficulties about the time, as the
notation of it [1] differed considerably in different
ships ; but the above hours are taken from the
Victory's log. At 4 A.M. the British fleet, or rather
its main divisions, wore and stood N. by E. As
the wind was about NW. by W., the ships were
close-hauled, and the leader of the ' lee-line,' i.e.

[1] Except the chronometers, which were instruments of
navigation so precious as always to be kept under lock and key,
there were no clocks in the navy till some years after I joined it.
Time on board ship was kept by half-hour sand-glasses.

Collingwood's flag-ship, was when in station two points abaft the *Victory's* beam as soon as the ' order of sailing ' in two columns—which was to be the order of battle—had been formed.

About 6 A.M. the enemy's fleet was sighted from the *Victory*, and observed to bear from her E. by S. and be distant from her ten or twelve miles. The distance is corroborated by observed bearings from Collingwood's flag-ship.[1] Viewed from the British ships, placed as they were relatively to it, the enemy's fleet must have appeared as a long single line-ahead, perhaps not very exactly formed. As soon as the hostile force was clearly made out, the British divisions bore up and stood to the eastward, steering by the *Victory's* compass ENE. The position and formation of the British main divisions were by this made exactly those in which they are shown in the diagram usually attached to the celebrated memorandum of 9th October 1805. The enemy must have appeared to the British, who were ten or twelve miles to windward of him, and on his beam, as if he were formed in line-ahead. He therefore was also in the position and formation assigned to him in that diagram.

At a time which, because of the variety in the notations of it, it is difficult to fix exactly, but somewhere between 7 and 8 A.M., the enemy's ships

---

[1] It would necessitate the use of some technicalities to explain it fully ; but it may be said that the bearings of the extremes of the enemy's line observed from his flag-ship prove that Collingwood was in the station that he ought to have occupied when the British fleet was in the Order of Sailing and close to the wind.

wore together and endeavoured to form a line to the
northward, which, owing to the direction of the
wind, must have been about N. by E. and S. by W.,
or NNE. and SSW. The operation—not merely
of wearing, but of both wearing and reforming the
line, such as it was—took more than an hour to
complete. The wind was light ; there was a
westerly swell ; the ships were under easy sail ;
consequently there must have been a good deal
of leeway, and the hostile or ' combined ' fleet headed
in the direction of Cadiz, towards which, we are
expressly told by a high French authority—Chevalier
—it advanced.

Nelson had to direct the course of his fleet so
that its divisions, when about to make the actual
attack, would be just opposite the points to which
the respective hostile ships had advanced in the
meantime. In a light wind varying in force a
direct course to those points could not be settled
once for all ; but that first chosen was very nearly
right, and an alteration of a point, viz. to E. by N.,
was for a considerable time all that was necessary.
Collingwood later made a signal to his division to
alter course one point to port, which brought them
back to the earlier course, which by the *Victory's*
compass had been ENE. The eight ships of
what has been referred to as the ' advance squadron '
were distributed between the two main British
divisions, six being assigned to Collingwood's and
two to Nelson's. They did not all join their
divisions at the same time, some—probably owing

to the distance at which they had been employed from the rest of the fleet and the feebleness of the breeze—not till several hours after the combined fleet had been sighted.

Collingwood preserved in his division a line-of-bearing apparently until the very moment when the individual ships pushed on to make the actual attack. The enemy's fleet is usually represented as forming a curve. It would probably be more correct to call it a very obtuse re-entering angle. This must have been largely due to Gravina's ' squadron of observation ' keeping away in succession, to get into the wake of the rest of the line, which was forming towards the north. About the centre of the combined fleet there was a gap of a mile. Ahead and astern of this the ships were not all in each other's wake. Many were to leeward of their stations, thus giving the enemy's formation the appearance of a double line, or rather of a string of groups of ships. It is important to remember this, because no possible mode of attack—the enemy's fleet being formed as it was—could have prevented some British ships from being ' doubled on ' when they cut into the enemy's force. On ' The First of June,' notwithstanding that the advance to the attack was intended to be in line-abreast, several British ships were ' doubled on,' and even ' trebled on,' as will be seen in the experiences on that day of the *Brunswick, Marlborough, Royal Sovereign,* and *Queen Charlotte* herself.

Owing to the shape of the hostile ' line ' at

Trafalgar and the formation in which he kept his
division, Collingwood brought his ships, up till the
very moment when each proceeded to deliver her
attack, in the formation laid down in the oft-quoted
memorandum. By the terms of that document
Nelson had specifically assigned to his own
division the work of seeing that the movements of
Collingwood's division should be interrupted as little
as possible. It would, of course, have been beyond
his power to do this if the position of his own division
in the echelon formation prescribed in the memorandum had been rigorously adhered to after Collingwood was getting near his objective point. In
execution, therefore, of the service allotted to his
division, Nelson made a feint at the enemy's van.
This necessitated an alteration of course to port,
so that his ships came into a line-of-bearing ' so
very oblique that it may well have been loosely
called a ' line-ahead.' Sir Charles Ekins says that
the two British lines ' *afterwards* fell into line-ahead,
the ships in the wake of each other,' and that this
was in obedience to signal. Collingwood's line
certainly did not fall into line-ahead. At the most
it was a rather oblique line-of-bearing almost
parallel to that part of the enemy's fleet which he
was about to attack. In Nelson's line there was
more than one alteration of course, as the *Victory's*
log expressly states that she kept standing for the
enemy's van, which we learn from the French
accounts was moving about N. by E. or NNE.
In the light wind prevailing the alterations of course

must have rendered it, towards the end of the forenoon, impossible to keep exact station, even if the *Victory* were to shorten sail, which we know she did not. As Admiral Colomb pointed out, ' Several later signals are recorded which were proper to make in lines-of-bearing, but not in lines-ahead.' It is difficult to import into this fact any other meaning but that of intention to preserve, however obliquely, the line-of-bearing which undoubtedly had been formed by the act of bearing-up as soon as the enemy's fleet had been distinguished.

When Collingwood had moved near enough to the enemy to let his ships deliver their attacks, it became unnecessary for Nelson's division to provide against the other's being interrupted. Accordingly, he headed for the point at which he meant to cut into the enemy's fleet. Now came the moment, as regards his division, for doing what Collingwood's had already begun to do, viz. engage in a ' pell-mell battle,'[1] which surely may be interpreted as meaning a battle in which rigorous station-keeping was no longer expected, and in which ' no captain could do very wrong if he placed his ship alongside that of the enemy.'

In several diagrams of the battle as supposed to have been fought the two British divisions just before the moment of impact are represented as converging towards each other. The Spanish diagram, lately reproduced by Mr. Newbolt, shows this, as well as the English diagrams. We may

[1] Nelson's own expression.

take it, therefore, that there was towards the end of the forenoon a convergence of the two columns, and that this was due to Nelson's return from his feint at the hostile van to the line from which he intended to let go his ships to deliver the actual attack. Collingwood's small alteration of course of one point to port slightly, but only slightly, accentuated this convergence.

Enough has been said here of Nelson's tactics at Trafalgar. To discuss them fully would lead me too far for this occasion.

I can only express the hope that in the navy the subject will receive fuller consideration hereafter. Nelson's last victory was gained, be it remembered, in one afternoon, over a fleet more than 20 per cent. his superior in numbers, and was so decisive that more than half of the hostile ships were taken. This was the crowning effort of seven years spent in virtually independent command in time of war —seven years, too, illustrated by more than one great victory.

The more closely we look into Nelson's tactical achievements, the more effective and brilliant do they appear. It is the same with his character and disposition. The more exact researches and investigations of recent times have removed from his name the obloquy which it pleased some to cast upon it. We can see now that his ' childlike, delighted vanity ' —to use the phrase of his greatest biographer— was but a thin incrustation on noble qualities. As in the material world valueless earthy substances

Q

surround a vein of precious metal, so through Nelson's moral nature there ran an opulent lode of character, unimpaired in its priceless worth by adjacent frailties which, in the majority of mankind, are present without any precious stuff beneath them. It is with minds prepared to see this that we should commemorate our great admiral.

Veneration of Nelson's memory cannot be confined to particular objects or be limited by locality. His tomb is wider than the space covered by dome or column, and his real monument is more durable than any material construction. It is the unwritten and spiritual memorial of him, firmly fixed in the hearts of his fellow-countrymen.

X

THE SHARE OF THE FLEET IN THE DEFENCE OF THE EMPIRE [1]

AT the close of the Great War, which ended in the downfall of Napoleon, the maritime position of the British Empire was not only predominant—it also was, and long remained, beyond the reach of challenge. After the stupendous events of the great contest such successes as those at Algiers where we were helped by the Dutch, at Navarino where we had two allies, and at Acre were regarded as matters of course, and no very grave issue hung upon any one of them. For more than half a century after Nelson's death all the most brilliant achievements of British arms were performed on shore, in India or in the Crimea. There were also many small wars on land, and it may well have seemed to contemporaries that the days of great naval contests were over and that force of circumstances was converting us into a military from a naval nation. The belief in the efficacy of naval defence was not extinct, but it had ceased to operate actively. Even whilst the necessity of that form of defence was far

[1] Written in 1907. (*Naval Annual*, 1908.)

more urgent, inattention to or ignorance of its true principles had occasionally allowed it to grow weak, but the possibility of substituting something else for it had not been pressed or even suggested. To this, however, we had now come ; and it was largely a consequence of the Crimean war. In that war the British Army had nobly sustained its reputation as a fighting machine. For the first time after a long interval it had met in battle European troops, and had come out of the conflict more renowned for bravery than ever. Nothing seemed able to damp its heroism—not scantiness of food, not lack of clothing amidst bitter cold, not miserable quarters, not superior forces of a valiant enemy. It clung to its squalid abodes in the positions which it was ordered to hold with a tenacious fortitude that had never been surpassed in its glorious history, and that defied all assaults. In combination with its brave allies it brought to a triumphant conclusion a war of an altogether peculiar character.

The campaign in the Crimea was in reality the siege of a single fortress. All the movements of the Western invaders were undertaken to bring them within striking distance of the place, to keep them within reach of it, or to capture it. Every battle that occurred was fought with one of those objects. When the place fell the war ended. The one general who, in the opinion of all concerned, gained high distinction in the war was the general who had prolonged the defence of Sebastopol by the skilful use of earthworks. It was no wonder that the attack and defence of fortified places assumed large importance in the eyes of the British people. The command of the sea held by the allied powers was so complete and all-pervading that no one stopped to think what the course of hostilities would have been without it, any more than men stop to think what the course of any particular business would be if there were no atmosphere to breathe in. Not a single allied soldier had been delayed on passage by the hostile fleet ; not a single merchant vessel belonging to the allies had been captured by a hostile cruiser. Supplies and reinforcements for the besieging armies were transported to them without escort and with as little risk of interruption as if the operations had been those of profound peace.

No sooner was the Crimean war over than another struggle took place, viz. the war of the Indian Mutiny, and that also was waged entirely on land. Here again the command of the sea was so complete that no interruption of it, even temporary, called attention to its existence. Troops and supplies were sent to India from the United Kingdom and from Hong-Kong ; horses for military purposes from Australia and South Africa ; and in every case without a thought of naval escort. The experience of hostilities in India seemed to confirm the experience of the Crimea. What we had just done to a great European nation was assumed to be what unfriendly European nations would wish to do and would be able to do to us. It was also assumed that the only way of frustrating their designs would be to do what had recently been done in the hope of frustrating ours, but to do it better. We must—it was said —depend on fortifications, but more perfect than those which had failed to save Sebastopol.

The protection to be afforded by our fleet was deliberately declared to be insufficient. It might, so it was held, be absent altogether, and then there would be nothing but fortifications to stand between us and the progress of an active enemy. In the result the policy of constructing imposing passive defence-works on our coast was adopted. The fortifications had to be multiplied. Dependence on that class of defence inevitably leads to discovery after discovery that some spot open to the kind of attack feared has not been made secure. We began by fortifying the great dockyard ports—on the sea side against a hostile fleet, on the land side against hostile troops. Then it was perceived that to fortify the dockyard ports in the mother country afforded very little protection to the outlying portions of the empire. So their principal ports also were given defence-works—sometimes of an elaborate character. Again, it was found that commercial ports had been left out and that they too must be fortified. When this was done spots were observed at which an enemy might effect a landing in force, to prevent which further forts or batteries must be erected. The most striking thing in all this is the complete omission to take note of the conditions involved in the command of the sea.

Evidently it had not been understood that it was

that very command which alone had enabled the armies of western Europe to proceed, not only without serious interruption, but also without encountering an attempt at obstruction, to the field in the Crimea on which their victories had been won, and that the same command would be necessary before any hostile expedition, large enough to justify the construction of the fortifications specially intended to repel it, could cross the sea and get within striking distance of our shores. It should be deeply interesting to the people of those parts of the British Empire which lie beyond sea to note that the defensive system comprised in the fortification of the coast of the United Kingdom promised no security to them in the event of war. Making all proper allowance for the superior urgency of defending the heart of the empire, we must still admit that no system of defence is adequate which does not provide for the defence of other valuable parts of the great body politic as well.

Again, the system of defence proved to be imperfect. Every part of the empire depended for prosperity—some parts depended for existence—on practically unrestricted traffic on the ocean. This, which might be assailed at many points and on lines often thousands of miles in length, could find little or no defence in immovable fortifications. It could not be held that the existence of these released the fleet from all duty but that of protecting our ocean commerce, because, if any enemy's navy was able to carry out an operation of such magnitude

and difficulty as a serious attack on our home
territory, it would assuredly be able to carry out the
work of damaging our maritime trade. Power to do
the latter has always belonged to the navy which
was in a position to extend its activity persistently
to the immediate neighbourhood of its opponent's
coast-line.

It is not to be supposed that there was no one to
point this out. Several persons did so, but being
mostly sailors they were not listened to. In actual
practice the whole domain of imperial strategy was
withdrawn from the intervention of the naval officer,
as though it were something with which he could not
have anything to do. Several great wars had been
waged in Europe in the meantime, and all of them
were land wars. Naval forces, if employed at all,
were employed only just enough to bring out how
insignificant their participation in them was. As
was to have been expected, the habit of attaching
importance to the naval element of imperial defence
declined. The empire, nevertheless, continued to
grow. Its territory was extended ; its population,
notably its population of European stock, increased,
and its wealth and the subsequent operations of
exchanging its productions for those of other
countries were enormously expanded. At the same
time the navy, to the strength and efficiency of
which it had to look for security, declined absolutely,
and still more relatively. Other navies were advancing : some had, as it were, come into existence. At
last the true conditions were discerned, and the

nation, almost with one voice, demanded that the
naval defences of the empire should be put upon a
proper footing.

Let no one dismiss the foregoing retrospect as
merely ancient history. On the contrary, let all
those who desire to see the British Empire follow
the path of its natural development in tranquillity
study the recent past. By doing this we shall be
able to estimate aright the position of the fleet in
the defence of the empire. We must examine
the circumstances in which we are placed. For
five-and-thirty years the nations of the world have
practically lived under the rule of force. The
incessant object of every great state has been to
increase the strength of its armed forces up to the
point at which the cost becomes intolerable.
Countries separated from one another only by
arbitrary geographical lines add regiment to regiment
and gun to gun, and also devise continually fresh
expedients for accelerating the work of preparing
their armies to take the field. The most pacifically
inclined nation must do in this respect as its neighbours do, on pain of losing its independence and
being mutilated in its territory if it does not. This
rivalry has spread to the sea, and fleets are increased
at a rate and at a cost in money unknown to former
times, even to those of war. The possession of a
powerful navy by some state which has no reason
to apprehend over-sea invasion and which has no
maritime interests, however intrinsically important
they may be, commensurate with the strength of its

fleets, may not indicate a spirit of aggression ; but it at least indicates ability to become an aggressor. Consequently, for the British fleet to fill its proper position in the defence of the empire it must be strong. To be strong more than large numbers will be required. It must have the right, that is the best, material, the best organisation, the best discipline, the best training, the best distribution. We shall ascertain the position that it should hold, if we examine what it would have to do when called upon for work more active than that of peace time. With the exception of India and Canada no part of the empire is liable to serious attack that does not come over-sea. Any support that can be given to India or Canada by other parts of the empire must be conveyed across the sea also. This at once indicates the importance of ocean lines of communication.

War is the method adopted, when less violent means of persuasion have failed, to force your enemy to comply with your demands. There are three principal ways of effecting this—invasion of his country, raids on his territory, destruction or serious damage of his sea-borne commerce. Successful invasion must compel the invaded to come to terms, or his national existence will be lost. Raids upon his territory may possibly so distress him that he would rather concede your terms than continue the struggle.[1] Damage to his sea-borne commerce may be carried so far that he will be ruined if he

---

[1] Though raids rarely, if ever, decide a war, they may cause inconvenience or local distress, and an enemy desiring to make them should be obstructed as much as possible.

does not give in. So much for one side of the account ; we have to examine the other. Against invasion, raids, or attempts at commerce-destruction there must be some form of defence, and, as a matter of historical fact, defence against each has been repeatedly successful. If we need instances we have only to peruse the history of the British Empire.

How was it that—whilst we landed invading armies in many hostile countries, seized many portions of hostile territory, and drove more than one enemy's commerce from the sea—our own country has been free from successful invasion for more than eight centuries, few portions of our territory have been taken from us even temporarily, and our commerce has increased throughout protracted maritime wars ? To this there can only be one answer, viz. that the arrangements for defence were effectual. What, then, were these arrangements ? They were comprised in the provision of a powerful, well-distributed, well-handled navy, and of a mobile army of suitable strength. It is to be observed that each element possessed the characteristic of mobility. We have to deal here more especially with the naval element, and we must study the manner in which it operates.

Naval war is sea-power in action ; and sea-power, taken in the narrow sense, has limitations. It may not, even when so taken, cease to act at the enemy's coast-line, but its direct influence extends only to the inner side of a narrow zone conforming to that line. In a maritime contest each side tries to control the ocean communications and to prevent the other from controlling them. If either gains the control, something in addition to sea-power strictly defined may begin to operate : the other side's territory may be invaded or harassed by considerable raids, and its commerce may be driven from the sea. It will be noticed that control of ocean communications is the needful preliminary to these. It is merely a variant of the often employed expression of the necessity, in war, of obtaining command of the sea. In the case of the most important portion of the British Empire, viz. the United Kingdom, our loss of control of the ocean communications would have a result which scarcely any foreign country would experience. Other countries are dependent on importations for some part of the food of their population and of the raw material of their industry ; but much of the importation is, and perhaps all of it may be, effected by land. Here, we depend upon imports from abroad for a very large part of the food of our people, and of the raw material essential to the manufacture of the commodities by the exchange of which we obtain necessary supplies ; and the whole of these imports come, and must come to us, by sea. Also, if we had not freedom of exportation, our wealth and the means of supporting a war would disappear. Probably all the greater colonies and India could feed their inhabitants for a moderately long time without sea-borne imports, but unless the sea were open to them their prosperity would decline.

This teaches us the necessity to the British

Empire of controlling our maritime communications, and equally teaches those who may one day be our enemies the advisability of preventing us from doing so. The lesson in either case is driven farther home by other considerations connected with communications. In war a belligerent has two tasks before him. He has to defend himself and hurt his enemy. The more he hurts his enemy, the less is he likely to be hurt himself. This defines the great principle of offensive defence. To act in accordance with this principle, a belligerent should try, as the saying goes, to carry the war into the enemy's country. He should try to make his opponents fight where he wants them to fight, which will probably be as far as possible from his own territory and as near as possible to theirs. Unless he can do this, invasion and even serious raids by him will be out of the question. More than that, his inability to do it will virtually indicate that on its part the other side can fix the scene of active hostilities unpleasantly close to the points from which he desires to keep its forces away.

A line of ocean communications may be vulnerable throughout its length ; but it does not follow that an assailant can operate against it with equal facility at every point, nor does it follow that it is at every point equally worth assailing. Lines running past hostile naval ports are especially open to assault in the part near the ports ; and lines formed by the confluence of two or more other lines—like, for example, those which enter the English Channel—

will generally include a greater abundance of valuable traffic than others. Consequently there are some parts at which an enemy may be expected to be more active than elsewhere, and it is from those very parts that it is most desirable to exclude him. They are, as a rule, relatively near to the territory of the state whose navy has to keep the lines open, that is to say, prevent their being persistently beset by an enemy. The necessary convergence of lines towards that state's ports shows that some portion of them would have to be traversed, or their traversing be attempted, by expeditions meant to carry out either invasion or raids. If, therefore, the enemy can be excluded as above mentioned, invasions, raids, and the more serious molestation of sea-borne commerce by him will be prevented.

If we consider particular cases we shall find proof upon proof of the validity of the rule. Three great lines—one from the neighbourhood of the Cape of Good Hope, one from the Red Sea, and a third from India and Ceylon—converge near the south-western part of Australia and run as one line towards the territory of the important states farther east. If an assailant can be excluded from the latter or combined line he must either divide his force or operate on only one of the confluents, leaving the rest free. The farther he can be pushed back from the point of confluence the more effectually will he be limited to a single line, because the combining lines, traced backwards, trend more and more apart, and it is, therefore, more and more difficult for him to keep detachments of his force within supporting distance of each other if they continue to act against two or more lines. The particular case of the approaches to the territory of the United Kingdom has the same features, and proves the rule with equal clearness. This latter case is so often adduced without mention of others, that there is some risk of its being believed to be a solitary one. It stands, however, exactly on all fours with all the rest as regards the principle of the rule.

A necessary consequence of an enemy's exclusion from the combined line as it approaches the territory to be defended is—as already suggested—that invasion of that territory and serious raids upon it will be rendered impracticable. Indeed, if the exclusion be absolutely complete and permanent, raids of every kind and depredations on commerce in the neighbourhood will be prevented altogether. It should be explained that though lines and communications are spoken of, it is the area crossed by them which is strategically important. A naval force, either guarding or intending to assail a line, does not necessarily station itself permanently upon it. All that it has to do is to remain, for the proper length of time, within the strategic area across which the defended or threatened line runs. The strategic area will be of varying extent, its boundaries being determined by circumstances. The object of the defence will be to make the area from which the enemy's ships are excluded as extensive as possible. When the enemy has been pushed back into his own waters and into his own ports the exclusion is strategically complete. The sea is denied to his invading and important raiding expeditions, and indeed to most of his individual cruisers. At the same time it is free to the other belligerent. To effect this a vigorous offensive will be necessary.

The immediate theatre of operations, the critical strategic area, need not be, and often ought not to be, near the territory defended by our navy. It is necessary to dwell upon this, because no principle of naval warfare has been more frequently or more seriously misapprehended. Misapprehension of it has led to mischievous and dangerous distribution of naval force and to the squandering of immense sums of money on local defence vessels ; that is, vessels only capable of operating in the very waters from which every effort should be made to exclude the enemy. Failure to exclude him from them can only be regarded as, at the very least, yielding to him an important point in the great game of war. If we succeed in keeping him away, the local defence craft of every class are useless, and the money spent on them has been worse than wasted, because, if it had not been so spent, it might have been devoted to strengthening the kind of force which must be used to keep the enemy where he ought to be kept, viz. at a distance from our own waters.

The demand that ships be so stationed that they will generally, and except when actually cruising, be within sight of the inhabitants, is common enough in the mother country, and perhaps even more common in the over-sea parts of the British Empire. Nothing justifies it but the honest ignorance of those who make it ; nothing explains compliance with it but the deplorable weakness of authorities who yield to it. It was not by hanging about the coast of England, when there was no enemy near it, with his fleet, that Hawke or Nelson saved the country from invasion, nor was it by remaining where they could be seen by the fellow-countrymen of their crews that the French and English fleets shut up their enemy in the Baltic and Black Sea, and thus gained and kept undisputed command of the sea which enabled them, without interruption, to invade their enemy's territory.

The condition insisted upon by the Australasian Governments in the agreement formerly made with the Home Government, that a certain number of ships, in return for an annual contribution of money, should always remain in Australasian waters, was in reality greatly against the interests of that part of the empire. The Australasian taxpayer was, in fact, made to insist upon being injured in return for his money. The proceeding would have been exactly paralleled by a householder who might insist that a fire-engine, maintained out of rates to which he contributes, should always be kept within a few feet of his front door, and not be allowed to proceed to the end of the street to extinguish a fire threatening to extend eventually to the householder's own dwelling. When still further localised naval defence—localised defence, that is, of what may be called the smaller description—is considered, the danger involved in adopting it will be quite as apparent, and the waste of money will be more obvious. Localised defence is a near relation of passive defence. It owes its origin to the same sentiment, viz. a belief in the efficacy of staying where you are instead of carrying the war into the enemy's country.

There may be cases in which no other kind of naval defence is practicable. The immense costliness of modern navies puts it out of the power of smaller states to maintain considerable sea-going fleets. The historic maritime countries—Sweden, Denmark, the Netherlands, and Portugal, the performances of whose seamen are so justly celebrated—could not now send to sea a force equal in number and fighting efficiency to a quarter of the force possessed by any one of the chief naval powers. The countries named, when determined not to expose themselves unarmed to an assailant, can provide themselves only with a kind of defence which, whatever its detailed composition, must be of an intrinsically localised character.

In their case there is nothing else to be done; and in their case defence of the character specified would be likely to prove more efficacious than it could be expected to be elsewhere. War is usually made in pursuit of an object valuable enough to justify the risks inseparable from the attempt to gain it. Aggression by any of the countries that have been mentioned is too improbable to call for serious apprehension. Aggression against them is far more likely. What they have to do is to make the danger of attacking them so great that it will equal or outweigh any advantage that could be gained by conquering them. Their wealth and resources, compared with those of great aggressive states, are not large enough to make up for much loss in war on the part of the latter engaging in attempts to seize them. Therefore, what the small maritime countries have to do is to make the form of naval defence to which they are restricted efficacious enough to hurt an aggressor so much that the victory which he may feel certain of gaining will be quite barren. He will get no glory, even in these days of self-advertisement, from the conquest of such relatively weak antagonists ; and the plunder will not suffice to repay him for the damage received in effecting it.

The case of a member of the great body known as the British Empire is altogether different. Its conquest would probably be enormously valuable to a conqueror ; its ruin immensely damaging to the body as a whole. Either would justify an enemy in running considerable risks, and would afford him practically sufficient compensation for considerable losses incurred. We may expect that, in war, any chance of accomplishing either purpose will not be neglected. Provision must, therefore, be made against the eventuality. Let us for the moment suppose that, like one of the smaller countries whose case has been adduced, we are restricted to localised defence. An enemy not so restricted would be able to get, without being molested, as near to our

territory—whether in the mother country or elsewhere—as the outer edge of the comparatively
narrow belt of water that our localised defences
could have any hope of controlling effectively. We
should have abandoned to him the whole of the
ocean except a relatively minute strip of coast-waters.
That would be equivalent to saying good-bye to the
maritime commerce on which our wealth wholly,
and our existence largely, depends. No thoughtful
British subject would find this tolerable. Every one
would demand the institution of a different defence
system. A change, therefore, to the more active
system would be inevitable. It would begin with
the introduction of a cruising force in addition to the
localised force. The unvarying lesson of naval history would be that the cruising division should gain
continuously on the localised. It is only in times of
peace, when men have forgotten, or cannot be made to
understand, what war is, that the opposite takes place.

If it be hoped that a localised force will render
coast-wise traffic safe from the enemy, a little knowledge of what has happened in war and a sufficiently
close investigation of conditions will demonstrate
how baseless the hope must be. Countries not yet
thickly populated would be in much the same
condition as the countries of western Europe a
century ago, the similarity being due to the relative
scarcity of good land communications. A part—
probably not a very large part—of the articles
required by the people dwelling on and near
the coast in one section would be drawn from

another similar section. These articles could be most conveniently and cheaply transported by water. If it were worth his while, an enemy disposing of an active cruising force strong enough to make its way into the neighbourhood of the coast waters concerned would interrupt the ' longshore traffic ' and defy the efforts of a localised force to prevent him. The history of the Great War at the end of the eighteenth century and the beginning of the nineteenth teems with instances of interruption by our navy of the enemy's coast-wise trade when his ocean trade had been destroyed. The history of the American War of 1812 supplies other instances.

The localised defence could not attempt to drive off hostile cruisers remaining far from the shore and meaning to infest the great lines of maritime communication running towards it. If those cruisers are to be driven off at all it can be done only by cruising ships. Unless, therefore, we are to be content to leave our ocean routes, where most crowded and therefore most vulnerable, to the mercy of an enemy, we must have cruisers to meet the hostile cruisers. If we still adhere to our localised defence, we shall have two distinct kinds of force—one provided merely for local, and consequently restricted, action ; the other able to act near the shore or far out at sea as circumstances may demand. If we go to the expense of providing both kinds, we shall have followed the example of the sage who cut a large hole in his study door for the cat and a small one for the kitten.

Is local naval defence, then, of any use ? Well, to tell the truth, not much ; and only in rare and exceptional circumstances. Even in the case of the smaller maritime countries, to which reference has been made above, defence of the character in question would avail little if a powerful assailant were resolved to press home his attack. That is to say, if only absolute belligerent considerations were regarded. In war, however, qualifying considerations can never be left out of sight. As the great Napoleon observed, you can no more make war without incurring losses than you can make omelettes without breaking eggs. The strategist —and the tactician also, within his province—will always count the cost of a proposed operation, even where they are nearly certain of success. The occupation of a country, which would be of no great practical value to you when you got it, would be a poor return for the loss to which you would have been put in the process. That loss might, and probably would, leave you at a great disadvantage as regards enemies more nearly on an equality with yourself. It would, therefore, not be the improbability of breaking down the local naval defence of a minor maritime state, but the pressure of qualifying and only indirectly belligerent considerations, that would prevent its being attempted.

In a struggle between two antagonists of the first rank, the circumstances would be different. Purely belligerent considerations would have fuller play. Mistakes will be made, of course, for war is full of mistakes ; but it may be accepted that an attack on any position, however defended, is in itself proof that the assailant believed the result hoped for to be quite worth the cost of obtaining it. Consequently, in a struggle as assumed, every mode of defence would have to stand on its intrinsic merits, nearly or quite unaided by the influence of considerations more or less foreign to it. Every scrap of local defence would, in proportion to its amount, be a diminution of the offensive defence. Advocates of the former may be challenged to produce from naval history any instance of local naval defence succeeding against the assaults of an actively aggressive navy. In the late war between Japan and Russia the Russian local defence failed completely.

In the last case, a class of vessel like that which had failed in local defence was used successfully, because offensively, by the Japanese. This and many another instance show that the right way to use the kind of craft so often allocated to local defence is to use them offensively. It is only thus that their adoption by a great maritime power like the British Empire can be justified. The origin and centre of our naval strength are to be looked for in the United Kingdom. The shores of the latter are near the shores of other great maritime powers. Its ports, especially those at which its fleets are equipped and would be likely to assemble on the imminence of war, are within reach of more than one foreign place from which small swift craft to be used offensively might be expected to issue.

The method of frustrating the efforts of these craft giving most promise of success is to attack them as soon as possible after they issue from their own port. To the acceptance of this principle we owe the origin of the destroyer, devised to destroy hostile torpedo-boats before they could reach a position from which they would be able to discharge with effect their special weapon against our assembled ships. It is true that the destroyer has been gradually converted into a larger torpedo-boat. It is also true that when used as such in local defence, as at Port Arthur, her failure was complete ; and just as true that she has never accomplished anything except when used offensively.

When, therefore, a naval country's coast is so near the ports of another naval country that the latter would be able with swift small craft to attack the former's shipping, the provision of craft of a similar kind is likely to prove advantageous. War between great powers is a two-sided game, and what one side can do the other will at least be likely to attempt. Nothing supports the view that it is well—either above or beneath the surface of the water—to stand on the defensive and await attack. Everything points to the superiority of the plan of beating up the enemy's quarters and attacking him before he can get far from them on his way towards his objective. Consequently the only justification of expending money on the localised vessels of which we have been speaking, is the probability that an enemy would have some of his bases within reach of those vessels' efforts. Where this condition does not exist, the money expended is, from the belligerent point of view, thrown away. Here comes in the greatest foe of belligerent efficiency, viz. political expediency. In time of peace it is thought better to conciliate voters than to prepare to meet an enemy. If local defence is thought to be pleasing to an inexpert electorate, it is only too likely to be provided, no matter how ineffectual and how costly in reality it will turn out to be.

Not only is the British Empire the first of naval powers, it is also the first of colonial powers. One attribute is closely connected with the other; neither, without the other, would be applicable. The magnitude of our colonial domain, and especially the imposing aspects of some of its greater components—the Dominion, the Commonwealth, South Africa, New Zealand—are apt to blind us to a feature of great strategical importance, and that is the abundance and excellence of the naval bases that stud our ocean lines of communication. In thinking of the great daughter states we are liable to forget these; yet our possession of them helps greatly to strengthen our naval position, because it facilitates our assuming a far-reaching offensive. By themselves, if not too numerous, they can afford valuable support to the naval operations that are likely to prove most beneficial to us. The fact that they are ours, and not an opponent's, also constitutes for us an advantage of importance. Of course, they have to be defended, or else they may fall into an opponent's hands. Have we here a case in which highly localised or even passive defences are desirable ? No doubt we did act for a time as though we believed that the question could only be answered in the affirmative ; but that was when we were under the influence of the feelings engendered by observation of the long series of land wars previously discussed.

Perhaps we have not yet quite shaken off the effects of that influence ; but we have at least got so far as to tolerate the statement of the other side of the question. It would be a great mistake to suppose that the places alluded to are meant to be ports of refuge for our ships. Though they were to serve that purpose occasionally in the case of isolated merchant vessels, it would be but an accident, and not the essence, of their existence. What they are meant for is to be utilised as positions where our men-of-war can make reasonably sure of finding supplies and the means of refit. This assurance will largely depend upon their power of resistance if attacked. Before we can decide how to impart that power to them we shall have to see the kind of attack against which they would have to be prepared. If they are on a continent, like, for example, Gibraltar, attack on them by a land force, however improbable, is physically possible. Against an attack of the kind a naval force could give little direct help. Most of our outlying naval bases are really or virtually insular, and are open to attack only by an expedition coming across the sea.

An essential characteristic of a naval base is that it should be able to furnish supplies as wanted to the men-of-war needing to replenish their stocks. Some, and very often all, of these supplies are not of native production and must be brought to the base by sea. If the enemy can stop their conveyance to it, the place is useless as a base and the enemy is really in control of its communications. If he is in control of its communications he can send against it as great an expedition as he likes, and the place will be captured or completely neutralised. Similarly, if we control the communications, not only can supplies be conveyed to it, but also no hostile expedition will be allowed to reach it. Thus the primary defence of the outlying base is the active, sea-going fleet. Moderate local defence, chiefly of the human kind, in the shape of a garrison, will certainly be needed. Though the enemy has not been able to obtain control of the communications of the place, fitful raids on it will be possible ; and the place should be fortified enough and garrisoned enough to hold out against the inconsiderable assaults comprised in these till our own ships can drive the enemy's away.

Outlying naval bases, though but moderately fortified, that contain depots of stores, docks, and other conveniences, have the vice of all immobile establishments. When war does come, some of them almost certainly, and all of them possibly, may not be in the right place with regard to the critical area of operations. They cannot, however, be moved. It will be necessary to do what has been done over and over again in war, in the latest as well as in earlier wars, and that is, establish temporary bases in more convenient situations. Thus much, perhaps all, of the cost and trouble of establishing and maintaining the permanent bases will have been wasted. This inculcates the necessity of having not as many bases as can be found, but as few as it is possible to get on with.

The control of ocean communications, or the command of the sea, being the end of naval warfare, and its acquisition being practicable only by the assumption of a vigorous offensive, it follows as a matter of course that we must have a strong and in all respects efficient mobile navy. This is the fundamental condition on which the continued existence of the British Empire depends. It is thoroughly well known to every foreign Government, friendly or unfriendly. The true objective in naval warfare is the enemy's navy. That must be destroyed or decisively defeated, or intimidated into remaining in its ports. Not one of these can be effected without a mobile, that is a sea-going, fleet. The British Empire may fall to pieces from causes as yet unknown or unsuspected : it cannot be kept together if it loses the power of gaining command of the sea. This is not a result of deliberate policy : it is inherent in the nature of the empire, scattered as its parts are throughout the world, with only the highway of the sea between them.

Such is the position of the fleet in the defence

of the empire : such are its duties towards it. Duties in the case are mutual, and some are owed to the fleet as well as by it. It is incumbent on every section of the empire, without neglecting its land forces, to lend zealous help in keeping the fleet efficient. It is not to be supposed that this can be done only by making pecuniary contributions to its maintenance. It is, indeed, very doubtful if any real good can be done by urging colonies to make them. It seems certain that the objections to this are greater than any benefit that it can confer. Badgering our fellow-subjects beyond sea for money payments towards the cost of the navy is undignified and impolitic. The greatest sum asked for by the most exacting postulant would not equal a twentieth part of the imperial naval expenditure, and would not save the taxpayer of the mother country a farthing in the pound of his income. No one has yet been able to establish the equity of a demand that would take something from the inhabitants of one colony and nothing from those of another. Adequate voluntary contribution is a different matter.

There are other ways in which every trans-marine possession of the Crown can lend a hand towards perfecting the efficiency of the fleet—ways, too, which would leave each in complete and unmenaced control of its own money. Sea-power does not consist entirely of men-of-war. There must be docks, refitting establishments, magazines, and depots of stores. Ports, which men-of-war must visit at least occasionally in war for repair or replenishment of supplies, will have to be made secure against the assaults which it has been said that a hastily raiding enemy, notwithstanding our general control of the communications, might find a chance of making. Moderate fixed fortifications are all the passive defence that would be needed ; but good and active troops must be available. If all these are not provided by the part of the empire in which the necessary naval bases lie, they will have to be provided by the mother country. If the former provides them the latter will be spared the expense of doing so, and spared expense with no loss of dignity, and with far less risk of friction and inconvenience than if her taxpayers' pockets had been nominally spared to the extent of a trifling and reluctantly paid money contribution.

It has been pointed out on an earlier page that a country can be, and most probably will be, more effectually defended in a maritime war if its fleet operates at a distance from, rather than near, its shores. Every subject of our King should long to see this condition exist if ever the empire is involved in hostilities. It may be—for who can tell what war will bring ?—that the people of some great trans-marine dependency will have to choose between allowing a campaign to be conducted in their country or forcing the enemy to tolerate it in his. If they choose the latter they must be pre-pared to furnish part at least of the mobile force that can give effect to their choice. That is to say, they must be prepared to back up our sea-power in its efforts to keep off the tide of war from the neighbourhood of their homes. History shows how rarely, during the struggle between European nations for predominance in North America, the more settled parts of our former American Colonies were the theatre of war : but then the colonists of those days, few comparatively as they were, sent strong contingents to the armies that went campaigning in the territory of the various enemies. This was in every way better—the sequel proved how much better—than a money contribution begged or extorted would have been.

Helping in the manner first suggested need not result in dissociating our fellow-subjects beyond the seas from participation in the work of the active sea-going fleet. It is now, and still would be, open to them as much as to any native or denizen of the mother country. The time has fully come when the people of the greater outlying parts of the empire should insist upon perfect equality of treatment with their home fellow-subjects in this matter. They should resent, as a now quite out-of-date and invidious distinction, any difference in qualification for entry, locality of service, or remuneration for any rank or rating. Self-respect and a dignified confidence in their own qualities, the excellence of which has been thoroughly tested, will prompt the King's colonial subjects to ask for nothing but equal chances in a force on which is laid so large a part of the duty of defending

the empire.   Why should they cut themselves off
from the promising career that service in the
Royal Navy opens to the capable, the zealous, and
the honourable aspirant of every grade ?   Some
of the highest posts in the navy are now, or lately
have been, held by men who not only happened to
be born in British Colonies, but who also belong to
resident colonial families.   Surely in this there is a
strong moral cement for binding and keeping the
empire together.   It is unnecessary to expatiate
on the contrast between the prospect of such a career
and that which is all that a small local service could
offer.   It would soon be seen towards which the
enterprising and the energetic would instinctively
gravitate.

In the defence of the British Empire the fleet
holds a twofold position.   To its general belligerent
efficiency, its strength and activity, we must look
if the plans of an enemy are to be brought to nought.
It, and it only, can secure for us the control of the
ocean communications, on the freedom of which
from serious interruptions the prosperity—indeed,
the existence—of a scattered body must depend.
In time of peace it can be made a great consolidating
force, fostering every sentiment of worthy local
patriotism whilst obliterating all inclination to
mischievous narrow particularism, and tending to
perfect the unity which gives virtue to national
grandeur and is the true secret of national independence and strength.

XI

NAVAL STRATEGY AND TACTICS AT THE TIME OF TRAFALGAR [1]

THE subject on which I have been invited to read a paper, and which is taken as the title of the latter, would require for anything like full discussion a much longer time than you can be expected to allot to it. To discuss it adequately, a volume of no diminutive size would be necessary. It may, however, be possible to indicate with the brevity appropriate to the occasion the main outlines of the subject, and to suggest for your consideration certain points which, over and above their historical interest, may furnish us with valuable guidance at the present day.

In taking account of the conditions of the Trafalgar epoch we have to note two distinct but, of course, closely related matters. These are the strategic plan of the enemy and the strategic plan adopted to meet it by the British. The former of these was described in the House of Commons by William Pitt at the beginning of the war in words which may be used without change at the present

[1] Written in 1905. (Read at Institute of Naval Architects.)

time. On 16th May 1803 the war, which had been interrupted by the unstable Peace of Amiens, was definitely resumed. The struggle was now to be a war not so much between the United Kingdom and the French nation as between the United Kingdom and the great Napoleon, wielding more than the resources of France alone. Speaking a week after the declaration of war, Pitt said that any expectation of success which the enemy might have must be based on the supposition that he could break the spirit or weaken the determination of the country by harassing us with the perpetual apprehension of descents on our coasts ; or else that our resources could be impaired and our credit undermined by the effects of an expensive and protracted war. More briefly stated, the hostile plan was to invade the United Kingdom, ruin our maritime trade, and expel us from our over-sea possessions, especially in the East, from which it was supposed our wealth was chiefly derived. The plan was comprehensive, but not easily concealed. What we had to do was to prevent the invasion of the United Kingdom and defend our trade and our outlying territories. As not one of the hostile objects could be attained except by making a maritime expedition of some kind, that is to say, by an expedition which had to cross more or less extensive areas of water, it necessarily followed that our most effective method of defence was the keeping open of our sea communications. It became necessary for us to make such arrangements that the maritime paths by which a hostile expedition could approach our home-coasts, or hostile cruisers molest our sea-borne trade, or hostile squadrons move to the attack of our trans-marine dependencies —that all these paths should be so defended by our navy that either the enemy would not venture to traverse them or, if he did, that he could be driven off.

Short as it is, the time at my disposal permits me to give a few details. It was fully recognised that defence of the United Kingdom against invasion could not be secured by naval means alone. As in the times of Queen Elizabeth, so in those of George III, no seaman of reputation contended that a sufficient land force could be dispensed with. Our ablest seamen always held that small hostile expeditions could be prepared in secret and might be able to slip through the most complete lines of naval defence that we could hope to maintain. It was not discovered or alleged till the twentieth century that the crew of a dinghy could not land in this country in the face of the navy. Therefore an essential feature of our defensive strategy was the provision of land forces in such numbers that an invader would have no chance of succeeding except he came in strength so great that his preparations could not be concealed and his expedition could not cross the water unseen.

As our mercantile marine was to be found in nearly every sea, though in greater accumulation in some areas than in others, its defence against the assaults of an enemy could only be ensured by the virtual ubiquity of our cruising force. This, of course, involved the necessity of employing a large number of cruisers, and of arranging the distribution of them in accordance with the relative amount and value of the traffic to be protected from molestation in different parts of the ocean. It may be mentioned here that the term 'cruiser,' at the time with which we are dealing, was not limited to frigates and smaller classes of vessels. It included also ships of the line, it being the old belief of the British Navy, justified by the experience of many campaigns and consecrated by the approval of our greatest admirals, that the value of a ship of war was directly proportionate to her capacity for cruising and keeping the sea.

If the ocean paths used by our merchant ships —the trade routes or sea communications of the United Kingdom with friendly or neutral markets and areas of production—could be kept open by our navy, that is, made so secure that our trade could traverse them with so little risk of molestation that it could continue to be carried on, it resulted as a matter of course that no sustained attack could be made on our outlying territory. Where this was possible it was where we had failed to keep open the route or line of communications, in which case the particular trade following it was, at least temporarily, destroyed, and the territory to which the route led was either cut off or seized. Naturally, when this was perceived, efforts were made to re-open and keep open the endangered or interrupted communication line.

Napoleon, notwithstanding his supereminent genius, made some extraordinary mistakes about warfare on the sea. The explanation of this has been given by a highly distinguished French admiral. The Great Emperor, he says, was wanting in exact appreciation of the difficulties of naval operations. He never understood that the naval officer—alone of all men in the world—must be master of two distinct professions. The naval officer must be as completely a seaman as an officer in any mercantile marine ; and, in addition to this, he must be as accomplished in the use of the material of war entrusted to his charge as the members of any armed force in the world. The Emperor's plan for the invasion of the United Kingdom was conceived on a grand scale. A great army, eventually 130,000 strong, was collected on the coast of northeastern France, with its headquarters at Boulogne. The numerical strength of this army is worth attention. By far the larger part of it was to have made the first descent on our territory ; the remainder was to be a reserve to follow as quickly as possible. It has been doubted if Napoleon really meant to invade this country, the suggestion being that his collection of an army on the shores of the Straits of Dover and the English Channel was merely a ' blind ' to cover another intended movement. The overwhelming weight of authoritative opinion is in favour of the view that the project of invasion was real. It is highly significant that he considered so large a number of troops necessary. It could not have been governed by any estimate of the naval obstruction to be encountered during the sea passage of the expedition, but only by the amount of the land force likely to be met if the disembarkation on our shores could be effected. The numerical strength in troops which Napoleon thought necessary compelled him to make preparations on so great a scale that concealment became quite impossible. Consequently an important part of his plan was disclosed to us betimes, and the threatened locality indicated to us within comparatively narrow limits of precision.

Notwithstanding his failure to appreciate all the difficulties of naval warfare, the Great Emperor had grasped one of its leading principles. Before the Peace of Amiens, indeed before his campaign in Egypt, and even his imposing triumphs in Italy, he had seen that the invasion of the United Kingdom was impracticable without first obtaining the command of the sea. His strategic plan, therefore, included arrangements to secure this. The details of the plan were changed from time to time as conditions altered ; but the main object was adhered to until the final abandonment of the whole scheme under pressure of circumstances as embodied in Nelson and his victorious brothers-in-arms. The gunboats, transport boats, and other small craft, which to the number of many hundreds filled the ports of north-eastern France and the Netherlands, were not the only naval components of the expedition. Fleets of line-of-battle ships were essential parts of it, and on their effective action the success of the scheme was largely made to depend. This feature remained unaltered in principle when, less than twelve months before Trafalgar, Spain took part in the war as Napoleon's ally, and brought him a great reinforcement of ships and important assistance in money.

We should not fail to notice that, before he considered himself strong enough to undertake the invasion of the United Kingdom, Napoleon found it necessary to have at his disposal the resources of other countries besides France, notwithstanding that by herself France had a population more than 60 per cent. greater than that of England. By the alliance with Spain he had added largely to the resources on which he could draw. Moreover, his strategic position was geographically much improved. With the exception of that of Portugal, the coast of western continental Europe, from the Texel to Leghorn, and somewhat later to Taranto also, was united in hostility to us. This complicated the strategic problem which the British Navy had to solve, as it increased the number of points to be watched ; and it facilitated the junction of Napoleon's Mediterranean naval forces with those assembled in his Atlantic ports by supplying him with allied ports of refuge and refit on Spanish territory—such as Cartagena or Cadiz—between Toulon and the Bay of Biscay. Napoleon, therefore, enforced upon us by the most convincing of all arguments the necessity of maintaining the British Navy at the 'two-power standard' at least. The lesson had been taught us long before by Philip II, who did not venture on an attempt at invading this country till he was master of the resources of the whole Iberian peninsula as well as of those of the Spanish dominions in Italy, in the Burgundian heritage, and in the distant regions across the Atlantic Ocean.

At several points on the long stretch of coast of which he was now the master, Napoleon equipped fleets that were to unite and win for him the command of the sea during a period long enough to permit the unobstructed passage of his invading army across the water which separated the starting points of his expedition from the United Kingdom. Command of the sea to be won by a powerful naval combination was thus an essential element in Napoleon's strategy at the time of Trafalgar. It was not in deciding what was essential that this soldier of stupendous ability erred : it was in choosing the method of gaining the essential that he went wrong. The British strategy adopted in opposition to that of Napoleon was based on the acquisition and preservation of the command of the sea. Formulated and carried into effect by seamen, it differed in some important features from his. We may leave out of sight for the moment the special arrangements made in the English Channel to oppose the movements of Napoleon's flotillas of gunboats, transport boats, and other small craft. The British strategy at the time of Trafalgar, as far as it was concerned with opposition to Napoleon's sea-going fleets, may be succinctly described as stationing off each of the ports in which the enemy's forces were lying a fleet or squadron of suitable strength. Though some of our admirals, notably Nelson himself, objected to the application of the term 'blockade' to their plans, the hostile ships were to this extent blockaded, that if they should come out they would find outside their port a British force sufficient to drive them in again, or even to defeat them thoroughly and destroy them. Beating them and thus having done with them, and not simply shutting them up in harbour, was what was desired by our admirals. This necessitated a close watch on the hostile ports ; and how consistently that was maintained let the history of Cornwallis's command off Brest and of Nelson's off Toulon suffice to tell us.

The junction of two or more of Napoleon's fleets would have ensured over almost any single British fleet a numerical superiority that would have rendered the defeat or retirement of the latter almost certain. To meet this condition the British strategy contemplated the falling back, if necessary, of one of our detachments on another, which might be carried further and junction with a third detachment be effected. By this step we should preserve, if not a numerical superiority over the enemy, at least so near an equality of force as to render his defeat probable and his serious maltreatment, even if undefeated, a certainty. The strategic problem before our navy was, however, not quite so easy as this might make it seem. The enemy's concentration might be attempted either towards Brest or towards Toulon. In the latter case, a superior force might fall upon our Mediterranean fleet before our watching ships in the Atlantic could discover the escape of the enemy's ships from the Atlantic port or could follow and come up with them. Against the probability of this was to be set the reluctance of Napoleon to carry out an eccentric operation which a concentration off Toulon would necessitate, when the essence of his scheme was to concentrate in a position from which he could obtain naval control of the English Channel.

After the addition of the Spanish Navy to his own, Napoleon to some extent modified his strategic arrangements. The essential feature of the scheme remained unaltered. It was to effect the junction of the different parts of his naval force and thereupon to dominate the situation, by evading the several British fleets or detachments which were watching his. Before Spain joined him in the war his intention was that his escaping fleets should go out into the Atlantic, behind the backs, as it were, of the British ships, and then make for the English Channel. When he had the aid of Spain the point of junction was to be in the West Indies.

The remarkable thing about this was the evident belief that the command of the sea might be won without fighting for it ; won, too, from the British Navy which was ready, and indeed wished, to fight. We now see that Napoleon's naval strategy at the time of Trafalgar, whilst it aimed at gaining command of the sea, was based on what has been called evasion. The fundamental principle of the British naval strategy of that time was quite different. So far from thinking that the contest could be settled without one or more battles, the British admirals, though nominally blockading his ports, gave the enemy every facility for coming out in order that they might be able to bring him to action. Napoleon, on the contrary, declared that a battle would be useless, and distinctly ordered his officers not to fight one. Could it be that, when pitted against admirals whose accurate conception of the conditions of naval warfare had been over and over again tested during the hostilities ended by the Peace of Amiens, Napoleon still trusted to the efficacy of methods which had proved so success-ful when he was outmanœuvring and intimidating the generals who opposed him in North Italy ? We can only explain his attitude in the campaign of Trafalgar by attributing to him an expectation that the British seamen of his day, tried as they had been in the fire of many years of war, would succumb to his methods as readily as the military formalists of central Europe.

Napoleon had at his disposal between seventy and eighty French, Dutch, and Spanish ships of the line, of which some sixty-seven were available at the beginning of the Trafalgar campaign. In January 1805, besides other ships of the class in distant waters or specially employed, we—on our side—had eighty ships of the line in commission. A knowledge of this will enable us to form some idea of the chances of success that would have attended Napoleon's concentration if it had been effected. To protect the passage of his invading expedition across the English Channel he did not depend only on concentrating his more distant fleets. In the Texel there were, besides smaller vessels, nine sail of the line. Thus the Emperor did what we may be sure any future intending invader will not fail to do, viz. he provided his expedition with a respectable naval escort. The British naval officers of the day, who knew what war was, made arrangements to deal with this escort. Lord Keith, who commanded in the Downs, had under him six sail of the line in addition to many frigates and sloops ; and there were five more line-of-battle ships ready at Spithead if required.

There had been a demand in the country that the defence of our shores against an invading expedition should be entrusted to gunboats, and what may be called coastal small craft and boats. This was resisted by the naval officers. Nelson had already said, ' Our first defence is close to the enemy's ports,' thus agreeing with a long line of eminent British seamen in their view of our strategy. Lord St. Vincent said that ' Our great reliance is on the vigilance and activity of our cruisers at sea, any reduction in the number of which by applying them to guard our ports, inlets, and beaches would, in my judgment, tend to our destruction.' These are memorable words, which we should do well to ponder in these days. The Government of the day insisted on having the coastal boats ; but St. Vincent succeeded in postponing the preparation of them till the cruising ships had been manned. His plan of defence has been described by his biographer as ' a triple line of barricade ; 50-gun ships, frigates, sloops of war, and gun-vessels upon the coast of the enemy ; in the Downs opposite France another squadron, but of powerful ships of the line, continually disposable, to support the former or attack any force of the enemy which, it might be imagined possible, might slip through the squadron hanging over the coast ; and a force on the beach on all the shores of the English ports, to render assurance doubly sure.' This last item was the one that St. Vincent had been compelled to adopt, and he was careful that it should be in addition to those measures of defence in the efficacy of which he and his brother seamen believed. Concerning it his biographer makes the following remark : ' It is to be noted that Lord St. Vincent did not contemplate repelling an invasion of gunboats by gunboats,' &c. He objected to the force of sea-fencibles, or 'long-shore organisation, because he considered it more useful to have the sea-going ships manned. Speaking of this coastal defence scheme, he said : ' It would be a good bone for the officers to pick, but a very dear one for the country.'

The defence of our ocean trade entered largely into the strategy of the time. An important part was played by our fleets and groups of line-of-battle ships which gave usually indirect, but sometimes direct, protection to our own merchant vessels, and also to neutral vessels carrying commodities to or from British ports. The strategy of the time, the correctness of which was confirmed by long belligerent experience, rejected the employment of a restricted number of powerful cruisers, and relied upon the practical ubiquity of the defending ships, which ubiquity was rendered possible by the employment of very numerous craft of moderate size. This can be seen in the lists of successive years. In January 1803 the number of cruising frigates in commission was 107, and of sloops and smaller vessels 139, the total being 246. In 1804 the numbers were : Frigates, 108 ; sloops, &c., 181 ; with a total of 289. In 1805 the figures had grown to 129 frigates, 416 sloops, &c., the total being 545. Most of these were employed in defending commerce. We all know how completely Napoleon's project of invading the United Kingdom was frustrated. It is less well known that the measures for defending our sea-borne trade, indicated by the figures just given, were triumphantly successful. Our mercantile marine increased during the war, a sure proof that it had been effectually defended. Consequently we may accept it as established beyond the possibility of refutation that that branch of our naval strategy at the time of Trafalgar which was concerned with the defence of our trade was rightly conceived and properly carried into effect.

As has been stated already, the defence of our sea-borne trade, being in practice the keeping open of our ocean lines of communication, carried with it the protection, in part at any rate, of our transmarine territories. Napoleon held pertinaciously to the belief that British prosperity was chiefly due to our position in India. We owe it to Captain Mahan that we now know that the eminent American Fulton—a name of interest to the members of this Institution—told Pitt of the belief held abroad that ' the fountains of British wealth are in India and China.' In the great scheme of naval concentration which the Emperor devised, seizure of British Colonies in the West Indies had a definite place. We kept in that quarter, and varied as necessary, a force capable of dealing with a naval raid as well as guarding the neighbouring lines of communication. In 1803 we had four ships of the line in the West Indian area. In 1804 we had six of the same class ; and in 1805, while the line-of-battle ships were reduced to four, the number of frigates was increased from nine to twenty-five. Whether our Government divined Napoleon's designs on India or not, it took measures to protect our interests there. In January 1804 we had on the Cape of Good Hope and the East Indies stations, both together, six sail of the line, three smaller two-deckers, six frigates, and six sloops, or twenty-one ships of war in all. This would have been sufficient to repel a raiding attack made in some strength. By the beginning of 1805 our East Indies force had been increased ; and in the year 1805 itself we raised it to a strength of forty-one ships in all, of which nine were of the line and seventeen were frigates. Had, therefore, any of the hostile ships managed to get to the East Indies from the Atlantic or the Mediterranean ports, in which they were being watched by our navy, their chances of succeeding in their object would have been small indeed.

When we enter the domain of tactics strictly so-called, that is to say, when we discuss the proceedings of naval forces—whether single ships, squadrons, or fleets—in hostile contact with one another, we find the time of Trafalgar full of instructive episodes. Even with the most recent experience of naval warfare vividly present to our minds, we can still regard Nelson as the greatest of tacticians. Naval tactics may be roughly divided into two great classes or sections, viz. the tactics of groups of ships, that is to say, fleet actions ; and the tactics of what the historian James calls ' single ship actions,' that is to say, fights between two individual ships. In the former the achievements of Nelson stand out with incomparable brilliancy. It would be impossible to describe his method fully in such a paper as this. We may, however, say that Nelson was an innovator, and that his tactical principles and methods have been generally misunderstood down to this very day. If ever there was an admiral who was opposed to an unthinking, headlong rush at an enemy, it was he. Yet this is the character that he still bears in the conception of many. He was, in truth, an industrious and patient student of tactics, having studied them, in what in these days we should call a scientific spirit, at an early period, when there was but little reason to expect that he would ever be in a position to put to a practical test the knowledge that he had acquired and the ideas that he had formed. He saw that the old battle formation in single line-ahead was insufficient if you wanted—as he himself always did—to gain an overwhelming victory. He also saw that, though an improvement on the old formation, Lord Howe's method of the single line-abreast was still a good deal short of tactical perfection. Therefore, he devised what he called, with pardonable elation, the ' Nelson touch,' the attack in successive lines so directed as to overwhelm one part of the enemy's fleet, whilst the other part was prevented from coming to the assistance of the first, and was in its turn overwhelmed or broken up. His object was to bring a larger number of his own ships against a smaller number of the enemy's. He would by this method destroy the part attacked, suffering in the process so little damage himself that with his whole force he would be able to deal effectively with the hostile remnant if it ventured to try conclusions with him. It is of the utmost importance that we should thoroughly understand Nelson's fundamental tactical principle, viz. the bringing of a larger number of ships to fight against a smaller number of the

T

enemy's. There is not, I believe, in the whole of the records of Nelson's opinions and actions a single expression tending to show that tactical efficiency was considered by him to be due to superiority in size of individual ships of the same class or—as far as *matériel* was concerned—to anything but superior numbers, of course at the critical point. He did not require, and did not have, more ships in his own fleet than the whole of those in the fleet of the enemy. What he wanted was to bring to the point of impact, when the fight began, a larger number of ships than were to be found in that part of the enemy's line.

I believe that I am right in saying that, from the date of Salamis downwards, history records no decisive naval victory in which the victorious fleet has not succeeded in concentrating against a relatively weak point in its enemy's formation a greater number of its own ships. I know of nothing to show that this has not been the rule throughout the ages of which detailed history furnishes us with any memorial—no matter what the class of ship, what the type of weapon, what the mode of propulsion. The rule certainly prevailed in the battle of the 10th August 1904 off Port Arthur, though it was not so overwhelmingly decisive as some others. We may not even yet know enough of the sea fight in the Straits of Tsushima to be able to describe it in detail ; but we do know that at least some of the Russian ships were defeated or destroyed by a combination of Japanese ships against them.

Looking back at the tactics of the Trafalgar epoch, we may see that the history of them confirms the experience of earlier wars, viz. that victory does not necessarily fall to the side which has the biggest ships. It is a well-known fact of naval history that generally the French ships were larger and the Spanish much larger than the British ships of corresponding classes. This superiority in size certainly did not carry with it victory in action. On the other hand, British ships were generally bigger than the Dutch ships with which they fought ; and it is of great significance that at Camperdown the victory was due, not to superiority in the size of individual ships, but, as shown by the different lists of killed and wounded, to the act of bringing a larger number against a smaller. All that we have been able to learn of the occurrences in the battle of the Japan Sea supports instead of being opposed to this conclusion ; and it may be said that there is nothing tending to upset it in the previous history of the present war in the Far East.

I do not know how far I am justified in expatiating on this point ; but, as it may help to bring the strategy and tactics of the Trafalgar epoch into practical relation with the stately science of which in our day this Institution is, as it were, the mother-shrine and metropolitical temple, I may be allowed to dwell upon it a little longer. The object aimed at by those who favour great size of individual ships is not, of course, magnitude alone. It is to turn out a ship which shall be more powerful than

an individual antagonist. All recent development
of man-of-war construction has taken the form of
producing, or at any rate trying to produce, a more
powerful ship than those of earlier date, or belonging
to a rival navy. I know the issues that such
statements are likely to raise ; and I ask you, as
naval architects, to bear with me patiently when
I say what I am going to say. It is this : If you
devise for the ship so produced the tactical system
for which she is specially adapted you must, in
order to be logical, base your system on her power
of defeating her particular antagonist. Consequently, you must abandon the principle of concentration of superior numbers against your enemy ;
and, what is more, must be prepared to maintain
that such concentration on his part against yourself
would be ineffectual. This will compel a reversion
to tactical methods which made a fleet action a
series of duels between pairs of combatants, and—
a thing to be pondered on seriously—never enabled
anyone to win a decisive victory on the sea. The
position will not be made more logical if you demand
both superior size and also superior numbers,
because if you adopt the tactical system appropriate
to one of the things demanded, you will rule out the
other. You cannot employ at the same time two
different and opposed tactical systems.

It is not necessary to the line of argument above
indicated to ignore the merits of the battleship class.
Like their predecessors, the ships of the line, it is
really battleships which in a naval war dominate the

situation. We saw that it was so at the time of Trafalgar, and we see that it has been so in the war between Russia and Japan, at all events throughout the 1904 campaign. The experience of naval war, down to the close of that in which Trafalgar was the most impressive event, led to the virtual abandonment of ships of the line [1] above and below a certain class.

[1] Experience of war, as regards increase in the number of medium-sized men-of-war of the different classes, tended to the same result in both the French Revolutionary war (1793 to 1801) and the Napoleonic war which began in 1803. Taking both contests down to the end of the Trafalgar year, the following table will show how great was the development of the line-of-battle-ship class below the three-decker and above the 64-gun ship. It will also show that there was no development of, but a relative decline in, the three-deckers and the 64's, the small additions, where there were any, being generally due to captures from the enemy. The two-deckers not 'fit to lie in a line' were at the end of the Trafalgar year about half what they were when the first period of the ' Great War ' began. When we come to the frigate classes we find the same result. In the

Classes of Ships	French Revolutionary War		Napoleonic War to the end of the Trafalgar year	
	Commencement of 1793	Commencement of 1801	Commencement of 1803	Commencement of 1806
3-deckers . . .	31	32	29	29
2-deckers of 74 guns, and above	76	111	105	123
64 and 60 gun ships .	46	47	38	38
2-deckers not ' fit to lie in a line '	43	31	21	22
Frigates 44 guns .	0	6	6	6
,, 40 ,, .	0	5	5	4
,, 38 ,, .	8	32	32	50
,, 36 ,, .	16	49	49	54
,, 32 ,, .	48	41	38	56
,, 28 ,, .	27	11	11	13

The 64-gun ships and smaller two-deckers had greatly diminished in number, and repetitions of them grew more and more rare.   It was the same with the three-deckers, which, as the late Admiral Colomb pointed out, continued to be built, though in reduced numbers, not so much for their tactical efficiency as for the convenient manner in which they met the demands for the accommodation required in flag-ships.   The tactical condition which the naval architects of the Trafalgar period had to meet was the employment of an increased number of two-deckers of the medium classes.

A fleet of ships of the line as long as it could keep the sea, that is, until it had to retreat into port before a stronger fleet, controlled a certain area of water. Within that area smaller men-of-war as well as friendly merchant ships were secure from attack. As the fleet moved about, so the area moved with it. Skilful disposition and manœuvring added largely

---

earlier war 11 frigates of 44 and 40 guns were introduced into our navy.   It is worth notice that this number was not increased, and by the end of the Trafalgar year had, on the contrary, declined to 10.   The smallest frigates, of 28 guns, were 27 in 1793, and 13 at the end of the Trafalgar year.   On the other hand, the increase in the medium frigate classes (38, 36, and 32 guns) was very large.   From 1793 to the end of the Trafalgar year the 38-gun frigates increased from 8 to 50, and the 36-gun frigates from 16 to 54.

The liking for three-deckers, professed by some officers of Nelson's time, seems to have been due to a belief, not in the merit of their size as such, but in the value of the increased number of medium guns carried on a ' middle ' deck.   There is, I believe, nothing to show that the two-deckers *Gibraltar* (2185 tons) and *Cæsar* (2003) were considered more formidable than the three-deckers *Barfleur* (1947), *Glory* (1944), or *Queen* (1876).   All these ships were in the same fleet, and fought in the same battle.

to the extent of sea within which the maritime interests that the fleet was meant to protect would be safe. It seems reasonable to expect that it will be the same with modern fleets of suitable battleships.

The tactics of 'single ship actions' at the time of Trafalgar were based upon pure seamanship backed up by good gunnery. The better a captain handled his ship the more likely he was to beat his antagonist. Superior speed, where it existed, was used to 'gain the weather gage,' not in order to get a suitable range for the faster ship's guns, but to compel her enemy to fight. Superior speed was also used to run away, capacity to do which was not then, and ought not to be now, reckoned a merit in a ship expressly constructed for fighting, not fleeing. It is sometimes claimed in these days that superior speed will enable a modern ship to keep at a distance from her opponent which will be the best range for her own guns. It has not been explained why a range which best suits her guns should not be equally favourable for the guns of her opponent; unless, indeed, the latter is assumed to be weakly armed, in which case the distance at which the faster ship might engage her would be a matter of comparative indifference. There is nothing in the tactics of the time of Trafalgar to make it appear that—when a fight had once begun—superior speed, of course within moderate limits, conferred any considerable tactical advantage in ' single ship actions,' and still less in general or fleet actions. Taking up a position ahead or astern of a hostile ship so as to be able to rake her was not facilitated by originally superior speed so much as by the more damaged state of the ship to be raked—raking, as a rule, occurring rather late in an action.

A remarkable result of long experience of war made itself clearly apparent in the era of Trafalgar. I have already alluded to the tendency to restrict the construction of line-of-battle ships to those of the medium classes. The same thing may be noticed in the case of the frigates.[1] Those of 44, 40, and 28 guns relatively or absolutely diminished in number ; whilst the number of the 38-gun, 36-gun, and 32-gun frigates increased. The officers who had personal experience of many campaigns were able to impress on the naval architects of the day the necessity of recognising the sharp distinction that really exists between what we should now call the ' battleship ' and what we should now call the ' cruiser.' In the earlier time there were ships which were intermediate between the ship of the line and the frigate. These were the two-deckers of 56, 54, 50, 44, and even 40 guns. They had long been regarded as not ' fit to lie in a line,' and they were never counted in the frigate classes. They seemed to have held a nondescript position, for no one knew exactly how to employ them in war any more than we now know exactly how to employ our armoured cruisers, as to which it is not settled whether they are fit for general actions or should be confined to commerce defending or other cruiser service. The

[1] See footnote, p. 277.

two-deckers just mentioned were looked upon by the date of Trafalgar as forming an unnecessary class of fighting ships. Some were employed, chiefly because they existed, on special service ; but they were being replaced by true battleships on one side and true frigates on the other.[1]

In conclusion, I would venture to say that the strategical and tactical lessons taught by a long series of naval campaigns had been mastered by our navy by the time of the Trafalgar campaign. The effect of those lessons showed itself in our ship-building policy, and has been placed on permanent record in the history of maritime achievement and of the adaptation of material means to belligerent ends.

[1] See footnote, p. 277.

XII

THE SUPPLY AND COMMUNICATIONS OF A FLEET [1]

A PROBLEM which is not an attractive one, but which has to be solved, is to arrange the proper method of supplying a fleet and maintaining its communications. In time of peace as well as in time of war there is a continuous consumption of the articles of various kinds used on board ship, viz. naval stores, ordnance stores, engineers' stores, victualling stores, coal, water, &c. If we know the quantity of each description of stores that a ship can carry, and if we estimate the progressive consumption, we can compute, approximately but accurately enough for practical purposes, the time at which replenishment would be necessary and to what amount it should be made up. As a general rule ships stow about three months' stores and provisions. The amount of coal and engineers' stores, measured in time, depends on the proceedings of the ship, and can only be calculated if we know during what portion of any given period she will be under way. Of course, this can be only roughly estimated. In peace time we know nearly exactly what the expenditure of ammunition within a given length of time—say, a quarter of a

[1] Written in 1902. (Read at the Hong-Kong United Service Institution.)

year—will be. For war conditions we can only form an estimate based upon assumptions.

The consumption of provisions depends upon the numbers of officers and men, and in war or peace would be much the same. The greater activity to be expected in war would lead to more wear and tear, and consequently to a larger expenditure of naval stores. In peaceful times the quarterly expenditure of ammunition does not vary materially. In case we were at war, a single action might cause us to expend in a few hours as much as half a dozen quarterly peace allowances. There is a certain average number of days that a ship of a particular class is under way in a year, and the difference between that number and 365 is, of course, the measure of the length of time she is at anchor or in harbour. Expenditure of coal and of some important articles of engineers' stores depends on the relation between the time that she is stationary and the time she is under way. It should be particularly noted that the distinction is not between time at anchor and time at sea, but between time at anchor and ' time under way.' If a ship leaves her anchorage to run an engine-trial after refit, or to fire at a target, or to adjust compasses, or to go into dock—she burns more coal than if she remained stationary. These occasions of movement may be counted in with the days in which the ship is at sea, and the total taken as the number of days under way. It may be assumed that altogether these will amount to six or seven a month. In time of war the period under way would probably be much longer, and the time spent in expectation of getting under way in a hurry would almost certainly be considerable, so that expenditure of coal and machinery lubricants would be greatly increased.

The point to be made here is that—independently of strategic conditions, which will be considered later —the difference in the supply of a given naval force in war and in peace is principally that in the former the requirements of nearly everything except provisions will be greater ; and consequently that the articles must be forwarded in larger quantities or at shorter intervals than in peace time. If, therefore, we have arranged a satisfactory system of peace supply, that system—defence of the line of communications being left out of consideration for the present—will merely have to be expanded in time of war. In other words, practice in the use of the system during peace will go a long way towards preparing us for the duty of working it under war conditions. That a regular system will be absolutely indispensable during hostilities will not be doubted.

The general principles which I propose to indicate are applicable to any station. We may allow for a squadron composed of—

    4 battleships,
    4 large cruisers,
    4 second-class cruisers,
    13 smaller vessels of various kinds, and
    3 destroyers,

being away from the principal base-port of the station for several months of the year. The number of officers and men would be, in round numbers, about 10,000.

In estimating the amounts of stores of different kinds required by men-of-war, it is necessary—in order to allow for proper means of conveyance—to convert tons of dead-weight into tons by measurement, as the two are not always exactly equivalent. In the following enumeration only estimated amounts are stated, and the figures are to be considered as approximate and not precise. It is likely that in each item an expert may be able to discover some variation from the rigorously exact ; but the general result will be sufficiently accurate for practical purposes, especially as experience will suggest corrections.

A thousand men require about 3·1 tons of victualling stores, packages included, daily. We may make this figure up to 3·5 tons to allow for ' medical comforts ' and canteen stores. Consequently 10,000 men require about 35 tons a day, and about 6300 tons for six months. The assumed squadron, judging from experience, would require in peace time about 600 tons of engineers' stores, about 400 tons of naval stores, and—if the ships started with only their exact allowance on board and then carried out a full quarterly practice twice—the quantity of ordnance stores and ammunition required would be about 1140 tons, to meet the ordinary peace rate of expenditure. We thus get for a full six months' supply the following figures :—

Victualling stores	6,300 tons.
Engineers' stores	600 ,,
Naval stores	400 ,,
Ordnance stores and ammunition .	1,140 ,,
Total . .	8,440 ,,

Some allowance must be made for the needs of the 'auxiliaries,'[1] the vessels that bring supplies and in other ways attend on the fighting ships. This may be put at 7 per cent. The tonnage required would accordingly amount in all to about 9000.

The squadron would burn in harbour or when stationary about 110 tons of coal a day, and when under way about 1050 tons a day. For 140 harbour-days the consumption would be about 15,400 tons; and for 43 days under way about 45,150 : so that for coal requirements we should have the following :—

Harbour consumption	15,400 tons.
Under-way consumption . . .	45,150 ,,
Total for fighting ships . . .	60,550 ,,
7 per cent. for auxiliaries (say) . .	4,250 ,,
Grand total . .	64,800 ,,

Some time ago (in 1902) a representation was made from the China station that, engine-room oil being expended whenever coal is expended, there must be some proportion between the quantities of each. It was, therefore, suggested that every collier should bring to the squadron which she was supplying a proportionate quantity of oil. This has been approved, and it has been ordered that the proportions will be 75 gallons of oil to every 100 tons

---

[1] The 7 per cent. mentioned in the text would probably cover nearly all the demands—except coal—of auxiliaries, which would not require much or any ammunition. Coal is provided for separately.

of coal.[1] It was also suggested that the oil should be carried in casks of two sizes, for the convenience of both large and small ships.

There is another commodity, which ships have never been able to do without, and which they need now in higher proportion than ever. That commodity is fresh water. The squadron constituted as assumed would require an average of about 160 tons of fresh water a day, and nearly 30,000 tons in six months. Of this the ships, without adding very inconveniently to their coal consumption, might themselves distil about one-half; but the remaining 15,000 tons would have to be brought to them ; and another thousand tons would probably be wanted by the auxiliaries, making the full six months' demand up to 16,000 tons.

The tonnage requirements of the squadron and its ' auxiliaries ' for a full six months' period would be about 74,000, without fresh water. As, however, the ships would have started with full store-rooms, holds, and bunkers, and might be expected to return to the principal base-port of the station at the end of the period, stores for four-and-a-half months', and coal to meet twenty weeks', consumption would be sufficient. These would be about 6750 tons of stores and ammunition and 46,000 tons of coal.[2]

---

[1] I was informed (on the 10th December 1902), some time after the above was written, that the colliers supplying the United States Navy are going to carry 100 gallons of oil for every 100 tons of coal.

[2] To avoid complicating the question, the water or distilling vessel, the hospital ship, and the repair vessel have not been considered specially. Their coal and stores have been allowed for.

The stores, &c., would have to be replenished twice and—as it would not be prudent to let the ships run right out of them—replenishment should take place at the end of the second and at the end of the fourth months. Two vessels carrying stores and ammunition, if capable of transporting a cargo of nearly 1700 tons apiece, would bring all that was wanted at each replenishment. To diminish risk of losing all of one description of supplies, if carried by itself in a separate vessel, it has been considered desirable that each supply - carrier, when employed, is to contain some ammunition, some stores, and some provisions. There are great advantages in having supply-carriers, including, of course, colliers, of moderate size. Many officers must have had experience of the inconvenience and delay due to the employment of a single very large vessel which could only coal one man-of-war at a time. Several vessels, each carrying a moderate amount of cargo, would permit much more rapid replenishment of the ships of a squadron. The inconvenience that would be caused by the loss or breakdown of a supply-carrier would be reduced by employing several vessels of moderate cargo-capacity instead of only one or two of great capacity.

Each battleship and large cruiser of the assumed squadron may be expected to burn about 1000 tons of coal in five weeks, so that the quantity to be used in that time by all those ships would be 8000 tons. The remaining ships, scattered between different places as most of them would probably be, would require about 3500 tons. Therefore, every five weeks or so 11,500 tons of coal would be required. Four replenishments would be necessary in the whole period, making a total of 46,000 tons. Each replenishment could be conveyed in five colliers with 2300 tons apiece.

Moderate dimensions in store- and coal-carriers would prove convenient, not only because it would facilitate taking in stores and coaling, if all the squadron were assembled at one place, but also if part were at one place and part at another. Division into several vessels, instead of concentration in a few, would give great flexibility to the system of supply. A single very capacious cargo-carrier might have to go first to one place and supply the ships there, and then go to supply the remaining ships lying at another anchorage. This would cause loss of time. The same amount of cargo distributed amongst two or more vessels would permit the ships at two or more places to be supplied simultaneously.

You may have noticed that I have been dealing with the question as though stores and coal were to be transported direct to the men-of-war wherever they might be and put straight on board them from the carrying-vessels. There is, as you all know, another method, which may be described as that of 'secondary bases.' Speaking generally, each of our naval stations has a principal base at which considerable or even extensive repairs of the ships can be effected and at which stores are accumulated. Visits to it for the sake of repair being necessary,

u

the occasion may be taken advantage of to replenish
supplies, so that the maintenance of a stock at the
place makes for convenience, provided that the
stock is not too large.   The so-called 'secondary
base' is a place at which it is intended to keep in
store coal and other articles in the hope that when
war is in progress the supply of our ships may
be facilitated.   It is a supply, and not a repairing
base.

   A comparison of the 'direct' system and 'secondary base' system may be interesting.   A navy
being maintained for use in war, it follows, as a
matter of course, that the value of any part of its
equipment or organisation depends on its efficiency
for war purposes.   The question to be answered is—
Which of the two systems promises to help us most
during hostilities?   This does not exclude a regard
for convenience and economy in time of peace,
provided that care is taken not to push economy
too far and not to make ordinary peace-time convenience impede arrangements essential to the proper
conduct of a naval campaign.

   It is universally admitted that a secondary base
at which stocks of stores are kept should be properly defended.   This necessitates the provision of
fortifications and a garrison.   Nearly every article
of naval stores of all classes has to be brought to
our bases by sea, just as much as if it were brought
direct to our ships.   Consequently the communications of the base have to be defended.   They would
continue to need defending even if our ships ceased

to draw supplies from it, because the communications of the garrison must be kept open. We know what happened twice over at Minorca when the latter was not done.

The object of accumulating stores at a secondary base is to facilitate the supply of fighting ships, it being rather confidently assumed that the ships can go to it to replenish without being obliged to absent themselves for long from the positions in which they could best counteract the efforts of the enemy. When war is going on it is not within the power of either side to arrange its movements exactly as it pleases. Movements must, at all events very often, conform to those of the enemy. It is not a bad rule when going to war to give your enemy credit for a certain amount of good sense. Our enemy's good sense is likely to lead him to do exactly what we wish him not to do, and not to do that which we wish him to do. We should, of course, like him to operate so that our ships will not be employed at an inconvenient distance from our base of supplies. If we have created permanent bases in time of peace the enemy will know their whereabouts as well as we do ourselves, and, unless he is a greater fool than it is safe to think he is, he will try to make us derive as little benefit from them as possible. He is likely to extend his operations to localities at a distance from the places to which, if we have the secondary base system of supply, he knows for certain that our ships must resort. We shall have to do one of two things —either let him carry on his operations undisturbed, or conform to his movements. To this is due the common, if not invariable, experience of naval warfare, that the fleet which assumes the offensive has to establish what are sometimes called ' flying bases,' to which it can resort at will. This explains why Nelson rarely used Gibraltar as a base ; why we occupied Balaclava in 1854 ; and why the Americans used Guantanamo Bay in 1898. The flying base is not fortified or garrisoned in advance. It is merely a convenient anchorage, in a good position as regards the circumstances of the war ; and it can be abandoned for another, and resumed, if desirable, as the conditions of the moment dictate.

It is often argued that maintenance of stocks of stores at a secondary base gives a fleet a free hand and at least relieves it from the obligation of defending the line of communications. We ought to examine both contentions. It is not easy to discover where the freedom comes in if you must always proceed to a certain place for supplies, whether convenient or not. It may be, and very likely will be, of the utmost importance in war for a ship to remain on a particular station. If her coal is running short and can only be replenished by going to a base, go to the base she must, however unfortunate the consequences. It has been mentioned already that nearly every item on our store list has to be brought to a base by sea. Let us ascertain to what extent the accumulation of a stock at a place removes the necessity of defending the communication line. Coal is so much the greater item that consideration of it will cover that of all the rest.

The squadron, as assumed, requires about 11,500 tons of coal every five weeks in peace time. Some is commonly obtained from contractors at foreign ports ; but to avoid complicating the subject we may leave contract issues out of consideration. If you keep a stock of 10,000 tons at your permanent secondary base, you will have enough to last your ships about four-and-a-half weeks. Consequently you must have a stream of colliers running to the place so as to arrive at intervals of not more than about thirty days. Calculations founded on the experience of manœuvres show that in war time ships would require nearly three times the quantity used in peace. It follows that, if you trebled your stock of coal at the base and made it 30,000 tons, you would in war still require colliers carrying that amount to arrive about every four weeks. Picture the line of communications with the necessary colliers on it, and see to what extent you are released from the necessity of defending it. The bulk of other stores being much less than that of coal, you could, no doubt, maintain a sufficient stock of them to last through the probable duration of the war ; but, as you must keep your communications open to ensure the arrival of your coal, it would be as easy for the other stores to reach you as it would be for the coal itself. Why oblige yourself to use articles kept long in store when much fresher ones could be obtained ? Therefore the maintenance of store depots at a secondary base no more releases you from the necessity of guarding your communications than it permits freedom of movement to your ships.

The secondary base in time of war is conditioned as follows. If the enemy's sphere of activity is distant from the base which you have equipped with store-houses and fortifications, the place cannot be of any use to you. It can, and probably will, be a cause of additional anxiety to you, because the communications of its garrison must still be kept open. If it is used, freedom of movement for the ships must be given up, because they cannot go so far from it as to be obliged to consume a considerable fraction of their coal in reaching it and returning to their station. The line along which your colliers proceed to it must be effectively guarded.

Contrast this with the system of direct supply to the ships-of-war. You choose for your flying base a position which will be as near to the enemy's sphere of action as you choose to make it. You can change its position in accordance with circumstances. If you cease to use the position first chosen you need trouble yourself no more about its special communications. You leave nothing at it which will make it worth the enemy's while to try a dash at it. The power of changing the flying base from one place to another gives almost perfect freedom of movement to the fighting ships. Moreover, the defence of the line communicating with the position selected is not more difficult than that of the line to a fixed base.

The defence of a line of communication ought to be arranged on the same plan as that adopted for the defence of a trade route, viz. making unceasing efforts to attack the intending assailant. Within the last few years a good deal has been written about the employment of cruisers. The favourite idea seems to be that peace-time preparation for the cruiser operations of war ought to take the form of scouting and attendance on fleets. The history of naval warfare does not corroborate this view. We need not forget Nelson's complaint of paucity of frigates : but had the number attached to his fleet been doubled, the general disposition of vessels of the class then in commission would have been virtually unaltered. At the beginning of 1805, the year of Trafalgar, we had—besides other classes—232 frigates and sloops in commission ; at the beginning of 1806 we had 264. It is doubtful if forty of these were attached to fleets.

It is sometimes contended that supply-carriers ought to be vessels of great speed, apparently in order that they may always keep up with the fighting ships when at sea. This, perhaps, is due to a mistaken application of the conditions of a land force on the march to those of a fleet or squadron making a voyage. In practice a land army cannot separate itself — except for a very short time — from its supplies. Its movements depend on those of its supply-train. The corresponding ' supply-train ' of a fleet or squadron is in the holds and bunkers of its ships. As long as these are fairly well furnished, the ships might be hampered, and could not be assisted, by the presence of the carriers. All that is necessary is that these carriers should be at the right place at the right time, which is merely another way of saying that proper provision should be made for ' the stream of supplies and reinforcements which in terms of modern war is called communications '—the phrase being Mahan's.

The efficiency of any arrangement used in war will depend largely on the experience of its working gained in time of peace. Why do we not work the direct system of supply whilst we are at peace so as to familiarise ourselves with the operations it entails before the stress of serious emergency is upon us? There are two reasons. One is, because we have used the permanent base method so long that, as usually happens in such cases, we find it difficult to form a conception of any other. The other reason is that the direct supply method is thought to be too costly. The first reason need not detain us. It is not worthy of even a few minutes' consideration. The second reason deserves full investigation.

We ought to be always alive to the necessity of economy. The only limit to economy of money in any plan of naval organisation is that we should not carry it so far that it will be likely to impair efficiency. Those who are familiar with the correspondence of the great sea-officers of former days will have noticed how careful they were to prevent anything like extravagant expenditure. This inclination towards a proper parsimony of naval funds became traditional in our service. The tradition has, perhaps, been rather weakened in these days of abundant wealth ; but we should do our best not to let it die out. Extravagance is a serious foe to efficient organisation, because where it prevails there is a temptation to try imperfectly thought-out experiments, in the belief that, if they fail, there will still be plenty of money to permit others to be tried. This, of course, encourages slovenly want of system, which is destructive of good organisation.

We may assume, for the purposes of our investigation, that our permanently equipped secondary base contains a stock of 10,000 tons of coal. Any proportionate quantity, however, may be substituted for this, as the general argument will remain unaffected. As already intimated, coal is so much greater in bulk and aggregate cost than any other class of stores that, if we arrange for its supply, the provision of the rest is a comparatively small matter. The squadron which we have had in view requires an estimated amount of 46,000 tons of coal in six months' period specified, and a further quantity of 4600 tons may be expected to suffice for the ships employed in the neighbouring waters during the remainder of the year. This latter amount would have to be brought in smaller cargoes, say, five of 920 tons each. Allowing for the colliers required during the six months whilst the whole squadron has to be supplied an average cargo of 2300 tons, we should want twenty arrivals with an aggregate of 46,000 tons, and later on five arrivals of smaller colliers with an aggregate of 4600 tons to complete the year.

The freight or cost of conveyance to the place need not be considered here, as it would be the same in either system. If we keep a stock of supplies at a place we must incur expenditure to provide for the storage of the articles. There would be what may be called the capital charges for sites, buildings, residences, jetties, tram lines, &c., for which £20,000 would probably not be enough, but we may put it at that so as to avoid the appearance of exaggeration. A further charge would be due to the provision of tugs or steam launches, and perhaps lighters. This would hardly be less than £15,000. Interest on money sunk, cost of repairs, and maintenance, would not be excessive if they amounted to £3500 a year. There must be some allowance for the coal used by the tugs and steam launches. It is doubtful if £500 a year would cover this ; but we may put it at that. Salaries and wages of staff, including persons employed in tugs and steam launches, would reach quite £2500 a year. It is to be noted that the items which these charges are assumed to cover cannot be dispensed with. If depots are established at all, they must be so arranged that the stores deposited in them can be securely kept and can be utilised with proper expedition. The total of the charges just enumerated is £6500 a year.

There are other charges that cannot be escaped. For example, landing a ton of coal at Wei-hai-wei, putting it into the depot, and taking it off again

to the man-of-war requiring it, costs $1 20 cents, or
at average official rate of exchange two shillings.
At Hong-Kong the cost is about 2s. 5d. a ton. The
charge at 2s. per ton on 50,600 tons would be
£5060. I am assured by every engineer officer
to whom I have spoken on the subject that the
deterioration in coal due to the four different
handlings which it has to undergo if landed in
lighters and taken off again to ships from the
coal-store cannot be put at less than 10 per cent.
Note that this is over and above such deterioration
as would be due to passing coal direct from the
hold of a collier alongside into a ship's bunkers.
If any one doubts this deterioration it would be
well for him to examine reports on coal and steam
trials. He will be unusually fortunate if he finds
so small a deterioration as 10 per cent. The
lowest that I can remember having seen reported
is 20 per cent. ; reports of 30 and even 40 per cent.
are quite common. Some of it is for deterioration
due to climate and length of time in store. This,
of course, is one of the inevitable conditions of
the secondary base system, the object of which is
to keep in stock a quantity of the article needed.
Putting the purchase price of the coal as low as
15s. a ton, a deterioration due to repeated handling
only of 10 per cent. on 50,600 tons would amount
to £3795.

There is nearly always some loss of coal due
to moving it. I say ' nearly always ' because it
seems that there are occasions on which coal being

moved increases in bulk. It occurs when competitive coaling is being carried on in a fleet and ships try to beat records. A collier in these circumstances gives out more coal than she took in. We shall probably be right if we regard the increase in this case as what the German philosophers call 'subjective,' that is, rather existent in the mind than in the external region of objective, palpable fact. It may be taken as hardly disputable that there will be less loss the shorter the distance and the fewer the times the coal is moved. Without counting it we see that the annual expenses enumerated are—

Establishment charges	£6,500
Landing and re-shipping . . .	5,060
Deterioration	3,795
	£15,355

This £15,355 is to be compared with the cost of the direct supply system. The quantity of coal required would, as said above, have to be carried in twenty colliers — counting each trip as that of a separate vessel — with, on the average, 2300 tons apiece, and five smaller ones. It would take fully four days to unload 2300 tons at the secondary base, and even more if the labour supply was uncertain or the labourers not well practised. Demurrage for a vessel carrying the cargo mentioned, judging from actual experience, would be about £32 a day ; and probably about £16 a day for the smaller vessels. If we admit an average delay, per collier, of eighteen days, that is, fourteen days more than the time necessary for removing the cargo into store, so as to allow for colliers arriving when the ships to be coaled are absent, we should get—

$$
\begin{array}{llllll}
20 \times 14 \times 32 & . & . & . & . & . & £8,960 \\
5 \times 14 \times 16 & . & . & . & . & . & 1,120 \\
\hline
& & & & & £10,080
\end{array}
$$

as the cost of transferring the coal from the holds to the men-of-war's bunkers on the direct supply system. An average of eighteen days is probably much too long to allow for each collier's stay till cleared : because, on some occasions, ships requiring coal may be counted on as sure to be present. Even as it is, the £10,080 is a smaller sum than the £11,560 which the secondary base system costs over and above the amount due to increased deterioration of coal. If a comparison were instituted as regards other kinds of stores, the particular figures might be different, but the general result would be the same.

The first thing that we have got to do is to rid our minds of the belief that because we see a supply-carrier lying at anchor for some days without being cleared, more money is being spent than is spent on the maintenance of a shore depot. There may be circumstances in which a secondary base is a necessity, but they must be rare and exceptional. We saw that the establishment of one does not help us in the matter of defending our communications. We now see that, so far from being more economical than the alternative method, the secondary base method is more costly. It might have been demonstrated that it is really much more costly than the figures given make it out to be, because ships obliged to go to a base must expend coal in doing so, and coal costs money. It is not surprising that consideration of the secondary base system should evoke a recollection of the expression applied by Dryden to the militia of his day :

In peace a charge ; in war a weak defence.

I have to say that I did not prepare this paper simply for the pleasure of reading it, or in order to bring before you mere sets of figures and estimates of expense. My object has been to arouse in some of the officers who hear me a determination to devote a portion of their leisure to the consideration of those great problems which must be solved by us if we are to wage war successfully. Many proofs reach me of the ability and zeal with which details of material are investigated by officers in these days. The details referred to are not unimportant in themselves ; but the importance of several of them if put together would be incomparably less than that of the great question to which I have tried to direct your attention.

The supply of a fleet is of high importance in both peace time and time of war. Even in peace it sometimes causes an admiral to pass a sleepless night. The arrangements which it necessitates are often intricate, and success in completing them occasionally seems far off. The work involved

in devising suitable plans is too much like drudgery
to be welcome to those who undertake it. All the
same it has to be done : and surely no one will care
to deny that the fleet which has practised in quiet
years the system that must be followed in war
will start with a great advantage on its side when
it is at last confronted with the stern realities of
naval warfare.

POSTSCRIPT

The question of ' Communications,' if fully dealt
with in the foregoing paper, would have made it
so long that its hearers might have been tired out
before its end was reached. The following summary
of the points that might have been enlarged upon,
had time allowed, may interest many officers :—

In time of war we must keep open our lines of
communication.

If we cannot, the war will have gone against us.

Open communications mean that we can prevent
the enemy from carrying out decisive and sustained
operations against them and along their line.

To keep communications open it is not necessary
to secure every friendly ship traversing the line
against attacks by the enemy. All that is necessary
is to restrict the enemy's activity so far that he
can inflict only such a moderate percentage of loss
on the friendly vessels that, as a whole, they will
not cease to run.

Keeping communications open will not secure a
friendly place against every form of attack. It

will, however, secure a place against attacks with large forces sustained for a considerable length of time. If he can make attacks of this latter kind, it is clear that the enemy controls the communications and that we have failed to keep them open.

If communications are open for the passage of vessels of the friendly mercantile marine, it follows that the relatively much smaller number of supply-vessels can traverse the line.

As regards supply-vessels, a percentage of loss caused by the enemy must be allowed for. If we put this at 10 per cent.—which, taken absolutely, is probably sufficient—it means that *on the average* out of ten supply-vessels sent we expect nine to reach their destination.

We cannot, however, arrange that an equal loss will fall on every group of ten vessels. Two such groups may arrive intact, whilst a third may lose three vessels. Yet the 10 per cent. average would be maintained.

This condition has to be allowed for. Investigations some years ago led to the conclusion that it would be prudent to send five carriers for every four wanted.

The word 'group' has been used above only in a descriptive sense. Supply-carriers will often be safer if they proceed to their destination separately. This, however, depends on circumstances.

For EU product safety concerns, contact us at Calle de José Abascal, 56–1°, 28003 Madrid, Spain or eugpsr@cambridge.org.

www.ingramcontent.com/pod-product-compliance
Ingram Content Group UK Ltd.
Pitfield, Milton Keynes, MK11 3LW, UK
UKHW040617240426
470322UK00010B/172